WITHDRAWN

Harry C. Trexler Library
Muhlenberg College

Paying the Costs of Austerity
in Latin America

Paying the Costs of Austerity in Latin America

EDITED BY
Howard Handelman
and Werner Baer

Westview Press
BOULDER, SAN FRANCISCO, & LONDON

Westview Special Studies on Latin America and the Caribbean

All rights reserved. No part of this publication may be reproduced or transmitted in any form or by any means, electronic or mechanical, including photocopy, recording, or any information storage and retrieval system, without permission in writing from the publisher.

Copyright © 1989 by Westview Press, Inc.

Published in 1989 in the United States of America by Westview Press, Inc., 5500 Central Avenue, Boulder, Colorado 80301, and in the United Kingdom by Westview Press, Inc., 13 Brunswick Centre, London WC1N 1AF, England

Library of Congress Cataloging-in-Publication Data
Paying the costs of austerity in Latin America/edited by Howard
   Handelman and Werner Baer.
     p. cm.—(Westview special studies on Latin America and the
Caribbean)
   Includes index.
   ISBN 0-8133-7422-7
   1. Latin America—Economic policy. 2. Latin America—Politics and
government—1980-   . 3. Debts, External—Latin America.
I. Handelman, Howard, 1943-   . II. Baer, Werner, 1931-   .
III. Series.
HC123.P39   1989
338.98—dc19   88-39013
                                                                    CIP

Printed and bound in the United States of America

The paper used in this publication meets the requirements of the American National Standard for Permanence of Paper for Printed Library Materials Z39.48-1984.

10   9   8   7   6   5   4   3   2   1

Contents

v

Introduction:
The Economic and Political Costs
of Austerity

Howard Handelman and Werner Baer

The 1980s have been years of hope and despair in Latin America. The decade has witnessed a series of transitions from authoritarian rule to more popularly based civilian government. During the same period, however, the region has experienced its most devastating economic and financial crisis since the great depression of the 1930s. In nations such as Argentina and Uruguay, political dissidents no longer face the horrible spectre of torture or death squads. More generally in low-income neighborhoods throughout Latin America, however, working-class families now face economic insecurity, declining living standards, and increased malnutrition.

As of early 1979 seven of the nine nations examined in this volume were governed by some form of military or quasi-military government. They ranged from highly repressive bureaucratic-authoritarian (B-A) regimes in Argentina and Chile, through Brazil's more open B-A regime and Nicaragua and Bolivia's venal kleptocracies, to the more benign military governments of Ecuador and Peru. Only Venezuela enjoyed a pluralist democracy, whereas Mexico's single-party-dominant regime combined elements of authoritarianism and democracy. Within only a few years, however, a mass-based revolution toppled the Somoza dictatorship in Nicaragua while elected governments assumed power in Argentina, Bolivia, Brazil, Ecuador, and Peru.[1]

In the economic realm, the trends among the nations studied here have been more varied. For the most part, Latin America sustained rather impressive rates of economic growth during the 1960s and 1970s. Overall gross domestic product (GDP) grew an average of 5.7 percent from 1961 to 1970 and 6.0 percent from 1971 to 1980.[2] But composite statistics for the region were skewed by rapid growth in the area's two largest economies, Brazil and Mexico. In the wake of the 1973 surge in world petroleum prices, the economies of oil exporters such as Venezuela, Mexico, Ecuador, and Boliva continued to expand at moderate to strong rates, while Brazil's growth rate remained among the highest in the hemisphere.[3] In Argentina, Chile, Nicaragua, and Peru, however, average annual growth for the 1970s ranged only from 1.5 to 3.5 percent, in some cases hardly keeping up with population growth. Even where growth was positive, rapidly spiraling inflation in several nations had led to decreased real wages by the late 1970s.

The roots of the current economic crisis lie, in part, with policies adopted in the 1970s. Military governments often showed themselves to be as capable of accumulating huge fiscal deficits as their populist predecessors had been. Civilian administrations in Mexico and Venezuela used their nations' petroleum reserves to secure large foreign debts. During an era of high liquidity in the international financial system, virtually all Latin American nations (with the notable exception of Colombia) availed themselves of cheap credit to finance current-accounts deficits. Private-sector borrowing kept pace with state indebtedness. As a consequence, the region's total debt rose from $59 billion to $331 billion between 1975 and 1982, and reached $410 billion by 1987.[4]

The 1979 oil price shock marked the beginning of the economic downturn. Deterioration in the terms of trade for commodity exporters, sharply higher interest rates, and decreased import demand from the economically stagnant industrialized nations all contributed to the debt crisis of 1982. With debt servicing accounting for an unacceptably high percentage of GDP and export revenue, and with major infusions of additional capital no longer available, nearly all the countries of Latin America were forced to consider some form of economic stabilization. Such programs were required to curtail domestic inflation and to correct excessive balance-of-payments deficits. As of the beginning of 1987, per capita GDP (in constant 1986 dollars) was 6.5 percent below 1980 levels. For a number of the nations examined in this volume—Argentina, Bolivia, Mexico, Nicaragua, and Venezuela—the declines were far greater, ranging from −11.9 percent in Mexico to −27.0 percent in Bolivia.[5]

The Economic Costs of Austerity

All stabilization and adjustment programs require considerable economic sacrifice from much of the population. Such programs usually try to contain the forces that have produced inflation and to correct distortions that have grown out of the inflationary process. Orthodox programs, favored by the International Monetary Fund (IMF) and by monetarist policymakers, involve some combination of currency devaluation, reduction of import controls, credit restrictions, reduction of government subsidies on basic consumer goods (including fuel and basic foods), higher prices for public utilities, freeing of prices, wage repression, reduction of public employment, and reduction of the fiscal deficit.[6]

These policies usually produce a slowdown of economic growth, or even a period of decline. Thus, stabilization confronts policymakers with the problem of how to allocate economic sacrifices. Should they be evenly shared by all socioeconomic groups, or should they be borne more heavily by specific sectors? Considerations of equity suggest placing the burden of sacrifice on the more privileged groups of society— especially in Latin America, with its notoriously inequitable distribution of wealth and income. Yet many orthodox economists maintain that economic efficiency requires lower income groups to bear a substantial share of the burden. As credit becomes more restricted, the private sector faces declining profit margins. Unless workers' wage levels are depressed, these analysts argue, many firms will face bankruptcy.

Policymakers must consider not only the distributional effects of stabilization on different socioeconomic classes but also the allocation of sacrifice between sectors: exporters versus importers, industry versus agriculture, the private sector versus the state. IMF stabilization and adjustment programs usually favor exporters, agricultural producers, and the private sector. Ultimately, government policy will be based not only on the regime's ideology and the orientation of its "economic team" but also on the relative ability of various interest groups to protect themselves in the "battle for shares" and on the capacity of the state to impose sacrifice on particular classes and sectors. Looking at the content of typical orthodox stabilization-austerity programs that periodically have been attempted in Latin America, we may assess their distributional impact.

Severe Fiscal Restraints. Fiscal restraints entail some combination of increased taxes and decreased government expenditures. If the former option consists of income taxes, they would fall most heavily on middle- and upper-income groups, which represent the most accessible tax base in most Latin American countries. But because about two-thirds of taxes are usually indirect, increasing revenues will likely necessitate raising sales and value-added taxes, which fall disproportionately on lower income groups. Either option will face strong opposition in open societies.

Decreasing expenditures also present complex implementation problems. Governments must divide such cuts between current and capital outlays. Reducing current expenditures usually entails decreasing government employment and/or lowering the real wages of state employees. But these options are politically risky, of course—given the large percentage of the economically active population normally employed by the government bureaucracy and state-owned enterprises, and considering their strategic location. Not suprisingly, then, governments find it easier politically to curtail capital outlays than to curtail current expenditures. These reductions in capital investment, however, obviously adversely affect long-term economic growth.

Reduced Subsidies and Increased Prices in Controlled Sectors. The controlled price sector in Latin America is very large, due to the widespread presence of state enterprises as well as to the tradition of controlling prices of some basic products produced by the private sector (especially food). For political and other reasons these prices are allowed to lag behind the general price level, thereby forcing reduced profits or losses in the firms concerned and obligating the government to provide subsidies. As inflation grows, these subsidies tend to increase, both absolutely and as a proportion of GDP, placing a burden on government finances and often further feeding the inflationary process as government deficits grow.

The sharp reduction or elimination of such subsidies, which are usually part of orthodox stabilization programs, produces higher prices of basic foodstuffs, transportation, utility rates, and other necessities. Since the relative burden of these price adjustments is usually borne more heavily by the poor, reduced subsidies frequently produce social tensions and political unrest. Urban middle-class consumers (university students, for example) may also voice their opposition to such austerity measures. Thus, increases in urban bus fares or the cost of milk, bread, rice, or sugar have often led to violent antigovernment demonstrations.

Credit Restrictions. Austerity programs frequently involve substantial reduction in the growth of credit and a corresponding rise in the cost of credit—often from negative to positive rates of (real) interest. Here the burden of adjustment is felt by the major debtor groups that had been favored by earlier credit subsidies—usually sectors that the government had promoted as part of its general development program and/ or as a means of gaining their political support. The tightening of credit, however, may favor the financial sector, which in turn may realize increased real earnings. Multinationals often gain as well, since their access to foreign financial capital may permit them to use periods of austerity as an opportunity to buy out their local competitors.

Exchange-Rate Adjustments. Stabilization programs generally involve currency devaluations in order to stimulate exports, restrain imports, and thus reduce trade deficits. Proponents of devaluation also argue that it will stimulate a return flow of capital from abroad. The gainers will be exporters and producers of import substitutes. In many countries these gainers are primarily traditional agro-exporters as well as new agribusiness groups (e.g., Argentine and Brazilian soybean producers), and strong domestic industrial groups (now encouraged to export non-traditional industrial products). Multinationals in the agricultural and industrial sectors are also likely to gain. The losers include firms that rely on imported inputs and the consumers who must pay the increased costs of imported food and fuel.

The growth of the foreign debt burden since the 1970s has brought about an additional cost of exchange-rate devaluation. Those firms that have incurred a large amount of foreign debt have suffered from a substantial increase in the local currency costs of financing those debt obligations. In the case of public-sector debt, devaluation increases the proportion of government expenditures that must go to servicing the external debt, thereby reducing outlays in other areas such as social and economic infrastructure.

Wage Restraints. Many austerity programs involve restraints in wage increases, whereby wages are allowed to rise only at a lower rate than the general price increase and real wages fall correspondingly. Even when programs have no specific gudelines on wages, the effect of government policies is to compress real wages. These declines in real earnings are further exacerbated by the increased cost of basic consumer items (due to reduced government subsidies) and the rise in unemployment (due to declining government and private-sector investment).

Critics of orthodox stabilization packages argue that the heaviest burden of austerity usually falls on the shoulders of the urban working class, which must sustain substantial declines in real wages and higher levels of unemployment.[7] Governments not wishing to unleash the political unrest often associated with orthodox stabilization programs—strikes, demonstrations, or even rioting—have often turned to less severe, heterodox programs. When alternative sources of refinancing their debts were available, they rejected IMF "conditionality"—that is, IMF standby loans with policy performance conditions. Instead, they addressed balance-of-payments deficits and domestic inflation through such measures as import restrictions, foreign exchange controls, and wage and price controls. Rosemary Thorp and Laurence Whitehead note that heterodox approaches have ranged from policies "that are almost orthodox, but allow a little more time to ease the process of adjustment and reduce associated political tensions, although the same final outcome is intended as under orthodox policies, to policies that only pretend to be attempts to stabilize, while essentially rejecting the underlying objectives of orthodox policies."[8] Critics of heterodox policies, whose criticisms seem to be supported by the recent failures of the Argentine Austral and Brazilian Cruzado plans, charge that such programs offer no coherent solution to economic disequilibria and are the products of governments that lack the political will or ability to impose the necessary harsh medicine of austerity.

Austerity and the Transition to Democracy

From the perspective of Latin America's newly established democratic regimes, the debt crisis could hardly have come at a more inauspicious time. Unable to escape the need for some form of stabilization and adjustment policy, they clearly did not relish the negative political fallout that such austerity programs inevitably entail. Indeed, much of the early literature on the stabilization programs of the 1960s and 1970s suggested a basic incompatibility between economic austerity and stable democratic government.

That argument took two forms. Some scholars maintained that attempts to impose economic stabilization programs tend to politically destabilize democratic regimes and contribute to the rise of authoritarian governments.[9] A second argument, related but conceptually distinct, contended that only authoritarian regimes can effectively impose unpopular austerity programs of an orthodox nature.[10] Accordingly, democratic regimes with a high degree of independent interest group activity might be expected to adopt heterodox adjustment packages with less deleterious distributional effects. Such heterodoxy would reflect both the democracies' greater responsiveness to interest group activity and their desire to avert mass-based protests that might provoke a military coup.

The presumed association between orthodox stabilization programs and authoritarian government stemmed largely from the experiences of the southern cone nations in the 1970s. In Chile, Uruguay, and, at times, Argentina (but not Brazil), bureaucratic-authoritarian regimes introduced orthodox economic adjustment programs as part of a broader policy of liberalizing the economy—that is, of reducing state intervention and artificial restraints on the price mechanism. Civilian regimes (particularly populist governments) in the 1960s and 1970s seemed more inclined to pursue expansionist economic policies. More recently, however, conventional wisdoms regarding regime type and stabilization policy have come under challenge. Stephan Haggard and Robert Kaufman note that "the few cross-national political comparisons of IMF programs that do exist . . . reveal no systematic association between either democracy or dictatorship and the ability to stabilize."[11] Thus, Karen Remmer's study of IMF Standby Programs from 1954 to 1984 found that "authoritarian regimes . . . are no more likely to initiate stabilization programs or to survive their political reverberations."[12] These findings raise the question of whether military takeovers are "irrelevant" to economic needs before or after the introduction of austerity packages.

In the wake of the 1982 debt crisis, governments throughout Latin America—regardless of regime type—were forced to adopt some form of economic adjustment and stabilization plan, with varying degrees of sacrifice for the population. Thus, although regime type and regime ideology obviously influence economic policy, any government—be it authoritarian or democratic, rightist or leftist—confronts a much narrower range of policy options during periods of severe economic crisis. Just as there is little empirical evidence to demonstrate that authoritarian regimes are more able to carry out coherent stabilization programs, it is equally unclear that democratic governments are able to administer more equitable ones. Jennifer McCoy's chapter in this volume presents cross-national data on real wages and real minimum wages, and concludes that "a relatively long-lived and stable democratic regime [Venezuela] does not guarantee any better distribution of the costs of austerity than do other regime types."

Austerity and Regime Type

The literature regarding the influence of regime type on the nature of government austerity programs has yielded contradictory findings;

the countries under examination in this volume were selected to shed further light on that issue. The nine case studies presented here offer opportunities for both within-nation comparisons across time and cross-national comparisions. In Argentina, Bolivia, Brazil, and Peru, stabilization policies were introduced by military regimes during the 1970s and by the civilian governments that succeeded them in the late 1970s and early 1980s. Were there any systematic differences between the adjustment policies of the military and civilian regimes examined here? David Schodt's study of Ecuador in this volume compares two democratic governments with very different ideological orientations. Did Febres Cordero's neo-conservative administration (with its strong links to economic elites) pursue a markedly different stabilization package than did Hurtado's left-of-center Christian Democratic government?

Obviously the precision of such longitudinal comparisons is limited, since internal economic disequilibria and external constraints are not constant over time. Thus, it is also useful to make cross-national comparisons of policy outputs in the 1980s, at a time when each of the nations examined here operated in a similar international environment. To what extent have the costs of austerity in the current economic crisis been distributed differently in varying regime types? Has Nicaragua's revolutionary socialist regime been able to distribute those burdens more equitably than have capitalist societies? Do more competitive party systems (as in Venezuela), with their high level of interest group representation, produce stabilization programs that are more equitable than Mexico's single-party-dominant system or Brazil's less mobilized society?

Here again, scientifically controlled testing of such hypotheses is not possible. At any point in time, the nations examined in this volume have faced very different economic constraints. Nicaragua, devastated by a tremendously destructive internal war (featuring a *contra* strategy of attacking economic targets) and a U.S. trade embargo, would have suffered severe declines in living standards no matter what type of government it had. Brazil and Mexico, with larger external debts, have been able to negotiate more favorable refinancing that have smaller debtors.[13] So too has Venezuela, which is viewed as more creditworthy by the banking community. Nations suffering more severe deterioration in their terms of trade might be forced to introduce more orthodox adjustment measures regardless of regime type or government ideology. In short, much hinges on the severity of the economic crisis facing a particular government and the space provided by international bargaining. Yet within these constraints, cross-national comparisons of the cases analyzed in this volume can help identify the political parameters of austerity policy.

Two of the country studies, Argentina and Chile, support the expectation that military authoritarian regimes are more likely than civilian governments to impose orthodox adjustment policies. René Cortázar's critical analysis of Chile indicates that Pinochet's repressive apparatus was a necessary (though not sufficient) condition for the long-term use of unpopular monetarist policies. Edward Epstein examines government taxation and expenditure in Argentina under the constraints of IMF stand-by agreements. He finds that, in times of austerity, Videla's military government (1976–1981) cut social welfare expenditures and raised taxes on production and consumption. In contrast, Alfonsín's populist civilian administration (1983–) was more prone to cutting military spending and increasing taxation on imports. In both Argentina and Chile, the existence of a police state obviously enabled the government to impose unpopular austerity measures. At the same time, however, authoritarianism alone does not dictate economic orthodoxy. Cortázar notes that the Pinochet regime could have opted for alternative policies had it chosen a civilian economic team less ideologically committed to "Chicago school" theories. Epstein examines the interaction between government policymakers and critical regime supporters under both military and civilian government as a means of explaining expenditure and tax policy during periods of austerity.

In their analysis of Brazilian austerity programs since the 1960s, Baer, Biller, and McDonald further refine comparisons between military and civilian governments. The transition from democratic to authoritarian rule in the 1960s seems to have confirmed the accepted paradigm. The three civilian governments that served prior to the 1964 coup found that "austerity programs attempted by democratic governments are politically suicidal." With the return of civilian government in 1985, President José Sarney's attempt to escape austerity through the expansionist Cruzado Plan paralleled Alfonsín's Austral Plan. Both programs featured wage and price controls and other heterodox stabilization measures. While both plans ultimately failed, they once again demonstrated the reluctance of democratic governments to face the political consequences of unpopular austerity measures. Conversely, General Castello Branco's authoritarian government (1964–1967) was able to stabilize the economy, but at a tremendous cost to the working class.

Baer et al. note, however, that although entrenched authoritarian regimes may opt for painful austerity measures, military governments that allow limited opposition or seek a graceful transition back to civilian rule are more likely to seek heterodox solutions to economic disequilibria. Thus, in the wake of opposition gains in the 1974 congressional elections, the Geisel regime chose economic expansion and further indebtedness, rather than austerity, as a reaction to the 1973 oil shock. Augusto Pinochet and even Jorge Videla faced no comparable constraints. Yet, the decision by the Figueiredo government to accept IMF-imposed orthodox measures during a key point in the democratic opening "presents a clear contradiction to the traditional paradigm." Here, Baer et al. look to explanations outside the realm of regime type. Indeed, regardless of regime type or ideology, stabilization and adjustment policies in most of the countries examined in this volume were influenced by the expectations of civil society and the likelihood of mass mobilization against austerity.

Paul Beckerman's discussion of Peru and Kenneth Jameson's analysis of Bolivia offer additional opportunities for within-nation comparisons of military and civilian regimes. Peru first experienced a serious balance-of-payments crisis in the mid-1970s during the military governments of Juan Velasco (1968–1975) and Francisco Morales Bermúdez (1975–1980), forcing each of those governments to adopt unpopular austerity measures. But both the left-leaning Velasco government and the more conservative Morales Bermúdez regime resisted IMF conditionality, and neither proved particularly capable of imposing a coherent stabilization package. In Velasco's case, the government had carefully tried to mobilize peasant and worker support for the regime. The Morales government, like its Brazilian counterpart, sought a graceful exit from military rule. Ironically, it was the succeeding democratic government of Fernando Belaúnde (1980–1985) that adopted the most painful orthodox austerity measures in recent Peruvian history, resulting in a devastating decline in real wages. Although Belaúnde proved that a democratic regime *can* impose a harsh stabilization package, he paid a political price. His Acción Popular party was annihilated in the 1985 national elections. His successor, Alan García (1985–) not only rejected austerity (like his civilian counterparts in Argentina and Brazil) but also stimulated economic growth and increased real wages while placing a lid on what Peru was willing to pay on its debt obligations. Unfortunately, that growth was mostly consumption driven and drew upon excess capacity. By the end of 1987, the economy had begun to falter as the government seemed unable to turn consumption-led expansion into investment-driven growth.

The Bolivian experience constitutes perhaps the most dramatic reversal of the expected paradigm. Jameson notes that a series of authoritarian military regimes were unable to impose a coherent stabilization program. It was left to the civilian administration of Victor Paz Estenssoro (1985–) to introduce an extremely harsh, orthodox austerity program. "Thus," argues Jameson, "the usual assumption that bureaucratic-authoritarian regimes are more able to impose austerity is reversed in Bolivia." One possible reason is that military rule in Bolivia did not fully subscribe to the B-A model. The highly clientelistic nature of military rule in Bolivia forced each government to deliver some economic benefits to its critical supporters. Furthermore, after the fall of the Banzer dictatorship, internal conflicts within the military created such instability that governments rose and fell with bewildering speed, none of them serving long enough to introduce any coherent economic program.

In sum, the cases presented in this volume reveal considerable variation in the economic policies of each regime type—whether authoritarian or democratic, military or civilian. Accordingly, regime type can only be a starting point for an examination of the political determinants of stabilization and adjustment policies. In trying to understand why a particular government either adopted or rejected orthodox policies, and in seeking to explain how well a regime was able to weather the discontent that austerity invariably brings, one must look beyond regime type to the relationship between civil society and the political order.

Inasmuch as individual political and economic structures vary from country to country, and because political-economic factors have impacted differently on each nation's recent history, the case studies in this volume cover somewhat diverse time periods (though all focus on the 1970s and 1980s) and sometimes stress different economic or political indicators. The specific variables discussed as a basis for explaining state economic policy also have differing impacts in each of the countries under study.

The Politics of Austerity

The Role of Trade Unions

Because of their negative distributional effects, orthodox austerity policies invariably precipitate some opposition from organized labor. The effectiveness of trade union opposition (or, conversely, the ability of the government to resist labor protest) will be influenced by the following factors: the proportion of the work force that is organized into unions, the strength of unions in strategic areas of the nation's economy, the capacity of the unions to sustain widespread or prolonged strike action, the degree of labor militancy, and the level of union autonomy from the state or from ruling political parties.

The countries examined here vary in terms of the mix of these factors and, hence, in terms of the level of trade union input into the policy process. As McCoy notes, in Venezuela, a nation with a relatively high level of unionization, the close linkage between the unions and the Acción Democrática party has enabled labor to temper slightly austerity policy. At the same time, however, Venezuelan unions have not been particularly militant during that nation's modern democratic era. Despite the rising labor unrest of late, Venezuela's workers usually have acquiesed to declines in real wages with relatively limited opposition. Here it is instructive to refer to Terry Karl's observation that the social pact that has guaranteed Venezuelan democratic stability since the 1950s has also placed limits on challenges to the nation's highly inequitable distribution of wealth and income.[14]

In Nicaragua, a very extensive Marxist trade union movement has accepted without challenge recent government austerity policies that have contributed to dramatic declines in real income. That acceptance is, in part, related to labor's recognition that the country is under siege and that the *contras* bear much of the blame for declining living standards. But, obviously, worker opposition to government policy has also been constrained by state control over most of the labor movement and by the state of emergency that prohibits strikes. Similarly, the incorporation of the Mexican trade union into the corporatist structure of the Institutional Revolutionary Party (PRI) not only affords labor guaranteed input into government economic policymaking but also reduces its ability to challenge policy decisions.

Finally, the southern tier nations of Argentina, Brazil, and Chile illustrate a continuum in the power of labor influence. In Argentina, the newly installed Alfonsín government faced one of the largest, most militant trade union movements in Latin America. Moreover, labor was intimately linked with the Peronist opposition. Given labor's history of bringing down military governments in the past, it is not surprising that Alfonsín opted for a heterodox stabilization policy. By contrast, the Brazilian labor movement has never had the strength or militancy of its Argentine counterpart. This may be one reason for which the outgoing Figueiredo government was willing to risk an IMF-style austerity package during a delicate period of democratic opening. Yet these measures ultimately increased strike activity. By 1985, Brazilian unions had become far more militant. Had Tancredo Neves lived to take office, he may have been in a position, with his strong popular mandate, to continue more orthodox stabilization policy. But Sarney, who was likely more wary of popular opposition, chose a heterodox approach. In Chile, where years of military repression have undermined the strength of a once-powerful union movement, the Pinochet government has been able to enforce unpopular austerity programs for a sustained period.

The Strength, Structure, and Ideology of Business Interests

The attitude of organized business interests toward economic austerity is more complex and less predictable. Restrictions on domestic credit and reduced (or negative) growth rates adversely affect a wide spectrum of the private sector. Various sectors of the economic elite, however, are affected differently by specific stabilization measures. Currency devaluation may help exporters and reduce the competition faced by import-substitution industry (ISI). But manufacturers who depend heavily on imported capital equipment or raw materials may be seriously harmed. So too would firms with large dollar debts. Finally, firms that depend heavily on popular consumption levels might suffer from sharp declines in real wages.

The relative political strength of each sector of the business community may influence both the type of austerity package that a government chooses and its effectiveness in implementing that program. Haggard and Kaufman note that the growth of the Argentine financial sector in the 1970s constrained Alfonsín's ability to employ heterodox policies. Conversely, in Brazil, the São Paulo industrial elite's support for expansionary credit and financial policies established an important base of support for Sarney's heterodox Cruzado Plan.[15]

It is important to recognize, however, that the reaction of economic elites toward adjustment and stabilization policies does not necessarily correspond to the economic impact of those programs. Business groups will respond according to their level of confidence in the long-term objectives of a particular administration. And that confidence level often hinges more on the ideological fit between the private sector and the regime than on the nature or impact of particular government policies. In Nicaragua, adjustment policies designed to benefit large agro-export growers in no way reduced that group's fierce opposition to the revolutionary regime. In Ecuador, similarly, the Hurtado administration's bailout of the private sector's dollar debt failed to diminish the business community's distrust of the president's alleged leftist tendencies. Conversely, import-substitution industrialists overwhelmingly supported Febres Cordero's candidacy in spite of clear evidence that his neoliberal policies would adversely affect them. As a long-time leader of the Guayaquil Chamber of Industry, Febres Cordero inspired *confianza* in the private sector as Hurtado never could. In Chile, the ISI sector has rather passively accepted the negative impact of government policy. Obviously, the Pinochet regime's iron grip inhibits private-sector opposition to the government's rigidly orthodox programs. At the same time, however, the polarization of Chilean politics and the business community's fear of a Marxist revival reinforces private-sector support for the government.

The ability of economic elites to influence government policy varies independently of regime type. Rightist authoritarian regimes may work closely with organized business interests, as exemplified by Minister of Economics Martínez de Hoz's strong linkages to Argentine financial and agro-export interests. Conversely, the Brazilian military government imposed orthodox stabilization policies in the mid-1960s despite opposition from the São Paulo industrial elite. Venezuela's democratic model has afforded organized business chambers effective institutionalized channels of communication with the state and both of the major political parties. In Ecuador, however, the restoration of democracy in 1979, coupled with constitutional reforms that reduced corporatist representation of the private sector, ushered in a period of intense conflict between economic elites and the Hurtado administration.

Regime Legitimacy

In her chapter on Venezuela, Jennifer McCoy indicates that the restoration of democracy in several Latin American nations led to short-term gains in real wages. At the same time, however, in countries such as Argentina, Brazil, Bolivia, and Nicaragua, the demise of highly discredited authoritarian regimes increased the legitimacy of (and popular support for) the democratic governments that succeeded them and afforded the new regimes greater political space for the introduction of adjustment and stabilization policies. In the short term, at least, that space seems to have granted them some protection from the pressures of newly mobilized political forces. In Nicaragua, where the Sandinistas' legitimacy rests, in part, on their role in liberating the nation from the Somocista dictatorship, and where the state was under attack from *contras* widely associated with Somocismo, significant portions of the urban population continue to support the revolution in spite of sharp declines in real incomes. Expanded educational opportunities as well as more equitable distribution of health care and other social services also help compensate for the costs of austerity. In Bolivia, the Paz government introduced extremely painful austerity measures with surprisingly little popular resistance. Here again, the government enjoyed greater political space because of the obvious corruption and incompetence of the preceding military regimes.

René Cortázar's analysis of Chile indicates that "international legitimacy" may also strengthen a government's hand. Despite the Pinochet regime's poor human rights record and its negative image abroad, its "Chicago school" economic team is respected by international organizations such as the IMF and by the international banking community. That linkage has facilitated debt refinancing; it has also helped the Chilean government to "stay the course" of painful orthodox policies. Conversely, Kenneth Jameson argues that, in the early 1980s, the Bolivian military government's involvement in the drug trade gave the regime such an "unsavory international reputation" that external debt refinancing became difficult. When the Paz administration introduced its tough austerity package in 1985, however, the civilian government's international position was strengthened by its economic team's links to Harvard. As David Schodt observes, Ecuadorian President Febres Cordero's high standing with the Reagan administration opened up channels to additional public loans.

Regime Unity

Because almost any austerity measure is likely to generate some opposition from civil society, a regime's ability to sustain a stabilization program will depend, in part, on the degree of internal unity within the ruling political coalition. In a competitive democratic system, political conflicts between the executive and legislative branches, particularly if each branch is controlled by different political parties, may weaken a government's capacity to successfully implement stabilization. Schodt notes that, in the face of congressional (and labor) opposition to his austerity measures, Febres Cordero chose "to eschew efforts to build consensus, relying instead on increasingly authoritarian tactics." In Mexico, opposition political parties presented no significant obstacles to government economic policy. But divisions between varying government agencies and ministries (some favoring orthodox and others more heterodox approaches) have contributed to the vacillation in stabilization policy.

Authoritarian governments might be expected to maintain greater internal unity in the fact of societal opposition to austerity. Despite recent divisions between branches of the Chilean military, Pinochet's continued firm control has allowed the economic team to rigidly pursue its orthodox stabilization policies. Other authoritarian regimes, however, have been crippled by internal divisions. From the close of the Banzer dictatorship in 1978 until the restoration of civilian government in 1982, no fewer than eight military governments (and one interim civilian president) held office in Bolivia. Internal military conflicts and constant changes of control contributed to the chaos in economic policy. Thus Paz Estenssoro's civilian government was able to introduce stringent austerity measures that the military regime had been unable to impose. During the late 1970s in Argentina, differences between military factions contributed to swings in adjustment policy. General Viola's government, seeking an opening toward civilian political forces, relaxed Martínez de Hoz's neoliberal economic policies. When Viola was replaced by General Galtieri's hard-line military faction, the government returned to harsh austerity measures.[16]

The Debt Crisis, Austerity, and the Politics of Acceptance

The decade of the 1980s has been a difficult time in which to govern in Latin America. Between 1980 and 1983 alone, real consumption per capita fell 8 percent in Brazil and Mexico, 14 percent in Peru, 17 percent in Argentina and Chile, and 39 percent in Nicaragua.[17] Real wages and consumption levels have continued to fall since that time. The Bolivian wage index, as Jameson notes, fell an incredible 82 percent from 1979 to 1986. Political leaders facing balance-of-payments and fiscal deficits have been caught in a dilemma. According to Joan Nelson, "Stabilization is inherently painful, but there is no avoiding the pain. The alternative to planned and guided adjustment is chaotic adjustment, entailing even higher costs in terms of controls, scarcities, inflation, unemployment, and atrophied output. . . . Politicians are 'damned if they do and damned if they don't' when it comes to the political consequences of their stabilization decisions."[18]

Small wonder that the last comparable economic decline—the depression of the 1930s—contributed to the fall of many governments in the region. Inasmuch as stabilization programs put particular strains on democratic governments, it is noteworthy that, to date, not a single democratic regime has been toppled by the current economic crisis. Throughout Latin America, unemployed workers, dismissed civil servants, and financially embattled business people have accepted their sacrifices with surprisingly little protest. Although most of the countries examined in this volume have experienced an increased incidence of strikes and other forms of labor protest, the general level of political unrest has been relatively limited. The reasons for this acceptance are obviously complex, but we can point to two sets of factors—one economic and one political—for partial explanation.

First, the urban poor have often proven remarkably resourceful in adapting to the economic crisis either by securing alternative income from the informal sector or, in some nations, by participating in illegal activities such as the drug trade. In Mexico, an undetermined (but very significant) portion of the urban population is involved in the informal economy. There, as in much of Latin America, official economic statistics probably overstate the decline in real incomes. Indeed, Kenneth Jameson has cited micro-level neighborhood studies in La Paz indicating that the deterioration of living standards for the Bolivian poor has been greatly ameliorated by informal sector activity.[19] In countries such as Argentina and Chile, the shift to the informal sector is part of a process of deindustrialization that has transpired over more than an decade. That shift in the work force has reduced the strength of the trade union movement and weakened its capacity to protest.

At the same time, as previously noted, both the newly established democratic regimes and Nicaragua's revolutionary government were given some political space when they assumed the reins of power. Nicaragua's revolutionary regime augmented its initial support with literacy and health-care campaigns; but it can blame the *contras* for the decline in living standards. Countries such as Argentina, Brazil, Bolivia, and Peru, and to a lesser extent Ecuador, have no desire to return to the discredited military regimes replaced by the current civilian governments. Given the magnitude of the current economic crisis, the armed forces may not wish to return to power at this point. Finally, it has been the very breadth of the crisis throughout the region and the widespread application of IMF conditionality that have enabled governments to escape some of the blame for deteriorating economic conditions. Governments can tell their constituents that their country is not alone in its suffering. Moreover, when nations are forced to sign IMF standby agreements, their political leaders can label that institution as the culprit.

Yet because hopes for an economic turnaround were recently crushed in Argentina, Brazil, Mexico, and Peru, the governments of these nations may face a rising tide of discontent and the prospects of political instability. The great hope held out for the leadership of Argentina's Raúl Alfonsín and Peru's Alan García has faded, and the possibility of renewed military intervention cannot be ruled out. The Venezuelan social pact has come under increasing strain. Ecuador's President Leon Febres Cordero became increasingly authoritarian. The PRI faces a rising challenge in Mexico and may choose to limit the political opposition. As Miguel Ramírez and Paul Beckerman argue in this volume, current stabilization programs offer little hope for renewed economic growth. Thus, both an exit from the economic crisis of the 1980s and a continuation of the democratic opening may depend on the kind of debt restructuring that Ramírez and Beckerman propose.

Notes

We are indebted to Stephan Haggard, Gary Wynia, and David Schodt for their comments on this chapter. Responsibility for any error rests with the authors.

1. For a discussion of the recent economic crisis, see Jonathan Hartlyn and Samuel Morley (eds.), *Latin American Political Economy: Financial Crisis and Political Change* (Boulder: Westview Press, 1986); on the transition to democracy, see Guillermo O'Donnell, Philippe Schmitter, and Laurence Whitehead (eds.), *Transitions from Authoritarian Rule: Latin America* (Baltimore: Johns Hopkins University Press, 1986).

2. Inter-American Development Bank, *Economic and Social Progress in Latin America: 1985 Report* (Washington, D.C.: IDB, 1985), p. 152.

3. Ibid. For the period 1971–1980, Brazil, Ecuador, and Mexico enjoyed average annual GDP growth of more than 6.5 percent, whereas Bolivia and Venezuela grew at annual rates of 4–5 percent.

4. Comisión Económica para América Latina y el Caribe (CEPAL), *Balance Preliminar de la Economiá Latinoamerica: 1987* (Santiago, December 31, 1987), pp. 1–2.

5. Inter-American Development Bank, *Economic and Social Progress in Latin America: 1987 Report* (Washington, D.C.: IDB, 1987), p. 2.

6. Wiliam Cline and Sidney Weintraub (eds.), *Economic Stabilization in Developing Countries* (Washington, D.C.: Brookings Institution, 1981); Rosemary Thorp and Laurence Whitehead, *Inflation and Stabilisation in Latin America* (London: Macmillan, 1979).

7. Alejandro Foxley, "Stabilization Policies and Their Effects on Employment and Income Distribution: A Latin American Perspective," in Cline and Weintraub (eds.), *Economic Stabilization*, pp. 191–233; Alejandro Foxley, *Latin American Experiments in Neoconservative Economics* (Berkeley: University of California Press, 1983).

8. Thorp and Whitehead, *Inflation and Stabilisation*, p. 17.

9. Thomas Skidmore, "The Politics of Economic Stabilization in Postwar Latin America," in James Malloy (ed.), *Authoritarianism and Corporatism in Latin America* (Pittsburgh: University of Pittsburgh Press, 1977), pp. 149–190.

10. Foxley, *Latin American Experiments*; Carlos Diaz-Alejandro, "Southern Cone Stabilization Plans," in Cline and Weintraub (eds.), *Economic Stabilization*, pp. 119–147.

11. Stephan Haggard and Robert Kaufman, "The Politics of Stabilization and Structural Adjustment," in Jeffrey Sachs (ed.), *Foreign Debt and Economic Performance: Selected Issues* (Chicago: University of Chicago Press, forthcoming). We are indebted to Haggard and Kaufman for sharing with us the manuscript of that chapter prior to its publication.

12. Karen L. Remmer, "The Politics of Economic Stabilization: IMF Standby Programs in Latin America, 1954–1984," *Comparative Politics* (October 1986), p. 20.

13. Haggard and Kaufman, "The Politics of Stabilization." Ecuador, however, has done quite well in its debt renegotiation, having received terms comparable to those of the larger debtors.

14. Terry Lynn Karl, "Petroleum and Political Pacts," in O'Donnell et al. (eds.), *Transitions from Authoritarian Rule*, pp. 196–219.

15. Haggard and Kaufman, "The Politics of Stabilization."

16. Andrés Fontana, *Fuerzas Armadas, Partidos Políticos y Transición a la Democracia en Argentina, 1981–1982* (Notre Dame, Ind.: Kellogg Institute, 1984).

17. Rosemary Thorp and Laurence Whitehead, "Review and Conclusions," in Thorp and Whitehead (eds.), *Latin American Debt and the Adjustment of Crisis* (Pittsburgh: University of Pittsburgh Press, 1987), p. 344.

18. Joan M. Nelson, "The Politics of Stabilization," in Richard E. Feinberg and Valeriana Kallab (eds.), *Adjustment Crisis in the Third World* (Washington, D.C.: Overseas Development Council, 1984), pp. 99, 103.

19. Kenneth Jameson, "The Effect of International Debt on Poverty in Bolivia and Alternative Responses," Paper presented at the Thirteenth National Congress of the Latin American Studies Association, Boston, 1986.

1

Austerity Under Different Political Regimes: The Case of Brazil

Werner Baer, Dan Biller, and Curtis T. McDonald

Introduction

Austerity programs to combat inflation usually require sacrifices in terms of economic growth, and the distribution of such sacrifices can affect the nature of a country's political regime, especially in the Third World. Distortions that occur during a prolonged period of inflation may make continued long-term growth increasingly difficult. Investments may decline or be applied to nonproductive areas. Savings may decline as capital markets become less efficient and fail to protect the real value of investors' assets. And price distortions may become increasingly evident as government-controlled prices (e.g., of public utilities and basic foods) lag behind general price increases, which result in government subsidies to state enterprises and to producers of basic foodstuffs. These subsidies, in turn, may increase the budget deficit, thereby reinforcing inflationary pressures. Finally, balance-of-payments difficulties may worsen as a result of an exchange rate that is increasingly overvalued.[1]

Traditional austerity programs constitute one method to deal with such a situation. These programs entail severe credit restrictions; drastic cuts in government expenditures; increases in taxation; severe wage repression; elimination of subsidies and a consequent rise of those prices which had been allowed to lag behind; and, finally, drastic devaluation.[2] The net result is a decline in growth (possibly a period of negative growth); growing unemployment; falling real wages, which are worsened by higher prices of public services and food products; and a general redistribution of income away from the wage-earning sector, and from those sectors depending on imported inputs, in favor of exporters and financial institutions.

The traditional belief regarding austerity programs is that their measures can achieve relative success only if carried out in a political environment characterized by an authoritarian/military government, as opposed to a democratic administration. Such programs, by their very nature, imply tremendous costs for society. The various economic tools used within a given austerity program will trigger strong negative reactions in many different sectors. Eventually various groups in society must be made to accept and absorb these costs in the interest of correcting the distortions that made the austerity program necessary to begin with.

Proponents of the traditional rationale claim that the political costs of austerity programs are too great for those who sponsor such measures in a democratic setting, where relative power is based on the appeasement of various pressure groups and constituents. Authoritarian regimes, on the other hand, normally draw their power from within and therefore find no need to win the approval of various support groups. Subsequently, they are able to proceed systematically through the different steps of an austerity program, essentially immune to the criticism of society at large.

Carlos Diaz-Alejandro, for instance, notes that inflationary expansionism has usually been associated with populist democratic regimes:

> Populist governments are likely to have witnessed substantial expansion in government expenditures not financed by tax collections, either because the opposition blocks efforts to raise taxes or because the government regards fiscal and monetary management as less important than structural reforms. Fiscal deficits are more likely to be financed by borrowing from the central bank than from either the domestic or foreign private sectors. Increased public expenditures will be channeled more toward consumption than investment. . . . Across-the-board massive wage increases also accompany . . . populist governments. Because these measures will be felt first in output expansion, especially of wage goods, rather than an acceleration of inflation, . . . the government will be confirmed in the wisdom of its heterodoxy. Pressure on the balance of payments in those early times can be handled by strengthening administrative import-repressing mechanisms, drawing down reserves, and seeking foreign loans.[3]

Ultimately, the general consensus will be that "'things cannot go on like this' and that something must be done. . . . Moderate technocrats may be able to attempt their own stabilization plans, which will come too late. The opposition will move for the kill, culminating in a military coup."[4]

Diaz-Alejandro further observes that after a coup the new authorities will have "some room to maneuver; for a considerable time, they can blame economic difficulties on the deposed populists, and a relieved bourgeoisie, with their property rights confirmed, will contemplate short-term economic hardships with equanimity. Entrepreneurs in particular will find the reestablishment of their authority within factories ample compensation for sluggish sales."[5]

Alejandro Foxley, in turn, notes that

Orthodox policies are being applied today by authoritarian military governments. The relative independence of these governments from popular pressure seems to solve what the monetarists saw as the reason for previous failure: the premature reversal of the policies, caused by the adverse reaction of the social groups most affected, mainly the workers. . . . Obviously, an authoritarian government should have no problem in disciplining the workers and controlling the political and social environment so that a sustained application of a consistent stabilization policy is made possible. Thus, authoritarianism is presented almost as a prerequisite for the success of the orthodox economic policies.[6]

Foxley believes that orthodox policies are the result of an alliance of capitalists and the military, and that the net result is a worsening of the distribution of income in favor of the capitalists. This "conclusion is familiar to political scientists: distribution of income and property rests . . . in the structure of power in society. If this is authoritarian and nonparticipatory and excludes important social groups from the political process, the outcome of the distributive process will almost necessarily be regressive."[7]

It is our purpose here to determine the extent to which these commonly accepted generalizations have been applicable to Brazil during the various periods in which austerity programs were called for—especially since the military takeover in 1964.

The Brazilian Austerity Program Prior to 1964

The implementation and orientation of the austerity program fielded by Brazil's first military government after the 1964 takeover, in contrast to the experiences of the previous democratic governments, provides us with a classic example in favor of the argument that austerity programs work only under authoritarian regimes.

In retrospect, the years of widespread populist support and general economic prosperity enjoyed by the Kubitschek administration (1956–1961) are uncharacteristic of the roughly three decades between World War II and the 1964 military takeover. Looking deeper, we find that Kubitschek was only harvesting the fruits of Brazil's recent and rapid industrialization phase, brought about by the full-fledged adoption of import-substitution industrialization policies.[8] The average yearly growth rate in the period 1956–1962 was an astounding 7.8 percent, and the even longer period of 1947–1962 yielded an average of more than 6 percent[9] (see Table 1.1). The Kubitschek years provided the added benefit of a brief respite from the political turmoil that burdened both previous and subsequent democratic regimes.

From a slightly different perspective, it is interesting to note that military opinion has played an important role in the success or failure of every regime since World War II. Looking specifically at the Kubitschek years, we can see that "the economic boom of the 1950's played a very

TABLE 1.1
Brazil: Annual Growth Rates and Rates of Inflation, 1948 - 1986

	Real GDP	Real Per Capita GDP	Industry	General Price Index
1948	7.4	4.7	11.2	8.3
1949	6.6	4.3	10.1	12.2
1950	6.5	4.0	11.3	12.4
1951	6.0	2.8	6.2	11.9
1952	8.7	5.6	5.0	12.9
1953	2.5	-0.5	8.7	20.8
1954	10.1	7.0	8.7	25.6
1955	6.9	3.7	10.6	12.4
1956	3.2	0.2	6.7	24.4
1957	8.1	4.9	5.7	7.0
1958	7.7	4.6	16.0	24.3
1959	5.6	2.4	11.0	39.5
1960	9.7	6.6	9.3	30.5
1961	10.3	7.2	10.5	47.7
1962	5.3	2.3	7.8	51.3
1963	1.5	-1.3	0.2	81.3
1964	2.9	0.0	5.5	91.9
1965	2.7	-0.4	-4.7	65.9
1966	5.1	1.8	11.7	41.3
1967	4.8	1.5	3.0	30.5
1968	8.4	5.0	13.2	25.5
1969	9.0	5.6	10.8	21.4
1970	9.5	6.0	11.1	19.8
1971	12.0	9.6	12.0	18.7
1972	11.1	8.7	13.0	16.8
1973	13.6	11.2	16.3	16.2
1974	9.7	7.3	9.2	33.8
1975	5.4	4.0	5.9	30.1
1976	9.7	7.3	12.4	48.2
1977	5.7	3.3	3.9	38.6
1978	5.0	2.7	7.2	40.5
1979	6.4	4.1	6.4	76.8
1980	7.2	3.8	7.9	110.2
1981	-1.6	-4.0	-5.5	95.2
1982	0.9	-1.5	0.6	99.7
1983	-3.2	-5.6	-6.8	211.0
1984	4.5	2.1	6.0	223.8
1985	8.3	5.9	9.0	235.1
1986	8.0	5.5	11.3	56.9

Source: *Conjuntura Economica*, various issues.

important part in reinforcing military confidence in civilian leadership and in the basic direction of the economy."[10]

By the beginning of the 1960s, however, the economic stability afforded by the industrialization boom was apparently coming to an end. The multiple problems inherent in rapid growth through industrial expansion could no longer be ignored. Inflation, as measured by the wholesale price index, had risen from 14.3 percent in 1957 to more than 50 percent in 1962[11] (see Table 1.1).

Brazil's foreign debt had already surpassed the $2 billion mark.[12] The internal deficit, bloated by bureaucratic inefficiency in many federal institutions and by high rates of growth-oriented spending, was accounting for an increasing proportion of GDP every year.[13]

Political stability began to erode as well. Even the Kubitschek administration was not immune, as evidenced by the fact that negotiations with the International Monetary Fund over monetary stabilization in late 1958 were broken off when it became clear that the political costs of continuing such a program were too high.[14]

Further attempts to correct structural distortions within the setting of a democratic regime were abandoned as well. Jânio Quadros, taking over the presidency in 1961 with 45 percent of the popular vote behind him,[15] immediately launched an ambitious and orthodox monetary stabilization program, which focused on tightening credit, freezing wages, streamlining government operations, and eliminating inflationary subsidies. He resigned in frustration just seven months later, as the unpopularity of his stabilization measures drew tremendous pressure from many of the same groups that had elected him—this in spite of the fact that the inflation rate was beginning to decline, indicating the relative success of the austerity measures being applied.[16] Tension over the crumbling socioeconomic situation within Brazil became acute after Quadros's resignation. Political and economic decay seemed to be proceeding at an increasingly rapid rate.

Unhappily, the incoming João Goulart administration was viewed by all as a regime with little or no legitimacy in a period of critical importance. Widespread strikes and violence became rampant as grassroots leftist movements and urban labor unions grew stronger, aided in part by the international attitude propagated by the Cuban Revolution.[17] Inflation, which reached more than 100 percent in the first quarter of 1964, spiraled out of control as the fight for shares accelerated. As Baer and Kerstenetzky note,

> There were half-hearted attempts at stabilization soon abandoned when Goulart could not resist the demands of labor leaders for rapid wage adjustments, the demand of the business community to refrain from painful credit restrictions, the pressure from many quarters not to abandon inflationary subsidy exchange rates for the importation of petroleum and wheat, and not to readjust public utility and transportation rates in accordance with the overall price increases.[18]

Goulart, Quadros, and many important civilians from both the Right and the Left began to declare that a basic change in the political system would be a prerequisite to avoiding profound structural damage to the system. The elite classes were becoming uncomfortable with the growing demand for land and other basic reforms. The middle classes watched their salaries erode as inflation progressed and became increasingly hostile toward labor and government, which they viewed as collaborators in worsening inflation.[19]

Within this period, the military was repeatedly called upon to quell violence related to strikes and general social unrest, and military discontent with government policy reached serious levels. According to Einaudi and Stepan, "The civilian population itself widely doubted the regime, and the military no longer trusted civilians to be able to solve the basic structural problems facing Brazil. Given these general socioeconomic trends, the military felt increasingly that the economic and political crisis was contributing to a security crisis and that they themselves might have to assume a much bigger role in the policy process."[20] These events and attitudes culminated in a military takeover at the end of March 1964.

The message, in general agreement with the standard rationale on austerity programs previously outlined, seems clear. Democratic governments, which draw their legitimacy from popular support, are not capable of implementing austerity measures, because of the short-run, net-negative effect that these policies have on the majority of socioeconomic groups, which are the legitimizers of power. In other words, austerity programs attempted by democratic governments are politically suicidal. Kubitschek, Quadros, and Goulart would probably agree.

This brief review of the pre-coup democratic administrations and their experience with austerity provides us with a relevant background against which to evaluate the stabilization program of the military/authoritarian regimes since 1964. The next step is to evaluate the austerity programs of the post-1964 regimes in order to determine if their experiences are also in accordance with the conventional wisdom.

The Post-1964 Stabilization Program
(1964–1967)

The military coup of March 31, 1964, signified the initiation of a radically new phase in the Brazilian experience. The Castello Branco administration (1964–1967), the first of the military authoritarian regimes, began the task of implementing a new brand of centralized authority, the likes of which had not been seen since the Getulio Vargas era of the thirties and forties.[21] Castello Branco and his colleagues within the military establishment had taken upon themselves to salvage a country on the brink of economic and political disaster, and they brought along a wealth of ideological and theoretical baggage upon which they depended heavily in their quest to transform Brazil into a respected player in the international arena.

Castello Branco was largely successful in achieving his goals. What was the formula for this success? How was his government able to organize the socioeconomic nightmare bequeathed to it by the populist predecessor governments? Who would pay the bill for revamping an economic machine stripped of efficiency by the contradictions of three-digit inflation? These and other queries must be dealt with if we are to come to a realistic understanding of the events that followed the 1964 coup.

In the interest of constructing a complete picture of the success or failure of the policies applied by the incoming military government, it is useful to look briefly at the nature of the group that took power. Fundamental changes had been taking place within the military since the end of World War II. Brazil's participation in that conflict would eventually have a dramatic effect on the course of Brazilian politics in the years to follow. Brazilian officers returned from the war having witnessed first-hand the efficiency of the American war machine. In addition, many of the officers in top decisionmaking positions in the Castello Branco and following regimes had attended military schools in the United States—training that was supplemented by attendance at the Superior War College (ESG).[22] After World War II, higher military education in Brazil was characterized by a new emphasis on the social sciences; it created officers who could be economic planners as well as battlefield strategists. The overall intellectual enlightenment that resulted from such training, in addition to a growing concern within the military over political and economic events in Brazil, helped promote the rise of a phenomenon described by Alfred Stepan as the "new professionalism."[23]

The "new professionals" differed from the traditional military in that they viewed threats to national security as having become internal; the assumption was that subversive movements emanated from a militarized Left, dedicated to the complete upheaval of society followed by radical reform. In contrast to the U.S. military, in which professionalism signifies rigid exclusion from the political arena, broadly trained Brazilian officers felt themselves increasingly competent to resolve the crisis associated with political confusion and economic stagnation, which they linked directly to internal security. In addition, military doctrine identified internal stability as a precursor for national growth and development, which were included within the scope of military concern.[24]

In light of these new attitudes, the military reaction to Brazil's internal troubles was predictable. As Stepan has observed, "In their studies of the political system the new professionals had, since the early 1960's, moved toward the position that (1) numerous aspects of the economic and political structures had to be altered if Brazil were to have internal security and rational economic growth, and (2) the civilian politicians were either unable or unwilling to make these changes."[25]

It was on the basis of this rationale that the Brazilian military not only intervened, as it had done on numerous occasions in the past, but also remained in power, identifying itself as the only institution capable of controlling the crisis and reforming the system.

The Castello Branco regime wasted no time in setting out to cure the economic woes of the country. Bringing into play the new power bestowed upon his regime by the "revolution," he entrusted the economic planning of the country to two civilian technocrats well-versed in the implementation of orthodox austerity measures: Roberto Campos and Octavio Bulhoes. In the space of just a few months, they hammered out the Programa de Ação Economico do Governo (PAEG), "a short-run economic policy program aimed at controlling inflation and correcting distortions which had developed in the economic system out of both the one-sided rapid Import Substitution Industrialization of the fifties and the long period of inflation."[26] This plan carried with it all the trappings of a classic stabilization program; as such, it almost automatically drew heavy criticism from a wide range of socioeconomic groups. The austerity measures adopted were not unlike those attempted (with little success) by the earlier democratic administrations. The vital difference in the 1964 experiment was the political shielding afforded Campos and Bulhoes by their association with the military regime, which was essentially immune to public opposition.

A brief examination of the stabilization measures and their ramifications will provide some insight into how Castello Branco and the technocrats succeeded where his democratic predecessors had failed.

Wage repression can probably be identified as the principal tool used by Campos and Bulhoes to fight inflation, which they saw as being pulled by excess demand. By allowing wage increases to lag behind increases in the cost of living, real wages were reduced by 20 to 25 percent in the three-year period from 1964 to 1967 (see Table 1.2). As Thomas Skidmore points out, "it is difficult to imagine how such a 'corrective' wage policy could have been carried out by a government that had to face a test at the polls. . . . Given the 'political cover' of a military regime, the technocrats were able to carry out a stabilization policy which weighed most heavily on one social sector—the working class."[27]

Having singled out the huge government deficit as another factor that fueled inflation, the Castello Branco administration began to eliminate the cost subsidies that had contributed to the individual deficits of state-owned enterprises, such as railroads, shipping, and the oil industry. In addition, public utility rates were corrected for inflation. These policies translated directly into increased expenses for individual consumers. It is highly unlikely that any democratically elected government could have withstood the tremendous public protest such a measure would have caused.[28]

In an attempt to force the private sector to purge itself of the bad habits it had adopted during inflationary periods, publicly subsidized credit from the Central Bank, normally applied during a liquidity crisis, was eliminated. This type of corrective stabilization prompted a severe "financial purification" of the business sector. Meanwhile, as foreign firms were not dependent on Brazilian government financing, they were not affected by these measures. As a result, various Brazilian businesses

TABLE 1.2
Brazil: Real Wages and Employment

(a)   Real Minimum Wage Index, 1949-1975

1949	57	1965	118	1972	103
1959	169	1966	110	1973	107
1960	137	1967	105	1974	101
1961	158	1968	107	1975	104
1962	139	1969	102		
1963	131	1970	100		
1964	129	1971	100		

(b)   DIEESE Index of Real Wages, 1961-1976

	1961	1966	1971	1976
Unskilled	100	70.2	58.9	58.2
Semiskilled	100	73.7	85.6	76.3
Skilled	100	86.5	94.1	108.3
Foremen	100	73.4	103.5	102.0
Managers	100	85.0	111.1	121.5

(c)   Index of Real Minimum Wages, 1969-1985

1969	100	1975	114	1981	118
1970	109	1976	115	1982	119
1971	109	1977	115	1983	107
1972	112	1978	118	1984	102
1973	116	1979	117	1985	105
1974	108	1980	119		

(d)   Yearly Growth Rate of Real Industrial Wages, 1976-1985

1976	17.6	1981	2.9
1977	5.4	1982	6.7
1978	13.5	1983	-16.2
1979	-0.2	1984	16.1
1980	13.6	1985	32.1

(e) Index of Industrial Employment, 1975-1985 (1978 = 100)

1975	89.7	1981	99.9
1976	95.5	1982	95.0
1977	97.3	1983	87.6
1978	100.0	1984	87.4
1979	103.5	1985	94.8
1980	107.3		

Sources: (a) Samuel Morley, Labor Markets and Inequitable Growth: The Case of Authoritarian Capitalism in Brazil (Cambridge: Cambridge University Press 1982), p. 184; (b) ibid., p. 187; (c) Conjunctura Economica and Boletim (Banco Central do Brasil, various issues); (d) ibid.; (e) ibid.

could be purchased with foreign capital, causing a widespread nationalistic outcry. This reaction, predictably, was ignored by the military establishment, but it is unlikely that such a move would even have been suggested in a democratic setting.[29]

In an effort to increase government receipts, Campos and Bulhoes embarked on an ambitious campaign to streamline the tax collection system, substantially augmenting the number of individual income tax payers. But, as one might deduce, the new taxpayers were unable to seriously resist this move in an environment of a military-authoritarian government.

In addition, substantial efforts were made to reform the country's export sector, attract foreign capital, woo the IMF and the U.S. government, and reshape government coffee policy. Each of the measures mentioned above contributed significantly to achievement of the goals of stabilization and long-run growth. But, as might have been predicted, each of these policies was highly criticized by the various sectors that stood to lose in the wake of their implementation.[30]

Was the Castello Branco government successful in its stabilization efforts? The answer is complex. Clearly the rate of inflation was reduced substantially, from more than 100 percent in the first quarter of 1964 to around 21 percent by the end of 1969 (see Table 1.1). In addition, many of the distortions caused by inflation were eliminated. The government budget deficit, which had significantly contributed to the high inflation rate, was brought down from 4.2 percent of GDP in 1963 to around 1.1 percent in 1966.[31] Campos and Bulhoes had been more or less successful in putting a damper on Brazil's demand-pull inflation. The measures implemented played an important role in creating a stable environment for the growth-oriented policies of the subsequent administrations. It is tempting to say that even the growth-boom of the late 1960s and early 1970s would not have occurred without the economic "sanitation" carried out by the Castello Branco government.

But such economic stability came with a price, and that price was paid by Brazil's working class. As mentioned earlier, one of the most important stabilization tools was wage repression. Although other factors contributed to the problem, the net result of this wage policy was to substantially worsen Brazil's distribution of income. Between 1960 and 1970, the lower 80 percent of the population lost almost 9 percent of its share in the national income, whereas the upper 5 percent increased its share by a similar amount.[32] In addition, one must weigh the importance of the substantial foreign takeover of domestic businesses.

The Impact of External Shocks
Under the Geisel Administration

The 1973 oil shock imposed some major changes on oil-dependent economies throughout the world and in Brazil. It marked the presidency of General Geisel. In Brazil, the incoming Geisel administration, whose term began in March 1974, had to deal with the resulting energy crisis. One immediate consequence of the shock was a gigantic deficit in the balance of payments, caused mainly by the quadrupling of oil prices. As Antonio Barros de Castro mentioned in his recent book *A Economia Brasileira em Marcha Forcada*, "The conventional economic wisdom takes into account two possible answers [to such an international shock]: financing or adjustment."[33] The latter, which would have avoided the huge trade deficit by means of a substantial decline of non-oil imports, would have implied a drastic decline of the country's rate of growth.

Brazil, however, opted for growth through international borrowing. This borrowing was facilitated by an abundant supply of petrodollars in the international banking system. In addition, industrial countries facing slowed growth rates due to adjustment policies decreased their demand for those funds.[34]

Brazil's option for growth was made clear in the Second National Development Plan (II PND), which was presented by the new government in 1974. It had the following main goals:

- "Consolidation of a modern economy through the implantation of new sectors, the creation and adaptation of new technologies.
- Adjustment to the world's new economic reality.
- New stage in the National Integration effort.
- A strategy of social development oriented towards (1) the assurance to all classes, in particular the middle and working classes, of substantial increases in real wages; and (2) the elimination in the short-run of any absolute misery."[35]

The Geisel administration was thus committed to promote a rise in the standard of living of the general population. This was to be achieved by raising real wages. However, in order to avoid having to force sacrifices on different sectors, the price-control agency (Conselho Interministerial de Preços, or CIP) allowed many prices to be adjusted in response to cost increases, especially those caused by higher labor and energy prices. Therefore, to avoid sectoral clashes within a climate of a gradual political opening, a rising level of inflation was tolerated. Moreover, in order to promote continued growth the government encouraged large investments in such sectors as energy, mining, and heavy industry. The government development bank (BNDES) helped to finance the expansion of the capital goods industry. In the field of energy, Petrobras (the government petroleum company) greatly increased oil extraction, both within Brazil and abroad, gradually making Brazil the third largest petroleum producer in Latin America (after Mexico and Venezuela). Huge projects to develop alternative sources of energy were also initiated, including the construction of massive hydroelectric dams (Itaipu and Tucurui) and large-scale investment in an alcohol program.

There is little doubt that in 1974 the Brazilian government decided to promote "growth at any cost" by means of foreign indebtedness, and that it was willing to accept a resurgence of inflation in order to keep social peace. The reasons for this choice are yet to be fully explained. One possibility was the general political situation. The opposition party had made significant gains in the November 1974 election, partly as a result of the initial recessive measures taken to absorb the first impact of the oil shock.[36] The Geisel administration, though still an authoritarian government, committed itself to a gradual political opening. This commitment, if associated with severe austerity measures, could have prompted considerable criticisms and pressures that might have made a continued political opening difficult.

Another explanation for the 1974 option was given by Antonio Barros de Castro, who referred to it as the "economic rationality." The "economic miracle" of the previous administration had left a number of projects only partially completed, and it made little sense to interrupt them. Such interruption would only have caused substantial losses and a general reversal of investment expectations. Moreover, the terms of trade severely deteriorated as a result of the shock. Although the costs of imports greatly increased, the ability to export remained the same. Brazil thus found it necessary to reduce its dependence on foreign products. The choice of financing entailed a long-run adjustment, since most of the projects of the Second Development Plan could be completed only by the end of the 1970s or early 1980s.[37]

The choice made in 1974 was a target of criticism as well. Several economists, including the twice-minister Delfim Netto, accused the Geisel administration of delaying problems by rejecting an immediate adjustment. Others pointed out that the increasing nationalization of some sectors of the Brazilian economy could quickly transform it into a socialist economy. Entrepreneurs also disagreed with government priorities. They placed greater emphasis on the Itaipu hydroelectric dam and the Steel Railroad (Ferrovia do Aço), whereas the government viewed oil extraction and steel industry expansion as more important. Finally, according to Antonio Barros de Castro, the economist Carlos Lessa criticized the Geisel administration for using the "State as subject and society as object." In other words, the Second National Development Plan had no real base, inasmuch as it was planned and implemented without any consultation of the society at large.[38]

It is difficult to imagine what would have happened if an immediate adjustment had been opted for in 1974. It is clear, however, that the chosen strategy prepared Brazil for the international disturbances of 1979.

The Geisel option still falls into the traditional paradigm. In this case, however, the situation is viewed from the opposite angle. Austerity in the mid-1970s would have called for substantially reduced growth so that resources could be transferred abroad to pay for oil through reduced imports. Increased unemployment as well as depressed wages and real income in many sectors would have been the result. And as this situation would have placed the gradual political opening in jeopardy, growth with increased foreign indebtedness and inflation was the option taken.

The Debt Crisis and Austerity (1981–1983)

The debt crisis of the early 1980s was brought about by three events—the second oil shock of 1979, the dramatic rise of world interest rates, and the world recession. Brazil's trade deficit increased from US$1 billion in 1978 to US$2.7 and US$2.8 billion in 1979 and 1980, respectively (see Table 1.3). Imports had risen by more than 70 percent, as a result of the drastic decline in the terms of trade, and petroleum rose to 45 percent of total imports in 1980. There was a steady decline of foreign exchange reserves, so that the net reserve/import ratio dropped from 71 percent in December 1978 to about 13 percent in September 1980. In addition, the rate of inflation had risen from 40.5 percent in 1978 to 76.8 and 110.2 percent in 1979 and 1980, respectively.

President Figueiredo took office in March 1979. His major political project was the final transition from military to democratic/civilian government. Given the increasingly precarious situation of the balance of payments and domestic prices, his economic team—under the leadership of Planning Minister Mario H. Simonsen—tried to implement a number of orthodox austerity measures, which would have implied a considerable slowdown of the economy.[39] Since his program found no political support, including that of the president, Simonsen resigned in August 1979 and was replaced by then Agricultural Minister Delfim Netto. The latter reversed policy gears by ruling out a recession to solve the foreign deficit and inflation problems. He cut nominal interest rates by 10 percent and proceeded with a strong stimulative program for agriculture as a major way of stopping inflation. Then, in October 1979, Congress approved a law proposed by the government that reduced the interval between wage adjustments from one year to six months. The law, which was to take effect in November, increased the degree of wage indexation at the same time that the economy was undergoing various inflationary shocks.

As the rate of inflation increased in the second half of 1979, a maxi-devaluation was decreed at the end of that year. This was followed in 1980 with various measures to fight inflation through a reversal of expectations; exchange-rate corrections and indexation for 1980 were pre-announced at 40 and 45 percent, respectively, and inflation was already past the 100 percent level. As 1980 progressed, most of the benefits of the maxi-devaluation were lost and savings declined drastically.

By the end of 1980, the government was forced to reverse gears again and institute orthodox austerity measures that led to an economic downturn. The austerity program consisted of decreases in capital ex-

TABLE 1.3
Brazil's Balance of Payments: Selected Items (Millions of US$), 1955 - 1986

	Exports	Imports	Trade Balance	Net Interest & Dividends	Current Account
1955	1,419	-1,099	320	-78	2
1956	1,483	-1,046	437	-91	57
1957	1,392	-1,285	107	-93	-264
1958	1,244	-1,179	65	-89	-248
1959	1,282	-1,210	72	-116	-311
1960	1,269	-1,293	-24	-145	-478
1961	1,405	-1,292	113	-145	-222
1962	1,214	-1,303	-90	-136	-389
1963	1,406	-1,294	112	-87	-114
1964	1,430	-1,086	344		140
1965	1,596	-941	655		-247
1966	1,741	-1,303	438	-197	54
1967	1,654	-1,441	213		-304
1968	1,881	-1,885	26		-530
1969	2,311	-1,993	318	-263	-312
1970	2,739	-2,507	232	-353	-583
1971	2,904	-3,245	-341	-420	-1,321
1972	3,991	-4,245	-244	-650	-1,494
1973	6,199	-6,191	7	-1,037	-1,715
1974	7,951	-12,641	-4,690	-1,618	-7,147
1975	8,670	-12,210	-3,540	-2,039	-6,964
1976	10,128	-12,383	-2,255	-2,419	-6,017
1977	12,120	-12,023	97	-2,917	-4,037
1978	12,659	-13,683	-1,024	-3,903	-6,990
1979	15,244	-17,961	-2,717	-5,983	-10,742
1980	20,132	-22,955	-2,823	-7,767	-12,807
1981	23,680	-22,086	1,594	-10,675	-11,734
1982	20,213	-19,396	817	-13,136	-16,311
1983	21,899	-15,429	6,470	-11,008	-6,838
1984	27,005	-13,916	13,089	-11,471	45
1985	25,639	-13,168	12,471	-11,191	-268
1986	22,393	-12,866	9,527	34	-2,519

(table continues)

penditures of state enterprises and a ceiling of 50 percent over the nominal values of December 1980 for loans to the private sector. In addition, interest rates were decontrolled (except for loans to agriculture, energy projects, and exports), and the growth of the money supply and the monetary base were limited to 50 percent. The basic goal was to reduce foreign exchange needs by reducing domestic absorption.

The effect of these measures on inflation was almost nil, as price increases continued at annual rates of about 100 percent. Although the trade balance improved (despite a further decline in the terms of trade), the rise of international lending rates by about 4 points caused interest payments to absorb about 40 percent of export earnings. The combination of government policies, rising world interest rates, and the world recession

TABLE 1.3 (cont'd.)

	Loans	New Direct Investment	Amortization	Reserves	Foreign Debt
1955			-140	491	
1956			-187	611	1,836
1957			-242	476	1,913
1958			-324	465	1,962
1959	439	124	-377	366	2,024
1960	348	138	-417	345	1,955
1961	579	108	-327	470	2,207
1962	325	69	-310	285	2,457
1963	250	30	-364	215	2,527
1964	363	28	-277	214	2,502
1965	266	154	-304	483	2,725
1966	508		-350	425	2,956
1967	530	115	-375	199	3,372
1968	583	61	-484	257	3,780
1969	1,023	177	-493	656	4,403
1970	1,433	132	-672	1,187	5,295
1971	2,037	168	-850	1,746	6,622
1972	4,299	318	-1,202	4,183	9,521
1973	4,495	940	-1,673	6,416	12,571
1974	6,886	887	-1,920	5,269	17,166
1975	5,932	892	-2,149	4,041	21,171
1976	7,772	959	-2,888	6,544	25,985
1977	8,424	810	-4,060	7,256	32,037
1978	13,811	1,071	-5,170	11,895	43,511
1979	11,228	1,491	-6,385	9,689	49,904
1980	10,596	1,121	-5,010	6,913	53,847
1981	15,553	1,584	-6,436	7,507	61,411
1982	12,515	991	-6,952	3,994	69,653
1983	6,708	664	-9,120	4,563	81,319
1984	10,401	1,077	-6,468	11,995	91,091
1985	7,010	710	-8,890	11,608	93,313

Sources: *Conjuntura Economica* (various issues); *Boletim* (Banco Central do Brasil, various issues).

caused Brazil to enter a deep recession (the worst since World War II). In 1981, real GDP declined by 1.6 percent and industrial production declined by 5.5 percent. Exports declined by US$3 billion due to a fall of export prices by 6 percent and of export quantum by 9 percent.[40] The overall situation remained essentially unchanged in 1982, although real GDP growth was a positive 0.9 percent. Per capita GDP declined by 1.5 percent, however (see Table 1.1).

The situation worsened in August 1982 with the Mexican debt moratorium, which closed international capital markets for Brazil (and most other debtor nations), and at the end of the year the country was forced to turn to the IMF (a move that authorities had previously declared unnecessary because of Brazil's supposed capacity to deal with the debt/inflation problem by itself).

When IMF supervision and approval of programs were named as the conditions for debt renegotiation, Brazil's policymakers became increasingly bound to follow IMF directives, which were listed in a series of letters of intent. In order to achieve balance-of-trade surpluses (a means of ensuring uninterrupted debt servicing) and to reduce the inflation rate, the IMF pressured the government to step up its recessive measures; which entailed (1) stepping up devaluation (leading to a new maxi-devaluation in February 1983); (2) cutting overall credit by 50 percent; (3) reallocating credit to the export- and import-substitution sectors, which caused credit shortages in other parts of the economy and extremely high real interest rates in nonfavored sectors; and (4) cutting government expenditures. As the government was viewed as complying insufficiently with IMF requirements (because it failed to reduce its deficit at a fast enough rate), a series of further negotiations and letters of intent kept up the pressure to step up restrictive policies, including a decline of wage indexation.[41]

The net result of the IMF-induced restrictive measures was a deepening of the recession: Real GDP declined by 3.2 percent in 1983, industrial production decreased by 6.8 percent (and capital goods by 20 percent); and employment, which had declined by 11.3 and 5.3 percent in 1981 and 1982, respectively, fell by 5.6 percent in 1983. The balance of payments recovered in 1983, however, when a trade surplus of US$6.5 billion was reached due to an export growth of US$1.7 billion and an import decline of US$4 billion (see Table 1.3). This latter decline was induced by the decrease in income and was also, in part, due to the results of the import-substitution investment process of the 1970s.

While Brazil was forced to undergo its worst recession since the 1930s, the political opening process continued unabated. Free congressional elections were held in November 1982 after censorship and repression disappeared, culminating in the transfer of executive power to an opposition civilian candidate in March 1985.

This period presents a clear contradiction to the traditional paradigm, as an extremely severe austerity program was carried out in a rapidly decompressing political atmosphere. There were no threats of severe general strikes and other types of resistance by economic groups, which might have led the military to reverse the democratization process.

What are the possible explanations? At this time we can offer only hypotheses that will have to be tested in the future as more information becomes available. First, after twenty-one years of military rule, during a decade in which a gradual, but continuous, political decompression occurred and President Figueiredo repeatedly promised to return the country to civilian rule at the end of his term in office, the expectations of most groups for a new regime were so high that none wanted to jeopardize its advent through provocative actions. Second, the economic crisis was seen by many as having been imposed by the outside world, thus reducing the responsibility of the government for the economic decline. As this crisis was essentially caused by the second oil shock, the rise of international interest rates, and the recession in the industrial countries, Brazilian policymakers had no alternative but to plunge the economy into a recession. Third, Brazil's capitulation to the IMF was not a unique event on the world scene; many other Latin American countries had also capitulated as a result of the general debt crisis. Convenient internal scapegoats were thus difficult to find. Fourth, Brazil's compliance with IMF conditions was slow and incomplete, thus salvaging the image of the Brazilian government somewhat. In other words, it was seen as very reluctant to impose austerity on the country. Finally, even if the government had found it necessary to use political repression, it would probably have been unable to do so as the political opening process had already gone past the point of reversal.

The Cruzado Plan: Adjustment Without Austerity?

Our last case study concerns the most recent attempt at economic stabilization with the introduction of the Cruzado Plan on February 28, 1986. In the last year of the military government (1984) and the first year of the new civilian government of President José Sarney (1985), the economy began to grow again. Real GDP grew at 4.5 and 8.3 percent in 1984 and 1985, respectively. As the high rate of growth in 1984 was linked to the rapid economic recovery of the U.S. economy, Brazilian exports increased by US$5 billion; the high growth rate of 1985 has been due to a 15 percent increase of real wages and a nearly 30 percent increase in the income of the wage sector, which led to a very rapid expansion of consumer sales. In both years the country managed to produce extremely favorable trade surpluses of US$13 and US$12.5 billion, respectively. The only negative factor was the continued high rates of inflation of 224 and 235 percent in 1984 and 1985.

As the inflationary situation seemed to be getting out of control in early 1986, approaching the yearly rate of almost 300 percent in February, President José Sarney issued Decree Law (DL) 2283 on February 28. It (and its revised version, DL 2284) imposed the following measures: (1) a general price freeze and a partial freeze of wages and other earnings;[42] (2) a prohibition of contracts of less than one year with indexation clauses; and (3) the creation of a new currency, the *cruzado*, which replaced the old *cruzeiro* (1 Cz$ = 1,000 Cr$). There was no specific reference in the decree laws to the exchange rate, but it appeared that the government was to keep it fixed at Cz$13.84 per US$1.00.[43]

The new plan reflected the influence of economists who diagnosed Brazil's inflation as being mainly of the "inertial" type.[44] They had gradually gained the upper hand in the new civilian government, against those groups who viewed inflation in an orthodox fashion and had pressured for traditional austerity measures leading to another recession, which was politically unacceptable.

The immediate impact of the plan was quite positive from both the economic and political points of view. The monthly general price index declined from a 22 percent increase in February 1986 to a fall of 1 percent in March, a further fall of 0.6 percent in April, a rise of 0.3 percent in May, and a rise of 0.5 percent in June. Meanwhile, economic growth accelerated in the first half of 1986—a surge that was led by consumer durables, automobiles, tractors, and so on.

The major aim of the plan's price freeze was to stop inflation. The freeze amounted to an incomes policy. Its drastic nature, coming after an inflation that seemed increasingly out of control, rallied the population behind the president, with millions of citizens volunteering as "Sarney's price inspectors" (*fiscais do Sarney*) to report on price cheating. This popular enthusiasm made an incomes policy quite feasible in the short run. That is, even those sectors caught behind at the time of the freeze were willing to remain briefly at a relative disadvantage for the sake of stabilization. Within a few months, however, a number of problems began to arise that seemed to seriously challenge the plan's ultimate success.

Although the freeze was supposed to reverse inflationary expectations and thus stop the inertial aspects of inflation, its negative side effect was to temporarily eliminate the functioning of the price mechanism as an allocator of resources. Maintaining the freeze too long would have resulted in serious distortions. The most worrisome aspect was the reaction of those sectors caught behind in their price readjustments at the time of the freeze and thus less and less inclined to continue at a disadvantage as time went on. Although all government economists agreed that the price freeze had to be temporary, there was considerable uncertainty over how and when the freeze would be lifted. The major fear was that a premature unfreezing would once again reintroduce inflationary expectations and bring about a renewed situation of inertial inflation.

By mid-1986 it had become increasingly clear that the continued price freeze, without readjustments, would bring along shortages (as was the case with meat and milk). Rather than change the relative price of such products, the government decided to import them. The policymakers were thus willing to spend foreign exchange reserves on food imports in order to preserve the price freeze instead of spending them on imported capital goods.

Public utility (especially electricity) prices were also caught behind by the freeze. As a result, the deficits of the state public utility companies increased, and pressure was placed on the government to subsidize both their current and capital projects. The latter could not be postponed if bottlenecks were to be avoided as rapid growth continued.

Finally, the government became increasingly preoccupied with various attempts to bypass the freeze. In particular, it raised prices by offering "new products," cheated on the contents of packages, and required "side-payments," or premiums (*agios*) to furnish various types of consumer durables or to supply components to manufacturing firms.

The Cruzado Plan contributed to a continuation (and even an acceleration) of economic growth, much of it based on consumer spending. The latter was stimulated by the substantial increase of real wages; the elimination of indexation from savings deposits, which caused a large exodus from savings banks (many of these funds were spent on consumer goods); and the price attractiveness of many goods whose relative prices were lagging at the time of the freeze.

As the boom continued, many sectors approached capacity, but there was little investment to increase it. Public investments had been cut back due to previous stabilization efforts, and the price freeze made it difficult for many public utility firms to generate internal funds to finance investments. Private investments were low due in part to lingering skepticism about the ultimate success of the plan and in part to the prejudicial position of the many firms caught behind the freeze.

The overall low investments of the mid-1980s were the result of a low savings rate. Whereas in the mid-1970s the investment/GDP ratio had reached 25 percent, it declined to 16 percent in the mid-1980s. Not only were savings low but, because of the foreign debt situation, Brazil had become a net exporter of capital amounting to about 5 percent GDP.

An interesting by-product of the Cruzado Plan was a rapid rise in the money supply. For instance, M_1, which declined by 6.3 percent in January and rose by 12.9 percent in February, suddenly increased by 76.9 percent in March and 20.4 percent in April. These surges reflected a rapid increase in the demand for money resulting from the sudden decline of inflation. Thus, to the extent that the increased money supply accommodated the increased demand for money, it had no inflationary impact; moreover, continued budget deficits financed by money creation had no immediately harmful inflationary effect. However, by mid-1986 the limits to such noninflationary money expansion had not been clearly defined.[45]

In spite of the growing supply problem resulting from the continued price freeze,[46] the government was determined to maintain the freeze. Aside from importing food products, it tried to meet some of the supply problems by lowering corporate taxes for firms that had fallen behind in the freeze rather than by allowing them to increase prices. The implied outcome, of course, was lower tax revenues. At the same time, the freeze on public utility rates, especially electricity, increased the deficit of state utility companies and led to larger government subsidies. Falling tax revenues, combined with rising expenditures, increased the government budget deficit.

In July, the government tried to cope with a number of accumulated problems. To increase investments and decrease consumption, it imposed a 25 percent tax on international travel and instituted a compulsory savings scheme that included a 30 percent "tax" on new cars and a 28 percent "tax" on gasoline. These "taxes" were considered to be loans, since they would be returned to the consumers of these products in the form of equity shares in a National Development Fund. The funds would then be invested in major development projects, thereby leading to a higher investment-to-GDP ratio.[47]

The refusal of the government to consider any price adjustment was probably motivated by two considerations. First, since the freeze came to symbolize the political success of the plan, President Sarney was reluctant to tamper with it, at least until after the crucial November elections to the new constituent assembly. Second, because the Cruzado Plan allowed wages to automatically rise every time that accumulated inflation reached 20 percent from a given starting point (at first, the date of the introduction of the Cruzado Plan), policymakers were afraid to permit price increases that might have triggered the adjustment.

As the elections approached, uncertainty grew; and continued shortages led the government to take certain inept actions. The worst example was its attempt to requisition livestock by sending the police to various cattle ranches. In addition, the rise of meat imports and other goods in short supply, and the diversion of exportable goods to the domestic market, reduced the trade surplus from about US$1 billion in August to US$145 million in October and US$107 million in November. The poor trade performance, resulting in a decline of reserves from more than $11 billion dollars at the time of the introduction of the Cruzado Plan to about $3.5 billion at the end of the year, placed Brazil in an increasingly weaker position with its creditors.

Shortly after the November 15 elections, the government announced a dramatic adjustment program that ended the price freeze on some key products. The prices of automobiles were raised by 80 percent; public utilities, such as electricity and telephone rates, by 35 percent; fuels by 60 percent; and cigarettes and alcoholic beverages by 100 percent. The "crawling peg" system of exchange-rate devaluation was reinstituted, and new tax incentives for savers were introduced.

The net result of these measures, combined in early 1987 with wage increases as the automatic trigger mechanism began to function, brought along a widespread resurgence of inflation. In December 1986, prices rose by 7.7 percent, in January 1987 by 16 percent, and in February 1987 by 14 percent. These prices did not include the widespread use of *agios*, which increased many prices to a higher level than the officially quoted ones. By February–March 1987, inflationary expectations had returned with a vengeance, as interest rates passed the yearly rate of 600 percent.

We can provisionally conclude that the Cruzado Plan failed for three reasons. First, the government waited too long to restore the market system. The result was a decline of the social consensus that had been reached at the time of the introduction of the Cruzado Plan, and the reappearance of the "fight for shares"—at first, in a hidden manner through the spread in the use of *agios* and, after November's unfreezing, in a more open way. Second, the manner in which the government tried to make adjustments, especially by excluding the new taxes from the price index, contributed to the crumbling of people's expectations. Third, by failing to control its budget disequilibrium, the government lost its chance of eliminating the non-inertial part of Brazil's inflation. The failure of the Cruzado Plan also led to a new crisis in the country's foreign debt servicing and to the declaration of a moratorium in March 1987.

Concluding Remarks

Until the 1980s, Brazil's experiences with austerity programs and political regimes followed the traditional paradigm, which associates successful austerity programs with politically repressive regimes. Because of political pressures, austerity was never successfully carried out in an open democratic setting. The Geisel administration was an example of a political decompression that could not afford economic regression.

The experiences of the 1980s, which seem to contradict the paradigm, might have been different given the special circumstances that existed at the time. The toleration of economic repression in the 1981–1983 period can be explained in part by the expectations that were raised as the end of the military regime approached and in part by the fact that the sacrifices of the country were shared generally throughout the world.

The Cruzado Plan's stabilization with growth was an initial success because of the willingness of a number of socioeconomic groups to accept a reduced share of the GDP and because of the consumer-based growth. Its collapse was due to the overextended maintenance of the freeze, which resulted in price and allocative distortions. Such distortions proved to be unsustainable from a socioeconomic point of view. The insistence on extending the duration of the price freeze was the result of political considerations. Since the price freeze had transformed Sarney from a position of weakness to one of strength and popularity, it was viewed increasingly as a political rather than just an economic instrument. The continued maintenance of the plan was viewed as a necessary tool to win the November 15th election.

These political benefits had a high cost, however. They undermined the continued viability of the plan. Gradual adjustments at an earlier stage might have sacrificed the ideal of zero inflation, but they prevented the return of inertial and/or fight-for-shares type of inflation. Ultimately, the tables were turned on President Sarney: The government party (PMBD) watched its strong mandate all but disappear following its abandonment of the plan a few days after the November elections.

Finally, if inflation is the reflection of an acute dissatisfaction with the way assets and incomes are distributed in a rapidly urbanizing and industrializing society, we may not see a longer period of economic stability, no matter what short-run experiments are devised to halt the rise of prices.

Notes

1. There is a vast literature on inflation in Latin America. See, for instance, Werner Baer, "The Inflation Controversy in Latin America," *Latin American Research Review* (Spring 1967); Werner Baer and Isaac Kerstenetzky (eds.), *Inflation and Growth in Latin America* (New Haven, Conn.: Yale University Press, 1970); Rosemary Thorp and Laurence Whitehead (eds.), *Inflation and Stabilization in Latin America* (New York: Holmes & Meier Publishers, 1979).

2. Thorp and Whitehead, *Inflation and Stabilization.*

3. Carlos F. Diaz-Alejandro, "Southern Cone Stabilization Plans," in *Economic Stabilization in Developing Countries,* edited by William R. Cline and Sidney Weintraub (Washington, D.C.: Brookings Institution, 1981), pp. 121–122.

4. Ibid., p. 122.

5. Ibid., p. 123.

6. See Alejandro Foxley, "Stabilization Policies and Their Effects on Employment and Income Distribution: A Latin American Perspective," in Cline and Weintraub, (eds.), *Economic Stabilization,* p. 197; see also Alejandro Foxley, *Latin American Experiments in Neo-Conservative Economics* (Berkeley: University of California Press, 1983).

7. Foxley, "Stabilization Policies," p. 225.

8. Werner Baer and Isaac Kerstenetzky, "The Brazilian Economy," in *Brazil in the Sixties,* edited by Riordan Roett (Nashville: Vanderbilt University Press, 1972), p. 105.

9. Werner Baer, *The Brazilian Economy: Growth and Development* (New York: Praeger Publishers, 1983), p. 80.

10. Luigi R. Einaudi and Alfred C. Stepan, *Latin American Institutional Development: Changing Military Perspectives in Peru and Brazil,* Report prepared for the Office of External Research, Department of State, funded by Rand Group (1971). See Part 3 and Conclusion, p. 76.

11. Baer and Kerstenetzky, in Roett (ed.), *Brazil in the Sixties,* p. 112.

12. Ibid., p. 113.

13. Ibid., p. 114.

14. Albert Fishlow, "Some Reflections on Post-1964 Brazilian Economic Policy," in *Authoritarian Brazil,* edited by Alfred Stepan (New Haven, Conn.: Yale University Press, 1973), p. 71.

15. Roett, *Brazil in the Sixties,* p. VII.

16. Baer and Kerstenetzky, in Roett (ed.), *Brazil in the Sixties,* p. 114.

17. Einaudi and Stepan, *Latin American Institutional Development,* p. 80.

18. Baer and Kerstenetzky, in Roett (ed.), *Brazil in the Sixties,* p. 114.

19. Einaudi and Stepan, *Latin American Institutional Development,* p. 77.

20. Ibid., p. 80.

21. Thomas E. Skidmore, "Politics and Economic Policy Making in Authoritarian Brazil, 1937–71," in Stepan (ed.), *Authoritarian Brazil,* pp. 37–38.

22. Riordan Roett, "A Praetorian Army in Politics: The Changing Role of the Brazilian Military," in Roett (ed.), *Brazil in the Sixties,* pp. 25–26.

23. Alfred Stepan, "The New Professionalism of Internal Welfare and Military Role Expansion," in Stepan (ed.), *Authoritarian Brazil*, pp. 47–65.

24. Ibid., pp. 48–53.

25. Ibid., p. 57.

26. Baer and Kerstenetzky, in Roett (ed.), *Brazil in the Sixties*, p. 115.

27. Skidmore, in Stepan (ed.), *Authoritarian Brazil*, p. 20.

28. Baer and Kerstenetzky, in Roett (ed.), *Brazil in the Sixties*, p. 116.

29. Skidmore, in Stepan (ed.), *Authoritarian Brazil*, p. 21.

30. Baer, *The Brazilian Economy*, pp. 96–97.

31. Andrea Maneschi, "The Brazilian Public Sector," in Roett (ed.), *Brazil in the Sixties*, p. 228.

32. Baer, *The Brazilian Economy*, p. 105.

33. Antonio Barros de Castro and Francisco Eduardo Pires de Souza, *A Economia Brasileira em Marcha Forcada* (Rio de Janeiro: Paz e Terra, 1985), p. 27.

34. Baer, *The Brazilian Economy*, pp. 156–157.

35. Castro and Souza, *A Economia Brasileira*, p. 30.

36. Dionisio Dias Carneiro, "Long-Run Adjustment, the Debt Crisis and the Changing Role of Stabilization Policies in the Recent Brazilian Experience," Pontifícia Universidad Católica (PUC)/Rio de Janeiro, *Texto Para Discussão*, No. 109 (June 1985), p. 34.

37. Castro and Souza, *A Economia Brasileira*, pp. 35–40.

38. Ibid., pp. 40–46.

39. Baer, *The Brazilian Economy*, pp. 124–125.

40. Imports stabilized in 1981 and began a dramatic decline the following year, thus enabling Brazil to achieve increasingly larger trade surpluses. The decline of imports was a function of both the recession and import substitution.

41. Edmar L. Bacha and Pedro S. Malan, "Brazil's Debt: From the Miracle to the Fund," PUC/Rio de Janeiro, *Texto Para Discussão*, No. 80 (November 1984), p. 26.

42. Wages and salaries were treated specially in that their average real value for the previous six months was estimated and then raised by 8 percent, and minimum wages were raised by 15 percent. See Gustavo Maia Gomes, "Monetary Reform in Brazil" (Recife, Pernambuco, May 1986), mimeo, pp. 10–11.

43. A full description of the Cruzado decree laws can be found in *Conjuntura Economica* (March 1986); the subsequent issue of this journal (April 1986) contained a lengthy discussion by many of Brazil's leading economists on various aspects of the Cruzado Plan.

44. Shortly after the introduction of the Cruzado Plan, some of its principal contributors (both within and outside the government) published books of essays that contained some of the ideas and theories that had gone into its formulation. See Francisco Lopes, *O Choque Heterodoxo: Combate a Inflacao a Reforma Monetaria* (Rio de Janeiro: Editora Campus Ltda., 1986); Persio Arida (ed.), *Inflacao Zero* (Rio de Janeiro: Paz e Terra, 1986). See especially the essay in the latter by Persio Arida and Andre Lara-Resende, "Inflacao Inercial e Reforma Monetaria," pp. 11–35. See also Eduardo Modiano, *Da Inflacao ao Cruzado* (Rio de Janeiro: Editora Campus, 1986).

45. Claudio R. Contador, "O espaco para o deficit publico em 1986," in *Conjuntura Economica* (April 1986), p. 46.

46. Some economists have also argued that the shortages were due to the redistribution of income that occurred under the Cruzado Plan. With the greater purchasing power of lower income groups, there was a change in the demand

profile; but since the production profile of Brazil was constructed in the light of a demand structure based on a very concentrated distribution of income, the new situation inevitably resulted in excessive demand relative to supply in many sectors. If this argument has a factual basis, the question remains as to how Brazil would face shortages—by rationing or by allowing prices to rise in order to reestablish equilibrium in the relevant sectors. The latter measure would rekindle inflation and thus possibly reverse the more favorable redistribution of income trend that the Cruzado Plan set in motion.

47. Controversy arose over whether the compulsory loans should be incorporated into the consumer price index. Arguing that the loans did not amount to a real price increase because the consumer would be repaid with participatory shares in the fund, the government decided to exclude such loans from its computation of the inflation rate.

2

Austerity Under Authoritarianism: The Neoconservative Revolution in Chile

René Cortázar

Introduction

In the last fifteen years Chile has again become a country of experimentation. A team of neoconservative economists has promised to build the conditions for a "free" economy under the patronage of a most repressive military regime.

This chapter deals with three aspects of this experiment. First, I analyze the main characteristics and distributive effects of the policies applied during this period. My argument is that these policies induced very high unemployment rates, low wages and pensions, a reduction of government expenditure in social sectors, and greater concentration in the distribution of income, consumption, and wealth.

Second, I analyze several aspects of the relationship among objective economic restrictions, the ideology of the economic team, and the characteristics of the political regime. In the third section I argue that at some points in time economic restrictions tended to dominate the agenda. These economic restrictions strongly influenced the more "reactive" aspects of these policies. But, during most of the period, economic policies have been strongly influenced by a neoconservative ideology that oriented the more "transformative" policies of the military regime.[1] The last thirteen years have witnessed a gradual unfolding of a deep neoconservative revolution in Chilean society.

I also argue that the military regime has been a necessary, though not sufficient, condition with respect to the characteristics of the policies applied. Another necessary condition has been satisfied by the existence of a coherent, highly homogeneous, and very well trained economic team. Finally, I comment on the apparent paradox of a weak social and political response to such an extremist experiment on the part of a society that traditionally has been considered very politicized and highly organized—at least when compared with other countries in Latin America.

Economic Policies and
Distributive Results (1973–1986)

I distinguish among three phases in the economic policies applied in Chile during the last thirteen years.[2]

Phase 1:
Deregulation, Privatization, and Closed Economy
Monetarism (September 1973–June 1976)

On September 11, 1973, the Chilean armed forces, led by General Augusto Pinochet, overthrew the Socialist (Unidad Popular) government of President Salvador Allende. When the military government took power, the inflation rate had climbed to a three-digit level, the public-sector deficit had reached 25 percent of GDP, and relative prices were grossly distorted as a consequence of the severely repressed inflation of the Allende years.

The first objective of the new economic policies was to correct the distortions in relative prices, the overvalued exchange rate, and the artificially low real-interest rate. Most prices were freed in October 1973, and the inflation rate for October alone climbed to 87.6 percent, compared to an average monthly rate of 14.6 percent between January and September.[3] Between September and October of 1973, the exchange rate was devalued by 230 percent.[4] Interest rates charged by banks were first raised sharply and then freed completely in 1975.

A second objective of economic policies in this period was to reduce the public-sector deficit—mainly by contracting government expenditures, thereby reducing the relative size of the government. These deficits were supposed to be the ultimate cause of the high growth rate of the money supply and, therefore, according to monetarism, of inflation. The public-sector deficit (including transfers to public-sector firms) decreased from 24.7 percent of GDP in 1973 to 10.5 percent in 1974 and to 2.6 percent in 1975.[5] And inflation dropped from 605.9 percent in 1973 to 369.2 percent in 1974 and to 343.3 percent in 1975.[6]

Even though these first two objectives were basically "reactive" in nature, the specific components of the policy package anticipated some of the elements that later characterized the more "transformative" phases of the military regime's economic policy.

A process of privatization was initiated when private property that had been taken over by workers or by the Allende government was returned to its previous owners. When the Allende government fell, more than 500 enterprises as well as some banks were publicly owned or intervened by the state. By 1980, no more than 15 of those enterprises remained in the hands of the public sector. By 1979, 30 percent of the land expropriated under Allende and Eduardo Frei (1964–1970) had been returned to its previous owners.

Across-the-board tariff reductions were announced at the beginning of 1974, when tariffs averaged almost 100 percent. In 1975, after average nominal tariffs had been reduced to almost half, the government indicated that no tariffs would be above 60 percent by 1977 or above 35 percent by the first semester of 1978. The latter goal was reached in the second semester of 1977; the government then announced the goal of a flat 10 percent (except for cars) for June 1979.

Another feature of the liberalization strategy was the deregulation of the domestic financial system. Interest ceilings were removed, and controls on portfolio composition and credit operations of banks and *financieras* were substantially loosened. In addition, collective bargaining was suppressed and unions were severely limited in the scope of their activities.

The distributive results of this first phase are summarized in Table 2.1. Real wages and pensions, which had been decreasing steadily since 1971, continued to fall.[7] Only minimum incomes experienced a recovery. Unemployment rates soared and social expenditures per capita fell sharply.

Wages and Pensions. The evolution of wages and pensions was basically determined by very restrictive government wage policies. The government decreed mandatory readjustments three or four times a year, and economic agents were not able to establish a significant degree of independence from this official incomes policy.[8]

The readjustment of wages and pensions scheduled to take place in October 1973 was postponed until January 1974, when the government decreed a readjustment of 400 percent relative to the level of January 1973. That was significantly below the rate of inflation in 1973, which, according to the official consumer price index (CPI), was estimated by the National Statistics Institute (INE) at 508.1 percent. It was much lower than the true inflation rate of 1973, which reached 605.9 percent.[9] This "error" in the computation of the inflation rate of 1973 was recognized afterward by government officials. Ramos, who detected this "error," called it "one of the most outlandish tampering operations in the history of the Chilean consumer price index."[10] He did not anticipate what was yet to come.

This statistical juggling was a major cause of the drop in real wages and pensions in 1974. Real wages fell almost 20 percent relative to the first eight months of 1973.[11] Minimum wages for blue-collar wages increased in 1974 as the result of a government policy that equalized minimum income for blue- and white-collar workers. Finally, even though pensions increased in 1974 as compared with their average level of 1973, they diminished when contrasted with those of the first eight months of that same year.[12]

In 1975, readjustments of remunerations were also determined by a discretionary policy that did not follow a predetermined policy rule. The restrictive character of these readjustments was the main cause of the additional drop in real wages and pensions of that year.

Unemployment. The rate of unemployment rose from less than 5 percent in 1973 to almost 22 percent in 1976. The main causes have been

TABLE 2.1
Chile: Economic Indicators

	Real Remunerations			Per Capita Government Social Expenditure	Unemployment Rate	Per Capita GNP	Inflation
	Average Wages	Minimum Income	Pensions Civilians				
	(1)	(2)	(3)	(4)	(5)	(6)	(7)
1970	100.0	100.0	100.0	100.0	5.9	100.0	36.1
1971	122.7	135.9	131.1	128.1	5.2	108.4	26.5
1972	96.1	98.2	83.8	104.0	4.1	105.9	260.0
1973	77.6[a]	83.6	48.3	NA	4.8	97.8	605.9
1974	65.0	102.7	51.3	91.6	9.1	96.7	369.2
1975	62.9	101.8	50.2	74.9	17.6	80.8	343.3
1976	64.7	102.6	52.3	71.1	21.9	82.8	197.9
1977	71.4	105.3	57.0	78.6	18.9	90.0	84.2
1978	76.0	119.3	62.1	78.9	18.0	95.6	37.2
1979	82.2	115.5	72.1	82.7	17.3	101.3	38.9
1980	89.3	115.7	74.3	83.4	16.9	107.0	31.2
1981	97.3	121.0	78.0	84.2	15.1	109.3	9.5
1982	97.6	119.7	83.5	86.8	26.1	89.5	20.7
1983	86.9	93.9	83.2	77.6	31.3	87.4	23.1
1984	87.1	82.2	89.7	76.5	24.7	NA	23.0
1985	83.2	76.6	NA	74.0	21.7	NA	26.4
1986	84.9	71.4	NA	NA	18.5[b]	NA	17.4

[a]First eight months of the year only
[b]Preliminary data

Sources: (1) Banco Central, Boletín Mensual (Santiago, various issues); R.
Cortázar and J. Marshall, "Indice de Precios al Consumidor en Chile, 1970-1978",
Colección Estudios CIEPLAN No. 4, (Santiago, 1980). (2) Superintendency of
Social Security; Banco Central, Boletín Mensual (Santiago, various issues); R.
Cortázar and J. Marshall, op. cit. The data reflect take-home minimum income for
a worker with three dependants. (3) Superintendency of Pension Fund
administrators; Banco Central, Boletín Mensual (Santiago, various issues); R.
Cortázar and J. Marshall, op. cit.; J. P. Arellano, "La situación social en
Chile", Notas Técnicas No. 94, CIEPLAN (Santiago, 1987) (4) M. Marcel, "Gasto
social del sector público en Chile 1979-1983", Notas Técnicas No. 66, CIEPLAN,
(Santiago, 1984); J. Marshall, "El gasto público en Chile 1969-1979: Metodología
y resultados", Notas Técnicas No. 33, CIEPLAN, (Santiago, 1980); J. P. Arellano,
op. cit. (5) E. Jadresic, "Empleo total, empleo sectorial y desempleo en Chile:
1970-85", CIEPLAN (Santiago, 1986) (6) Central Bank, Official National Accounts
(Santiago, various issues). (7) Data for 1970-1978 are revised figures drawn
from R. Cortázar and J. Marshall, op. cit.; data for 1979-1986 from Banco
Central, Boletín Mensual (Santiago, various issues).

mentioned above: a drastic cut in the public-sector deficit and a reduction in the real wage. Both elements, together with the attempt to reduce the rate of expansion in the money supply, triggered a sharp contraction in aggregate demand. Per capita income stagnated in 1974 and dropped almost 15 percent in 1975.

In assessing the employment situation in underdeveloped countries, we must go beyond unemployment statistics and consider the evolution of underemployment. First, self-employed workers in Chile (who represent around one-third of the labor force, as compared with less than 10 percent in most developed countries) do not get laid off during recessions. Normally, hours of work and their average incomes are reduced, and they become underemployed. But they do not increase the unemployment rate as measured by conventional statistics.

Second, because of the partial coverage and low levels of unemployment compensation benefits, many salaried workers who get laid off reenter the labor force as self-employed workers. One characteristic of self-employment and family business in such sectors as commerce and services is the "ease of entry." It is possible to start producing in the market without great amounts of capital, technology, or education. These newcomers increase underemployment among the self-employed, who have to share a reduced level of sales among an even larger number of workers but do not get counted as unemployed.

Hence, the unemployment rate tends to underestimate the employment problems that occur during deep recessions. Unfortunately there is a lack of reliable statistics on underemployment. It is important, however, that we keep this dimension in mind; even if we do not arrive at precise estimates, we must at least consider the potential biases involved in more conventional estimations.

In a country like Chile, with almost no unemployment compensation benefits, the social impact of high and persistent unemployment has been devastating. Unemployment occurs more often among blue-collar workers and the poor than among white-collar workers and professionals, and it is probably one of the most significant distributive results of economic policy in this period.

Social Expenditures. Per capita government social expenditure decreased more than 22 percent from 1974 to 1976 (see Table 2.1). As a result, public programs in several sectors such as education, health, social security, and housing deteriorated. The main cause of this decline was the sharp cut in total government expenditure, as a proportion of total output.[13]

Wealth. In 1970 Chile had 46 public enterprises. And as we have seen, by 1973 around 500 firms had been nationalized or placed under official control by the Allende government. By 1977 no more than 70 of those enterprises remained under the control of the public sector.[14] Foxley has shown that the assets sold to the private sector were severely undervalued because firms were hurriedly privatized in the midst of a huge recession (GNP decreased 13% in 1975), during which liquid assets were very concentrated and access to foreign credit was rationed.[15] Although it is difficult to assess the magnitude of this transfer, indirect evidence (such as the statements made to *Fortune* magazine by Javier Vial, chairman of one of the two largest private conglomerates) is highly suggestive. In the second half of 1981, Vial asserted that "the assets he acquired from the government about six years before were now [in 1981] worth eight times what he paid."[16]

Phase 2:
Recovery, Open Economy Monetarism, and
Institutional Change (June 1976–mid-1981)

Phase 2 was initiated to counter both a recession that was deeper and longer than expected and an upsurge of inflation in early 1976. Stabilization policies changed the emphasis from demand restriction and austerity to curbing cost pressures by revaluing the exchange rate in June 1976 (by 10 percent) and then again in March 1977 (by another 10 percent). The program of tariff reductions continued at an accelerated pace. As a way of influencing inflationary expectations, the government began pre-announcing the exchange rate for subsequent months. At the beginning of 1978, for instance, the value of the exchange rate was pre-announced for the next eleven months.[17]

These policies have been considered the dominant cause of the deceleration of inflation from 197.9 percent in 1976 to 38.9 percent in 1979. But a second cause of the reduction in the rate of expansion of costs and prices was, surprisingly, the manipulation of the consumer price index by the National Statistics Institute. The official CPI indicated rates of inflation for 1976, 1977, and 1978 of 174.3 percent, 63.5 percent, and 30.3 percent, respectively. The corrected CPI showed rates of 197.9 percent, 84.2 percent, and 37.2 percent, respectively.[18] The incidence of these errors was specially important because throughout all these years wages were indexed with respect to the official CPI. The exchange rate was also indexed during most of 1976 and 1977. Therefore, the errors in the computation of the official CPI affected nominal wages and the nominal exchange rate, thus contributing to the reduction in the rate of growth of costs and prices. Moreover, these errors in the computation of the official CPI were responsible for more than half of the reduction in the inflation rate that took place during Phase 2.[19]

In June 1979, after the government had reduced tariffs from an average of almost 100 percent in 1973 to a flat 10 percent (except for cars), the exchange rate was fixed in nominal terms. The government expected domestic inflation to converge rapidly upon world inflation, as predicted by the monetary approach to the balance of payments. But inflation did not respond to what orthodoxy had prescribed. Accordingly, from June 1979 to June 1982, when the first devaluation took place, there was a loss in international competitiveness of some 50 percent.

This loss in competitiveness—together with a deterioration in the terms of trade, a rise in world interest rates, and an increase in spending as the result of a wave of excessive, indeed heady, optimism (stimulated by government officials and foreign banks)—led to the balance-of-payments crisis of 1982.

During this second phase, per capita GNP recovered at more than 5 percent a year. Inflation decelerated. The unemployment rate decreased, though at a very slow pace. There was a gradual recovery in the purchasing power of wages. Pensions and per capita social expenditure also grew, though at a slower rate than per capita income or wages (see Table 2.1).

The presence of an overvalued exchange rate—together with an increase in consumption, investment, output, and employment—made some observers qualify the Chilean economic performance as an economic miracle. The sharp increase in the price of assets, though largely the result of a speculative process, further heightened the optimism of the business community. Prices of stocks, for example, increased ten times in real terms from 1975 to 1980.[20]

The overt enthusiasm of many observers made them overlook the fact that several of these variables had not recovered to the levels of the early 1970s, and that below the surface there were serious disequilibria (an obvious example being the enormous current account deficit). The high unemployment rates and the accumulated deficit of investment, which during the 1970s averaged 25 percent less than historical levels, were less frequently mentioned but certainly not less serious.

Wages and Pensions. Throughout Phase 2, most wages were determined by wage policies that followed a 100 percent indexation rule.[21] The new labor laws of 1979, which made collective bargaining possible for about 10 percent of the labor force, also guaranteed full indexation as the "floor" to wage negotiations.

Decelerating inflation rates, together with wage increases over and above the indexation "floor," induced a gradual recovery in the purchasing power of wages and pensions that more than compensated for the wage reductions produced by the manipulation of the official CPI. By 1981, per capita GNP was 9 percent above its 1970 level, whereas average real wages had barely reached the purchasing power of 1970 and real pensions were still 22 percent below those of the beginning of the 1970s. Only the minimum income for blue-collar workers rose more than the average income (see Table 2.1).

Unemployment. After the depression of 1975, employment grew along with output. Again, as in Phase 1, the evolution of employment was related more to shifts in effective demand than to variations in the cost of labor. Still, the unemployment rate never fell below 15 percent—that is, three times the rate of the pre-1973 period.

Social Expenditure. Even though per capita government social expenditure also recovered slowly during this period, mainly as the result of

TABLE 2.2
Average Monthly Consumption Per Household in Santiago
(in U.S. dollars of June 1987)

Household	1969	1978
20% low income	136.7	94.4
20% lower-middle income	212.2	168.8
20% middle income	280.5	246.9
20% upper-middle income	368.6	379.4
20% high income	800.2	925.8
Average	359.6	363.1

Sources: INE, Household Budget Surveys; Banco Central, Boletín Mensual
(Santiago, various issues); R. Cortazar and J. Marshall, "Indice de Precios al
Consumidor en Chile, 1970-1978", Colección Estudios CIEPLAN No. 4, (Santiago,
1980); Consumer Price Index of the U.S.

the overall increase in economic activity, as of 1981 it was still 16 percent
below the level of 1970.

Consumption. Reliable data are lacking on the changes in income
distribution during this period. But an approximation is possible if we
utilize data on the distribution of consumption.

The INE undertook Household Budget Surveys in Santiago in 1969
and 1978. As Table 2.2 indicates, average consumption was the same
in both years. But its distribution underwent important changes. Whereas
the consumption level of the lower and middle classes deteriorated, the
standard of consumption of the top 20 percent improved significantly.
Even though the starting date for this comparison precedes the Allende
government and thus cannot be used as a demonstration of the changes
in income distribution during the Pinochet regime, it is highly suggestive
of the income inequality that prevailed in Chile by the end of the 1970s.

Wealth. The process of privatization of public-sector firms continued
during this second phase. By 1980 the number of firms under the control
of the public sector had been reduced to 15.[22]

A gradual financial opening of the economy also took place during
these years, however, and until mid-1979 important quantitative restrictions on foreign borrowing prevailed. These restrictions contributed to
the gap between foreign and domestic interest rates. From 1976 to 1979
the cost of foreign credit was less than 10 percent a year, whereas

domestic short-run interest rates reached more than 50 percent a year (in dollars).[23] Those firms and banks that had access to foreign credit (i.e., the largest ones) were able to collect huge rents, thereby contributing to a more skewed distribution of wealth in the private sector.

Finally, the reform of the social security system (to be discussed) also contributed to the concentration of wealth in the private sector.

Institutional Reforms. The improved economic situation injected into the regime a high degree of confidence. The economic team had been tested in its capacity to overcome its initial crisis. And according to the regime, which at this point was dominated by Pinochet himself, it passed the test.

Conditions seemed ripe for the government to turn to the "transformative" aspects of its economic strategy.[24] Its structural objectives began to take on a life of their own. Deregulation, reduction in the scope of government action, new labor laws based on a free market ideology, and the opening up of the economy were presented as objectives in themselves, not merely as means to attain short-run targets such as a reduced rate of inflation. A new ideology—a more doctrinaire view of neoconservative policies—also emerged.

The government announced a set of institutional changes (the "seven modernizations"), which involved labor institutions, social security, education, health, regional decentralization, agriculture, and justice. These changes were intended to bring about decentralization of public institutions, privatizations, and greater scope for the action of the market.

We shall now examine both the new labor laws and the reforms of the social security system. In June 1979, new labor legislation—the so-called Plan Laboral, was put into effect. As a "floor" in collective negotiations, it initially guaranteed workers the conditions in their previous contract—but it readjusted these conditions according to the rate of inflation. Collective bargaining was restored for the private sector at the enterprise level, but labor federations were not allowed to bargain collectively. In practical terms, then, most workers in the agricultural, construction, and commerce sectors were excluded from collective bargaining. Before the military coup, collective bargaining in agriculture took place at the regional level; in construction, it occurred at the sectoral level. Given the small size of enterprises in those sectors, it was very difficult for workers to negotiate at the firm level, as the law required. Workers in the public sector and certain services were also excluded from collective bargaining.

The right to strike has been formally guaranteed to most workers, but under very severe restrictions—especially when compared to the labor laws that existed before the military takeover. The maximum period for a strike was sixty days. After this period workers were assumed to have voluntarily quit their jobs. Firms could hire replacements during the lapse of the strike. The legal protection of union leaders was also restricted. And the employer's cost of firing a worker, in terms of severance payments was sharply reduced. The motivation underlying all of these reforms was to let market forces reign and to prevent the labor union movement from being resurrected as a strong actor in the political scene.

The social security system was changed, in May 1981, from a pay-as-you-go system to an individual savings scheme.[25] Mandatory social security contributions had to be deposited in private firms that were specially created for this purpose. Over the next ten years, these funds will represent more than 20 percent of GDP.

"Let Competition Regulate Social Security" was the slogan of reformers. In fact, the new system ended up costing more to operate than the old one.[26] Moreover, during the first months of implementation of the new scheme, the two biggest private conglomerates concentrated 75 percent of the funds.[27]

In January 1983, as a result of a crisis in the financial sector, the government assumed control of several banks and financial institutions, the two biggest private conglomerates, and the administrations of the pension funds of 80 percent of the workers.[28] After the intervention, the main firms in charge of administrating the social security system ended up under the control of foreign investors. But the main objective of the reformers (or should we call them revolutionaries?) had been attained. They reduced the size of the state, increased the amount of funds to be intermediated by the financial system, and helped to deregulate the workings of the economy.

Phase 3:
Debt Crisis and Orthodox Adjustment Policies (1982–1986)

The external debt crisis in Chile was triggered by the well-known external shocks of 1981 and 1982, which involved a sharp cutback of new lending, a deterioration of the terms of trade, and a drastic increase in world interest rates.[29]

But the crisis was to a large extent also the result of domestic policies that had led to ever-increasing current-accounts deficits. By 1981 the deficit had reached 15 percent of GDP, starting from about 6.4 percent in 1979. The average during the 1960s and 1970s was 3.5 percent of GDP.[30]

A dramatic turning point in government policy took place in June of 1982. After three years of a fixed nominal exchange rate, the government devalued several times, increasing the real exchange rate during the second semester of that year by almost 50 percent. In so doing, it experimented with several exchange-rate regimes. First, it announced a once-and-for-all devaluation, then a clean float, afterward a dirty float, and finally a crawling peg. At the same time it was creating this uncertainty, the government lifted exchange controls, inducing a huge and perfectly avoidable capital flight.[31]

The increase in the exchange rate contributed to a doubling of the rate of inflation, whereas the devaluation together with restrictive monetary and fiscal policies induced a sharp recession.[32] Per capita GNP fell in 1982 by 18 percent (see Table 2.1).

Serious problems also emerged in the financial sector because firms were not able to repay debts that had been growing during the previous six years at annual real interest rates of more than 30 percent. The real magnitude of the stock disequilibria and financial mess did not reveal itself until the government intervened several banks in 1983. Balance sheets indicated that only 2.3 percent of bank loans needed to be characterized as nonperforming assets. After the intervention, however, it was revealed that more than 24 percent of bank loans fell under that classification. The two largest private banks, which channeled one-third of all bank loans, had lost between five and six times their capital.[33]

The government signed a stand-by agreement with the IMF for the period 1983–1984. This agreement required a reduction in government expenditure and restrictive monetary and wage policies.[34] The Extended Fund Facility Agreement with the IMF for the years 1985–1987 had similar characteristics.[35] These agreements were reinforced by a Structural Adjustment Loan from the World Bank. Many countries have had to take similar measures; among them, Chile has followed IMF recommendations most closely.[36]

A new reduction in per capita GNP took place in 1983. From 1984 on, we lack data on GNP; but per capita GDP has been recuperating at a rate of about 1.5 percent a year. Even though inflation accelerated after 1982, it reached a new plateau of about 20 percent, certainly a low rate when compared with most countries in Latin America.

During the period 1982–1986, pensions recovered slowly, average wages dropped 15 percent, and minimum income fell around 40 percent (Table 2.1). Per capita government social expenditure fell by about 15 percent during 1982–1985. Finally, unemployment rates soared, reaching more than 30 percent in 1983. From 1985 on, however, the economic recovery induced a gradual reduction of open unemployment.[37]

Again, as occurred after the depression of 1975, economic recovery has induced a wave of optimism in the business community. The deteriorated confidence of the economic team was boosted also by the open support of the IMF, the World Bank, and the "international business community." The Chilean Economic Experiment, which was declared dead by the end of 1983, had been resurrected with minor modifications. The economic team used this new influx of legitimacy to try to finish the structural reforms that had been interrupted by the crisis of 1982–1983. They focused especially on the process of privatization.

Wages and Pensions. The evolution of wages and pensions was, again, in great measure the result of governmental incomes policies. The government agreed with the IMF that nominal wage increases for the public sector would be held below the projected rate of inflation. Wage settlements in the private sector were to be determined mainly through collective bargaining or individual agreements. (Very high unemployment rates prevailed during this period, as indicated in Table 2.1.) The 100 percent indexation "floor" for workers who bargain collectively was eliminated from labor legislation.

As a result of these policies, average real wages dropped about 15 percent from 1982 to 1985, and rose very slightly in 1986. Minimum income suffered an even more dramatic drop, because of official readjustments. Between 1981 and 1986, minimum income fell 30 percent as compared to average wages (see Table 2.1). Pensions were the object of a more generous readjustment policy and thus continued to recuperate during the crisis (see Table 2.1).

Unemployment. Unemployment increased sharply during the depression of 1982–1983 (see Table 2.1). The policy package of the IMF—which included restrictive income, monetary, and fiscal policies—induced this recession, as it has done all over the rest of Latin America. The main difference in the Chilean case is the intensity and puritanism with which these policies have been applied. From 1985 to 1986, as output began to recover, the rate of unemployment started to fall again.

Social Expenditure. As a result of the general trend in the government budget, per capita social expenditure, which had risen steadily from its low point in 1975 through 1982, dropped once again in 1983, aggravating the difficulties in sectors such as health, housing, and education. By 1985, per capita government social expenditure was 26 percent below the level of 1970.

Wealth. As noted earlier, by the beginning of the 1980s the majority of domestic capitalists were heavily indebted. This situation gave the government tremendous power, given its control of the financial system and its subsidies to debtors. Paradoxically, state control over the private sector became greater than that attained by Allende's socialist reforms.

The magnitude of the subsidies to some of those highly indebted sectors have produced a very significant, and regressive, redistribution of wealth. For example, the cost of the subsidies given to debtors in foreign currency amounts to more than 30 percent of GDP.[38]

During Phase 3, the government has started a new phase in the process of reducing the number of public-sector firms. The plebiscite announced for 1988 may be the beginning of a process of re-democratization. And, not surprisingly, the economic team prepares a state apparatus that is as weak and as absent from socioeconomic decisions as possible.

Regime, Ideology, and Economics:
A Tentative Interpretation

Are the distributive results we have discussed in the previous section the natural outcome of economic restrictions, external shocks, and the need to surmount the macroeconomic disequilibria inherited from the previous regime? Most members of the economic team—in particular those of the so-called Chicago school—would answer affirmatively. According to this view, the economic policies applied were the corollary of an adequate understanding of the basic laws that govern the workings of the economy. The "Chicago school" perceives economics as a solid science with a hard core of very robust theorems. For each problem a precise answer is provided by "the theory." Bad outcomes and economic crises are normally the result of unavoidable shocks, vested interests, or ignorant politicians that impede the application of "sound" economic policies.

In this last section, we shall take a different perspective. The argument here is that the policies applied resulted not only from the reaction to the initial conditions but also from the attempt to provoke a deep revolution—a transformation that went beyond the workings of the economy to redefine many other dimensions of social life.

In short, economic policies were the result of the interplay of three main elements: technical propositions, the ideology of an economic team, and the characteristics of the political regime.

The Unfolding of a Revolution

Phase 1:
Deregulation, Privatizations, and Closed Economy
Monetarism (September 1973–June 1976)

At first the government pursued a "reactive" strategy.[39] The magnitude of the macroeconomic disequilibria it inherited from the Allende period strongly conditioned the design of economic policy. Certain trends had to be reversed: The huge government deficit had to be reduced, price controls that maintained a situation of repressed inflation had to be lifted, and the exchange rate had to be devalued. Given these initial conditions, government officials viewed their policies as the natural implications of technical propositions. There was some debate regarding the proper mechanisms to perform these tasks. But the discussion was certainly of a very technocratic blend.

At the beginning of 1975, inflation began to accelerate, reaching a monthly rate of 21.6 percent in April. At the same time, the drop in the price of copper, among other factors, triggered a balance-of-payments crisis. Monetarists inside the government proposed their standard solution: very restrictive monetary, fiscal, and wage policies. Other supporters of the regime did not agree with the specifics of their policy proposal; they voiced their support for a more gradual stabilization and adjustment program, but were unable to present a coherent policy package backed by an alternative "economic team." The monetarists had won this first round in the struggle for hegemony inside the government.

Gradually it became more evident that economic policy was oriented by a certain ideology—monetarism. Such policy was not just a technical reaction to initial disequilibria. This more ideological interpretation was expressed through the initial reforms undertaken by the regime (described in the previous section): privatization, liberalization, and the suppression of both collective bargaining and a legitimate space for union activity.

At this stage Pinochet had managed to control most of the levers of power of the regime, putting not only the army but the rest of the armed forces as well entirely under his control. Therefore, to attain hegemony the economic team had to convince Pinochet to back its views. If it achieved that end, it would be able to apply a very coherent strategy since no other power group seemed capable of opposing the government's will.

During the first months of 1975, as it prepared to combat inflation, the economic team was faced with the task of overcoming a severe balance-of-payments crisis, partly induced by insufficient external finance. Its restrictive monetary, fiscal, and wage policies produced a dramatic recession that reduced per capita GNP by over 16 percent. The social costs were enormous. But the economic team was able to overcome the crisis of the external sector. It had passed its first exam.

Phase 2:
Recovery, Open Economy Monetarism, and
Institutional Change (June 1976–1981)

Phase 2 started with a new task for the economic team. It had to overcome stubborn inflation. Inflation did not return to its historical level until 1978. Again we could argue that the social costs of the policy were excessive, that the deep recession of 1975 could have been avoided, and that part of the "success" of the stabilization policy was the result of the manipulation of the official CPI. But the fact remains that the "Chicago school" was perceived by Pinochet as having passed its second exam. The "hegemonic bloc" formed by the economic team and Pinochet had been consolidated.[40]

An implicit (or explicit?) division of labor took place. Pinochet would be in charge of the political and military aspects of the regime, and the "Chicago boys" would be in charge of socioeconomic transformations. A surprising aspect of this alliance was the fact that the economic team perceived itself as "liberal" but, at the same time, was willing to accept the obvious inconsistency of attempting to construct a "free society" by means of a ruthless dictatorship. In fact, it was willing to accept a lack of political freedom and a severe restriction of civil rights, including basic human rights, as the price for implementing its neoconservative policies. If pressed, it would argue that economic freedom was a precondition for political freedom, and that it was using this dictatorship to create the "material basis" of a more stable democracy for the future.

During this second phase, a recovery in most economic indicators began to take place. This situation increased the prestige, confidence, and power of the economic team. The "hegemonic bloc" began arguing publicly about the need for a profound revolution. Up to this point it had presented all of its recommendations as the "technical" solution to specific economic problems. Phase 2 was a time of institution building aimed at changing the workings of the economy and other aspects of social life. The "seven modernizations" encompassed labor legislation and unions, social security, education, health, regional decentralization, agriculture, and justice. At this point it was fairly obvious that the government, particularly the economic team, had a "transformative" program, a historical project, that reached far beyond the original targets of overcoming the initial macroeconomic disequilibria. Even though the proposals in this second phase included many technical (or ideologically "neutral") aspects, they were intertwined with strong ideological views that could no longer be denied.

Phase 3:
Debt Crisis and Orthodox Adjustment Policies (1982–1986)

Phase 3 began with a deep crisis. The confidence of the economic team seemed deeply eroded. And a certain consensus emerged; the excessive orthodoxy of economic policies appeared to be at least partly responsible for the crisis. The fixed nominal exchange rate derived from the monetary approach to the balance of payments had decreased competitiveness and helped to induce the debt crisis; and the excessive liberalization of the financial sector had induced the domestic financial crisis. The situation seemed ripe for a more pragmatic policy design. For the first time in eight years, Pinochet named a finance minister (Luis Escobar) who did not agree with the "Chicago school" and who pursued a more heterodox policy. The economy began to recover, though at the cost of a deteriorating external balance. But, more notably, Escobar was not able to establish a new economic team and had to rely on the same technocrats that had dominated the government during the previous years.

As the crisis in the external sector worsened, Pinochet returned power to the economic team. A new generation of technocrats had replaced many of the old ones. Even though their views were basically the same as those of the old economic team, the crisis of 1982–1983 had reduced their dogmatism. They had come to accept the need to regulate certain areas of the economy, such as the financial system. They had learned the advantages of stabilizing certain prices, such as those of wheat and other crops. They had learned about the convenience of a high and stable exchange rate. But they still shared with the old economic team the emphasis on reducing the size of the state, on pursuing further privatizations, and on letting market forces reign in almost all economic and social areas.

They regained the confidence of Pinochet, partly because they had helped him out of another external sector crisis in the past (1975), but also because they were rivaled by no other coherent economic team capable of replacing them.

After 1984, the economy began to recover. Inflation leveled off, and the economy seemed again to be under control. As had occurred after the depression of 1975, a wave of optimism swept among the capitalists and the members of the upper-middle class, who had helped to support the comeback of the economic team.

Another contribution to the resurrection of the "Chicago boys" came from the support they received from international organizations, specifically the IMF and the World Bank. These institutions have granted support to the economic policies pursued by the government at least since Phase 2. Pinochet is aware that his economic team is certainly his best credential in an otherwise adverse international environment, and the foreign bankers as well as the high officials of the international organizations are his best diplomats.

During this third phase, international organizations have not only helped reconsolidate the economic team; they have also contributed to the implementation of the team's favorite policies. The obvious example is that of privatization. As mentioned earlier, the government is pursuing a new round of privatizations, in part because of the political uncertainties of the next few years. This ideological objective of the regime is being backed and legitimized by an equally ideological emphasis on privatizations on the part of the World Bank and other supporters of the Baker Plan.

Capitalists and Workers:
The Silent Civil Society

One of the most striking aspects of this period has been the relative silence of civil society, particularly of capitalists and workers, in the midst of a process of deep socioeconomic transformations.

The workers' silence has been mostly the result of the repressive character of the regime but also, to a certain extent, the result of their own weakness. Between 1973 and 1983 the rate of unionization, as a proportion of the labor force, fell from 27 percent to under 8 percent. It is illustrative to note that, whereas in 1973 there existed more than ten times more unionized workers than unemployed workers, in 1983 the unemployed were triple the number of those who belonged to a union.[41]

To this I should add that, since power in the regime has been concentrated in the hands of Pinochet and his economic team, the labor movement soon realized that it had no possibility whatsoever of influencing governmental decisions. At the same time, it did not have the power to overthrow the government. Thus it ended up opposing the reforms and policies that had been imposed on them from the pinnacle of power.

I must temper this pessimistic diagnosis by pointing out that trade unionism has remained strong in some key sectors such as mining, gas, water, and electricity. Even in the cases of industry and transport, despite their sharp declines, the rate of union membership is still higher than Latin American averages. The labor movement, too, was able to reorganize many of the federations and confederations that had been dismantled and to create new national confederations. Despite setbacks, it was precisely the labor movement that was critical in promoting the national protest mobilizations of 1983 and 1984.

Capitalists also remained fairly silent during most of this period. But, in contrast to labor, they have openly supported governmental policies. In part, this is because policies have, in general, favored capitalist classes. But even during those years in which policies hurt the interests of important segments of the business community, business people did not challenge the government openly. This was the case, for example, during the process of trade liberalization, when the abrupt reduction of tariffs meant that a great number of firms, especially in the industrial sector, went bankrupt.

It is also worth noting that in contrast to what occurred in several other countries in Latin America, the debt crisis did not help to create significant support for democracy among capitalists. It is true that certain sectors of small business supported the social mobilizations against the regime that began in 1983. But, as the movement seemed to radicalize, they rapidly de-politicized again.

Why is this so? One of the reasons for the support that capitalists have granted to the regime is to be found in the characteristics of economic policies. Even though some specific policies could damage specific segments of the business community, privatization, deregulation, and the repression of the labor movement were perceived as favoring capitalists in general (i.e., as a class).[42]

Another reason for this support of the regime derives from the characteristics of the Chilean opposition and the traumatic experiences of the past.[43] Business people have perceived a threatening opposition. According to their view, there exists a strong Leninist Left under the hegemony of the Communist party that seems to represent between one-fourth and one-third of the vote. The same Left, with less than 35 percent of the vote, was able to elect Allende as president of Chile—a traumatic experience that the capitalists are not willing to forget. The other strong political party in the opposition is the Christian Democratic party, which represents about one-third of the vote. Although it currently does not seem threatening to private property and the vital interests of capitalists, the Christian Democratic party has a long history of collaboration with the left and conflicts and lack of mutual trust toward the business community.

Under these conditions of fear and uncertainty, capitalists and their organizations have preferred to remain either silent or loyal to Pinochet and his regime rather than to return to the uncertainties inherent in the reconstruction of democracy.

Regime, Ideology, and Economic Restrictions

In the previous sections I have referred to the interplay of ideology and economic restrictions. The initial stages of Phases 1 and 3 were dominated by the need to overcome acute macroeconomic disequilibria. Consequently, most of the government's attention was concentrated on solving these short-run imbalances. These were the "reactive" aspects of the strategy. But, especially during Phase 2 and in the latter years of Phase 3, the more "transformative" elements of the strategy began to dominate. Here, ideological perspectives played a more crucial role.

But what about the regime? Could we argue that the characteristics of the regime are independent of the economic policies applied? We have already referred to the "division of labor" that took place between Pinochet and the economic team. On the other hand, it seems fairly obvious that, given the levels of social and political organization in Chilean society, and given the political preferences of its electorate in the past, policies such as those applied during these years could not have been pursued in an open political system. The economic team could specialize in the socioeconomic aspects of the strategy, but they needed the repressive apparatus Pinochet was more than willing to provide, to make their policies viable from a political point of view.

This is not to say that the presence of an authoritarian regime is a sufficient condition to explain the neoconservative characteristics of the policies applied during these years. It is obvious that there are several "transformative" strategies consistent with a military regime, such as that of Pinochet. As noted by some of the members of the economic team who feel uncomfortable collaborating with a ruthless dictatorship to build what they believe are the preconditions of a free society, "Had we not been there, someone else would have taken our place." The authoritarian regime was certainly a necessary condition, but another necessary one was the presence of a large team of economists who had been trained in the neoconservative perspective for years, first at the Catholic University and then, after the military coup, at the University of Chile.[44]

Finally, just as the neoconservative economists in Chile required an authoritarian regime to impose their views, Pinochet benefited from the high degree of consistency of their policies, from the strength of their team, and from their strong ideological link with international organizations and the banking community. They helped him attain the legitimacy he required to remain in power, to maintain the enthusiasm of business, and to gain some support, or at least tolerance, from the international community.

Notes

The basic research for this paper was part of CIEPLAN's research program on macroeconomics, which is supported by the International Development Research Center (IDRC) of Canada. The author wishes to thank the editors of this book for their comments. The usual caveats apply.

1. M. A. Garretón, "The Political Evolution of the Chilean Military Regime and Problems in the Transition to Democracy," in *Transitions from Authoritarian Rule: Prospects for Democracy*, edited by G. O'Donnell, P. Schmitter, and L. Whitehead (Baltimore: Johns Hopkins University Press, 1986).
2. See J. P. Arellano, R. Cortázar, and A. Solimano, "Adjustment Policies in Chile: 1981–1985" (1986), mimeo; A. Foxley, *Latin American Experiments in Neoconservative Economics* (Berkeley: University of California Press, 1983); R. Cortázar, "Distributive Results in Chile, 1964–1982," in *The National Economic Policies of Chile*, edited by G. Walton (Greenwich, Conn.: JAI Press, 1985); J. Ramos, *Neoconservative Economics in the Southern Cone of Latin America, 1973–1983* (Baltimore: Johns Hopkins University Press 1986).
3. R. Cortázar and J. Marshall, "Indice de Precios al Consumidor en Chile, 1970–1978," *Collección Estudios Cieplan*, No. 3 (Santiago, 1980).
4. Banco Central, *Boletín Mensual* (December 1973).
5. Banco Central, *Boletín Mensual* (various issues).
6. The inflation rate is measured as the variation in the consumer price index as corrected in Cortázar and Marshall, 1980, *op. cit.* The official index was grossly manipulated by government authorities to understate the level of inflation in 1973 as well as in 1976–1978.
7. After a sharp increase in 1971, real wages and pensions started to decline. Wages, which had normally been readjusted every twelve months, were readjusted on the first of October 1972, after nine months, and again in May 1973, after only seven months. The amount of the readjustments, as a proportion of inflation, also increased. All of these increases, however, were insufficient. The rapid acceleration of the inflation rate of the Allende years produced a reduction in the purchasing power of wages and pensions. See R. Cortázar, "Wages in the Short Run: Chile, 1964–1981," *Notas Técnicas Cieplan*, No. 57 (Santiago, 1983).
8. Cortázar, 1983, *op. cit.*
9. Cortázar and Marshall, 1980, *op. cit.*, p. 198.
10. J. Ramos, "The Economics of Hyperinflation: Stabilization Policy in Post-1973 Chile," *Journal of Development Economics*, Vol. 7, No. 4 (1980), p. 472.
11. Real wages averaged 80.4 for the first eight months of 1973.
12. No readjustments in pensions took place in the last quarter of 1973, and inflation accelerated sharply. Under these conditions, simple arithmetic calculations indicate that the average of real pensions during the first eight months of 1973 was higher than that of 1974.
13. Cortázar, 1985, *op. cit.*, p. 97.
14. Foxley, 1983, *op. cit.*, p. 62.
15. Foxley, 1983, *op. cit.*, p. 66.
16. *Fortune* (November 2, 1981), p. 142.
17. R. French-Davis, "Las Experiencias Cambiarias en Chile: 1965–79," *Collección Estudios Cieplan*, No. 2 (Santiago, 1979).
18. Cortázar and Marshall, 1980, *op. cit.*, p. 161.
19. Cortázar, 1983, *op. cit.*, p. 204.

20. Banco Central, *Boletín Mensual* (various issues).

21. Cortázar, 1983, *op. cit.*

22. Foxley, 1983, *op. cit.*, p. 62.

23. R. French-Davis and J. P. Arellano, "Apertura Financiera Externa: La Experiencia Chilena en 1973–1980," *Colección Estudios Cieplan*, No. 5 (Santiago, 1981), p. 27.

24. Garretón, 1986, *op. cit.*

25. For a discussion of the reforms of the social security system in Chile, see J. P. Arellano, *Políticas Sociales y Desarrollo: Chile 1924–1984* (Santiago: CIEPLAN, 1985).

26. Arellano, 1985, *op. cit.*, pp. 168–171.

27. Foxley, 1983, *op. cit.*, p. 106.

28. Arellano, 1985, *op. cit.*, p. 183.

29. The deterioration of the terms of trade in Chile was the worst in Latin America. They dropped about 15 percent from 1979 to 1981, reaching about half their 1970 level. See Comisión Económica para América Latina y el Caribe (CEPAL), *Estudio Económico de América Latina 1981* (Santiago, 1983).

30. Banco Central, *Boletín Mensual* (various issues).

31. J. P. Arellano and J. Ramos, "Capital Flight in Chile" (Washington, D.C.: Institute for International Economics, 1986), mimeo.

32. Empirical research on Chile, as well as on many other Latin American countries, reveals that devaluations are contractionary, at least in the short run. See A. Solimano, "Aspectos Conceptuales Sobre Política Cambiaria Relevantes Para América Latina", in CIEPLAN, *Políticas Macroeconómicas: Una Perspectiva Latinoamericana* (Santiago: CIEPLAN, 1986).

33. Arellano, Cortázar, and Solimano, 1986, *op. cit.*, p. 9.

34. The 1983–1984 stand-by agreement contemplated the following policy goals: A reduction was called for in the current-account deficit from 11 percent of GDP in 1982 to 7 percent in 1983; nominal wage increases for the public sector were to be held below the projected rate of inflation, whereas wage settlements in the private sector were to be determined through collective bargaining or individual agreement; explicit indexation mechanisms were ruled out for the private sector; the monetary policy stance was expected to be determined by the credit requirements of the subsidized domestic financial system and the monetary counterpart of medium-term borrowing from foreign banks; and, finally, the deficit for the nonfinancial public sector was expected to drop to 2 percent of GDP in 1983 and to approach equilibrium in 1984. See Arellano, Cortázar, and Solimaro, 1986, *op. cit.*

35. The Extended Fund Facility Agreement for 1985–1986 involved the following policy goals: The current-account deficit was reduced from 11.2 percent in 1984 to 4.5 percent in 1987; the wage policy stance continued its previous terms of partial wage indexation for the public sector and decentralized collective bargaining and individual agreements for the private sector; monetary policy was expected to accommodate growth and inflation prospects, producing a positive interest rate; and, finally, a balanced budget for the nonfinancial public sector was to be reached by 1987. See Arellano, Cortázar, and Solimano, 1986, *op. cit.*

36. Arellano, Cortázar, and Solimano, 1986, *op. cit.*

37. As argued earlier, unemployment statistics do not consider the incidence of underemployment, a drawback of great importance in countries where a great proportion of the labor force is self-employed.

38. Arellano, Cortázar, and Solimano, 1986, *op. cit.*

39. My discussion of Phases 1 and 2 has been strongly influenced by T. Moulian and P. Vergara, "Estado, Ideología y Políticas Económicas en Chile: 1973–1978," *Colección Estudios Cieplan*, No. 3 (June 1980); Foxley, 1983, *op. cit.;* and Garretón, 1986, *op. cit.* (See the latter, in particular, regarding the "reactive" strategy.)

40. Garretón, 1986, *op. cit.*

41. G. Campero and R. Cortázar, "Logic of Union Action in Chile," *Working Paper No. 85* (Notre Dame, Ind.: Kellogg Institute, 1986).

42. Moulian and Vergara, 1980, *op. cit.*, p. 105.

43. R. Cortázar, "Dos Hipótesis sobre la No-Transición a la Democracia en Chile, y las Oportunidades del Plebiscito," *Coleccion Cieplan*, No. 22 (Santiago, 1987).

44. The best students were normally encouraged to pursue graduate studies at the University of Chicago.

3

What Difference Does Regime Type Make? Economic Austerity Programs in Argentina

Edward C. Epstein

During the last decade, an increasing number of Latin American countries have been forced to respond to the economic crises provoked by oil shocks, currency inflation, and record levels of international debt with drastic changes in their normal economic programs. Austerity policy has usually included major cuts in government spending and, on occasion, increases in taxation. Given the obvious impact of these measures on the relative income of various social groups, such adjustments almost invariably have been the center of considerable political controversy. Consequently, the study of austerity programs offers a means of evaluating the distributional policies of individual governments and regimes.

This chapter deals with Argentina's recent experience with austerity policy. In particular, it asks whether the type of political regime in power has made any significant difference in the allocation of required sacrifice.[1] Even more specifically, by examining Argentine history since World War II, it asks whether "bureaucratic-authoritarian" military dictatorships[2] have been more inclined than populist democracies[3] to thrust a disproportionate share of the burden of sacrifice on the working class. An underlying rationale in support of such a view is that most military regimes will be less concerned about the ill-will to be expected from such a policy choice because of the absence of elections as a mechanism for removing an unpopular government. A contrary finding, however, could be explained in terms of the common external constraints felt by all regime types at a particular time. For example, any regime in sufficient need of financial assistance to sign the usual stand-by agreement with the International Monetary Fund (IMF) might be expected to implement a similar socially regressive program.[4]

TABLE 3.1
Regimes and Governments in Argentina (1966-present)

Regime*	Government	Years
Military	Onganía	1966-1970
	Levingston	1970-1971
	Lanusse	1971-1973
Civilian (Peronist)	Cámpora	1973
	J.D. Perón	1973-1974
	M.E. Perón	1974-1976
Military	Videla	1976-1981
	Viola	1981
	Galtieri	1981-1982
	Bignone	1982-1983
Civilian (Radical)	Alfonsín	1983-present

*Although the generic labels of "military" and "civilian" are used here to delimit particular regimes, the specific governments within each category are not presumed to have similar public policies.

The contrast of military authoritarian and populist democratic regimes is particularly interesting in Argentina, where each has repeatedly alternated in power in fairly rapid succession. During the relatively short interval of the last twenty years, Argentina has experienced four distinct regimes—two military and two populist (see Table 3.1).

In this chapter I shall examine the purported correspondence that has existed over the years between particular regimes and particular economic policies. The military has supported orthodox policies of currency devaluation, free capital flow, and foreign borrowing; the populists, in their turn, have opted for economic expansion through greater government spending, price controls, subsidized interest.[5] In particular, I shall examine the relationship between austerity policies and the pattern of beneficiaries of each regime.

A basic question to be asked here is why the economic policies of each regime type tend to favor particular social groups. My argument is that economic policy evolves, at least in part, from the interaction between policymakers and the individual interest groups that constitute a coalition of regime supporters. Obviously, the particular groups involved and the degree of decisionmaker autonomy will vary according to the nature of the coalition at any specific time. Analysts of democratic politics have long related policy outputs to coalitional maintenance requirements;[6] this chapter suggests that such analysis may be similarly helpful in explaining politics within military regimes. Although the rule of generals is likely to be less subject to political pressures from society than that of party politicians, total military isolation from civilian interest groups would be surprising. External support is necessary for any type of regime if it is to endow its policies with sufficient legitimacy to sustain government cohesion.[7]

If all regimes are based on external group support in varying degrees, it is important to know the identities of the core members of such political coalitions. It is these groups whose interests need to be served if the coalition is to be preserved as a meaningful political entity. In the case of regime crisis, I will argue that those in power are likely to use public policy as a means of favoring these critical supporters. The solutions sought will be most beneficial (or least harmful) to them, as compared to peripheral or nonmembers of the same coalition. Only in the case of overwhelming external pressure are those in power likely to consider departing from this pattern; but in such a case, the regime itself, deprived of most of its internal support, becomes extremely unstable and subject to collapse.

The first part of this chapter examines the differences between regimes by comparing two of the most recent regimes facing the need for austerity; it then looks at other administrations governing under less restrictive economic conditions. The second part examines the linkages between state and society in each of the four Argentine regimes under discussion in an effort to evaluate public policy as a response to coalitional politics. Finally, it draws a contrast between these domestic political factors, and the international pressures on policymakers—specifically the influence of the International Monetary Fund.

Public Policy and Regime

The military authoritarian regime that took power in March 1976 and its democratic populist successor of December 1983 each faced an economic crisis of major proportions, though with different characteristics. In 1976, the major problems were the balance of payments and the recently elevated level of inflation. In 1983 inflation continued, but the earlier trade deficit was replaced by a huge foreign debt. The government of General Jorge Videla negotiated two stand-by agreements with the IMF in August 1976 and April 1977, respectively; after seeking unsuccessfully to solve its international debt problem without the Fund's assistance, the civilian Alfonsín government felt compelled to sign a similar IMF agreement in December 1984. Although the military successfully implemented its commitments to the Fund, Alfonsín had difficulty accomplishing the same. The 1984 agreement was suspended by the Fund on grounds of noncompliance shortly after the release of the first tranche of the IMF loan. It would be reactiviated in a modified form only after Alfonsín's appointment of a new economic team and the emergence in June 1985 of a new anti-inflation program, the "Austral Plan."[8]

Our concern here is a comparison of the austerity policies developed in the most recent versions of authoritarian and democratic regimes—

TABLE 3.2
Budgetary Size (in Constant Currency) and Percentage of Allocations

Year	Budget Size Index (100=1960)	Defense	Education	Health	Social Security & Welfare	Housing
1970	136.81	09.6	10.2	03.8	28.7	00.6
1971	135.90	09.7	06.0	03.7	27.6	00.9
1972	145.64	09.0	09.3	03.3	24.5	00.3
1973	181.93	09.9	13.1	03.7	27.4	01.4
1974	220.70	07.7	12.0	02.5	28.1	02.5
1975	222.08	07.9	10.9	02.6	23.7	02.4
1976	204.47	10.7	07.4	04.1	20.6	03.0
1977	198.68	11.7	08.6	02.8	23.7	02.5
1978	214.21	13.6	09.7	02.2	29.6	04.3
1979	223.21	14.0	08.3	01.7	34.4	00.3
1980	240.31	11.9	08.9	01.7	35.5	00.4
1981	251.00	11.4	07.3	01.4	33.9	00.3
1982	182.15	11.0	06.2	01.1	28.6	00.6
1983	180.87	09.1	07.6	01.4	33.4	00.6
1984	148.06	08.8	09.5	01.8	37.8	00.5
1985	127.60*	05.2	06.0	01.3	32.6	00.4

*Through November 1985 only.

Note: The sources cited do not contain figures for foreign debt servicing, which constituted a significantly increasing percentage of the budget from the late 1970s onward.

Sources: Figures relating to budget size for 1970-1981 were taken from World Bank, Argentine Economic Memorandum (Washington, D.C.: 1985), p. 334; figures relating to budget size for 1982-1984, and 1985 through November were taken from Fundación de Investigaciones Económicas Latinoamericanas (FIEL), Indicadores de Coyuntura (June 1986), p. 67, deflated by average of Cost of Living and Non-Agricultural Wholesale Price Indices, FIEL, op. cit. (November, 1985): 40, 44, and (June, 1986): 38, 42. Figures relating to budgetary allocations were taken from IMF, Government Finance Statistics Yearbook (1981, 1986, and 1987), pp. 50, 103, and 213, respectively.

a comparison that focuses on the early years of the Videla and Alfonsín governments when each regime was politically at its strongest. The major policy instruments to be examined are budgetary allocations and taxation, given that particular types of spending and taxes normally benefit or penalize certain social groups more than others.

Table 3.2 presents data on central government spending since 1970. As can be seen, the budgets in both 1976–1977 and 1984–1985 represented the significant cutbacks that would be expected from austerity.[9] Measured in constant pesos, such spending fell to 10.54 percent for Videla and 29.45 percent for Alfonsín. Declining total expenditure meant that budget making occurred in a zero-sum environment, in which relative increases for one set of specific programs meant large reductions for others.

The same table provides figures on the allocation of these shrinking real funds. Comparing the two austerity programs, one sees that the

TABLE 3.3
Austerity versus Non-Austerity Budget Shares (Percentages)

	(1)Social Spending	(2)Defense	Ratio 1: 2
Austerity Years:			
Videla (1976-1977)	36.4	11.2	3.3: 1
Alfonsín (1984-1985)	45.0	07.0	6.4: 1
Nonausterity Years:			
1970-1972 Military	39.6	09.4	4.2: 1
1978-1981 Military	45.0	12.7	3.5: 1
1973-1975 Peronists	43.4	08.5	5.1: 1

Sources: Calculated from data in IMF, Government Finance Statistics Yearbook
(1981, 1986, and 1987), pp. 50, 103, and 213, respectively.

Videla administration spent a lower proportion in the combined social areas of education, health, social security and welfare, and housing than did Alfonsín's (i.e., an average of 36.4 percent in 1976–1977 to 45.0 percent in 1984–1985). Funding for social security/welfare and education, in particular, was sacrificed by Videla, whereas that for health and housing was kept at levels higher than occurred later on. Alfonsín reversed most of these specific priorities in social expenditure. In its turn, the military not surprisingly allocated more to defense than did the Radical party government (11.2 percent versus 7.0 percent for the same years). The major benefits from such social spending went to middle- and lower-class groups, which were more apt to use such government services than the very affluent. In terms of military spending, the bigger and better equipped armed forces that were forthcoming with a general in the presidency satisfied the self-perceived institutional needs of the officer corps better than would have occurred with civilians in office. As for the direct economic benefits linked to greater or lesser budgetary shares, such cash other than that going to salaries probably ended up in the hands of foreign arms dealers or domestic suppliers. An additional perspective on spending in each of the two austerity programs under study derives from the comparison of such budgetary allocations with the averages of nonausterity years, grouped by regime. Table 3.3 provides such data.

In terms of overall social spending, the low figures for the 1976–1977 Videla austerity program represented sharp cuts from the levels of the previous Peronist government in social security/welfare and in education. The recipients of such programs were deemed low priority so that their interests could be sacrificed to the needs of budgetary contraction. Whereas the reduced percentage spent for education was fairly typical of all the military governments in the period examined, the amount for social security represented a temporary deviation to be remedied once austerity had passed. In turn, the emphasis given to social spending within the constraints of Alfonsín's small 1984–1985 austerity budgets reflected a return of the social security share to the already higher percentages of the late 1970s and a temporary restoration of some of education's relative importance in the 1984 budget, if not that of 1985. Renewed civilian rule under the Radical party did little in relative terms for either public health or housing. Such an omission probably reflects the different needs of a middle-class populist constituency as compared with the predominantly working-class Peronists.

The pattern for defense spending was less complex than that for social programs. Seizing power in 1976, General Videla clearly exempted the military from the need for any direct sacrifice. He rationalized such liberality in a time of overall austerity by referring to the threat posed by leftist guerrillas, but such claims were rather exaggerated and meant to win favor with his fellow officers. As in the earlier military period, the share of the budget in 1976–1977 going to the armed forces was considerably above that found under any civilian administration. The Alfonsín Radical government, on the other hand, made a point of lowering military allocations, thereby capitalizing on the huge loss of prestige suffered by the generals after their ignominious defeat in the 1982 Malvinas/Falklands War. The effect of such a noticeable cut in spending upon the military must have been devastating given the now much smaller overall budget size.

When combined with spending cuts, increased tax revenue often constitutes a second aspect of austerity policy. In Table 3.4, three different time series are presented as estimates of total taxation for particular years so as to cover the entirety of the 1970–1985 period. Although these data are divergent where the years overlap, the overall tendencies toward increases or decreases are usually consistent. The combined sharp increases in revenue of 42.54 percent in 1976 and 1977 (55.37 percent if the period is extended to 1978) and 30.21 percent in 1984 and 1985 are consistent with notions of austerity.

As with spending, our focus is on the particular breakdown or mix of taxes over time. To simplify the presentation of three separate data sets, Table 3.5 classifies all taxes into three categories: income and wealth taxes, consumption and production taxes, and foreign trade taxes.

Comparing the austerity program of 1976–1977 with that of 1984–1985, one sees that, regardless of the data source used, Alfonsín placed slightly more emphasis on consumption and production taxes and considerably less on income and wealth taxes than Videla. The small share of total tax revenue accounted for by income and wealth taxes seems a most important finding. In terms of taxes on foreign trade, little difference appears between the two sets of years.

Somewhat different results emerge if the 1976 data, which appear quite divergent from those for the rest of the Videla period, are excluded. There is no longer any suggestion that Alfonsín relied slightly more on consumption and production taxes, and his previously small edge in

TABLE 3.4
Indices of Total Central Government Tax Revenue, 1970-1985

Year	A Index	%v	B Index	%v	C Index	%v
1970	100.00					
1971	86.22	-13.78				
1972	85.17	-01.22				
1973	87.18	+02.36				
1974	115.11	+32.04				
1975	75.67	-34.26				
1976	91.61	+21.07	100.00			
1977	107.86	+17.74	148.10	+48.10		
1978	117.57	+09.00	145.12	-01.68		
1979	115.39	-01.85	143.39	-01.19	100.00	
1980	119.62	+03.67	172.58	+20.36	124.42	+24.42
1981	94.15	-21.29	202.33	+17.24	111.28	-10.56
1982	84.35	-10.41	186.35	-07.90	90.45	-18.72
1983			185.60	-00.40	86.24	-04.65
1984					96.55	+11.96
1985					112.30	+16.32

Note: Each series has been deflated to correct for inflation.

Sources: The "A" figures were calculated as a percentage of GDP from Sindicatura General de Empresas Públicas (SIGEP), Indicadores económicos, financieros y sociales (Buenos Aires, 1984): 93-94, with GDP in 1970 pesos, also from SIGEP, op. cit.: 7; The "B" figures were calculated as a percentage of GDP from the World Bank, Argentine Economic Memorandum (Washington, D.C., 1985): 341, with GDP in 1970 pesos from SIGEP, op. cit. 7; The "C" figures were calculated as current australes from FIEL, op. cit. (September, 1984): 74, and (June, 1986): 66, deflated by Non-Agricultural Wholesale Price Index, FIEL, op. cit. (September, 1984): 46, and (1986): 42.

the use of foreign trade taxes is transformed into a considerable one. Furthermore, if the Videla year of 1977 is compared only with the second Alfonsín year of 1985, when the Plan Austral went into effect, it is now clearly Videla who made the greater use of consumption and production taxes, whereas Alfonsín's use of foreign trade duties is now far more important.

The earlier discussion of the relative reliance on particular types of taxes is important because it relates to possible shifts in income. In theory, income and wealth taxes should weigh more on the affluent than on middle- and lower-class taxpayers. In a similar fashion, consumption and production taxes (e.g., value-added and sales taxes) are normally paid disproportionately by those with smaller incomes. Alfonsín's lesser use of the income and wealth tax than Videla suggests that the Radical party leader was not very interested in using taxes to penalize the rich, as would have been expected on the part of earlier populists such as the Peronists. In this sense, Radicals and Peronists appear to be variants on what we have been calling populists.

TABLE 3.5
Revenue Composition by Tax, 1970 - 1985

Year	Income & Wealth A	B	C	Consumption & Production A	B	C	Foreign Trade A	B	C
1970	35.0			44.3			16.8		
1971	29.7			47.8			18.7		
1972	26.0			45.5			25.2		
1973	29.9			43.4			22.6		
1974	30.3			48.8			17.4		
1975	16.0			58.5			22.3		
1976	19.6	15.5		52.1	44.1		25.6	40.5	
1977	23.2	21.6		60.0	56.1		13.9	22.4	
1978	22.2	20.6		63.8	63.8		11.3	16.0	
1979	20.0	18.3	18.5	63.4	60.8	55.2	13.2	20.7	
1980	21.0	18.7	18.6	60.7	58.6	58.5	14.7	22.7	23.0
1981	[19.8]	16.5	16.2	64.0	62.2	62.9	13.6	21.3	20.9
1982	[21.9]	17.2	16.1	62.5	59.9	61.2	13.2	22.9	22.7
1983	[19.2]	14.2	14.1	[54.2]	54.1	53.1	[19.1]	31.7	32.8
1984	[13.3]	[9.9]	9.8	[63.8]	[63.7]	62.5	[16.1]	[26.8]	27.7
1985	[15.3]	[11.4]	11.3	[49.9]	[49.8]	48.9	[23.1]	[38.5]	39.8

Note: The bracketed figures in columns A and B represent the author's interpolations based on the changes in C for the same years.

Sources: "A" figures are from CEPAL, Estadísticas económicas de corto plazo. Vol. V: Moneda, crédito y finanzas públicas (Buenos Aires, 1984), p. 137; the "B" figures are from World Bank, Argentine Economic Memorandum (Washington, D.C., 1985), p. 341; and the "C" figures are from FIEL, Indicadores de Coyuntura (September 1984) and (June 1986), pp. 73 and 66, respectively.

Our discussion of taxes and income transfer has missed one important point because the data have been presented jointly on all types of foreign trade taxes. Table 3.6 disaggregates that category into import duties and export taxes. Comparing the 1976–1977 and 1984–1985 periods, we find that the marginally greater use of all trade taxes by Alfonsín mentioned earlier now reveals both his smaller use of import duties and his far greater reliance on export taxes. In fact, by 1977 Videla was dramatically reducing export taxes. Alfonsín, in turn, stressed taxes on exports more in 1985 than in 1984. By the time Videla had reached his second year in power, his tax policy seemed to greatly favor the predominantly agricultural export sector; at the same stage in his administration, Alfonsín was moving in the opposite direction, making grain and cattle producers pay a far larger proportion of the total tax bill.

As with earlier spending allocations, a comparison of the overall pattern of taxation during the austerity and nonausterity years should provide a useful longer-term perspective. Table 3.7 simplifies this task by grouping the data by selected years. Although all governments have relied most on consumption and production taxes for revenue, there are some important distinctions to be made. More recent administrations

TABLE 3.6
Import Duties and Export Taxes

Year	Import Duties A	B	Export Taxes A	B
1976	13.2		27.0	
1977	14.6		7.5	
1978	14.5		1.1	
1979	19.0	20.0	0.6	0.7
1980	21.8	22.5	0.5	0.5
1981	18.1	18.4	2.5	2.6
1982	12.9	13.2	9.4	9.6
1983	12.4	12.9	19.1	19.9
1984	[10.0]	10.4	[16.6]	17.3
1985	[11.7]	12.2	[26.5]	27.6

Note: (1) A third category of foreign trade taxes accounting for only a small amount of the total has been omitted; (2) Bracketed material represents interpolations made by this author based on the changes in B.

Sources: "A" figures were taken from World Bank, Argentine Economic Memorandum (Washington, D.C., 1985), p. 341; "B" figures were taken from FIEL, Indicadores de Coyuntura (September 1984) and (June 1986), pp. 73 and 66, respectively.

TABLE 3.7
Austerity Versus Nonausterity Taxation (Percentage)

	Income & Wealth	Consumption & Production	Foreign Trade
Austerity Years:			
Videla (1976-1977)	21.4	56.1	19.8
Alfonsín (1984-1985)	14.3	56.9	19.6
Nonausterity Years:			
1970-1972 Military	30.2	45.9	20.2
1978-1981 Military	20.8	63.0	13.2
1973-1975 Peronists	25.4	50.2	20.8

Sources: The figures for 1970-1983 are from CEPAL, Estadísticas económicas de corto plaza Vol. V: Moneda, Crédito y finanzas públicas (Buenos Aires, 1984), p. 137; The figures for 1984-1985 represent this author's interpolations based on the changes for those years in FIEL, Indicadores de Coyuntura (September, 1984) (June 1986), pp. 73 and 66, respectively.

seem to have relied more on this type of tax than those in the past. Just the opposite appears true in relation to income and wealth taxes. In this context, the earlier governments were more prone toward such usage. One possible explanation relates to the greater difficulties of collecting income/wealth taxes under the conditions of high inflation so prevalent in Argentina since 1975. As for foreign trade taxes, the major exception in use appears to be the 1978–1981 military, which placed a very low emphasis on this tax source. Once again, the low figure reflects the curtailment of export duties through 1980.[10]

Public Policy and Political Pressures

Central government spending and taxation were discussed earlier as key aspects of the austerity policies imposed in 1976–1977 during the Videla military regime and in 1984–1985 with respect to the new democracy inaugurated by Alfonsín. These years corresponded to periods in which the existing governments signed stand-by agreements with the IMF in return for new loans. Although both Videla and Alfonsín were subject to Fund restrictions of a similar kind,[11] each proceeded to implement the necessary financial cutbacks and new taxes in different ways. Whereas the military cut social spending, the civilians reduced defense. The former raised taxes on production and consumption while the latter raised foreign trade taxes, especially those on exports. My purpose here is explain why such differences occurred.

As I suggested earlier, my explanation will focus on the relation between the governments in question and political coalitions. Clearly, certain groups benefited more than others from the two austerity programs under study. But such winners and losers were not random; rather, they reflect to some degree the extent of government commitment to or alienation from these groups.[12] Given the need for sacrifices, we would expect the government to impose the heaviest burden on those furthest politically from the decisionmakers. What is meant here by *coalition* is an informal alliance of sympathies as well as interests. Although coalitions may take the form of public arrangements of mutual support, such explicitness is not really necessary. As long as all participants share certain political goals, the degree of mutual obligation may be left vague. The resulting ambiguity allows those in charge of the policy process not only greater flexibility of action but also the pretense of high-minded impartiality, of supposedly acting only in the national interest.

The Videla and Alfonsín coalitions were obviously very different in composition. In the former case, the most important entities were the armed forces themselves, represented by General Videla, as well as many of the upper-class civilian technocrats in charge of the economic policy area.[13] A number of these office holders—including Martínez de Hoz, the minister of economics for the entirety of the Videla government— had extensive personal ties to export agriculture, finance, and, to a lesser degree, multinational industry. Because of the friendship between Martínez de Hoz and the minister of agriculture, Cadenas Madariaga, agriculture was especially well represented until 1978, when the original coalition began to disintegrate.[14] In the case of the Alfonsín coalition, interest group linkages were probably less important than the relatively unorganized individuals represented by the Radical party. Judging from the results of the 1983 elections, these included various members of the urban middle class as well as highly skilled industrial workers.[15] The absence of particular ties with such groups as organized labor suggests that the Radical coalition was weaker than its Peronist predecessor had been in terms of mobilizing support.

Another indication of the behavior of these coalitions was the policy result in economic areas other than austerity. Under Videla, agricultural exporters benefited from the three large devaluations of 1976 and 1977.[16] Financial interests took advantage of the possibilities for short-term speculation in government financial instruments in 1976 and the return to positive interest rates made possible with the 1977 financial reform.[17] Factory owners did less well: Although they benefited from the low labor costs fixed by the government, part of that advantage was eroded by reduced tariff protection. Alfonsín, in turn, responded to the needs of his constituents by deciding early in his administration to continue the economic recovery begun in 1983 through generous government-decreed wage increases. As he stated in his speech of January 25, 1984, higher real wages could be expected to result in more consumption and lower unemployment.[18]

As can be seen in Table 3.8, which provides figures for each government on real wages in the manufacturing sector, Alfonsín's administration offered this relatively better-off part of the working class a return of buying power from the lows of the military dictatorship begun in 1976, almost to the level achieved during the Peronist period.

Later on, because it needed to control rapidly rising inflation, the Alfonsín government responded with a policy of price freezes for key products and indexation of wages and public-sector charges.[19] With the first stage of the Plan Austral introduced in mid-1985, Alfonsín imposed a generalized price-wage freeze that lasted until early 1986.[20] Given Alfonsín's political need to protect his supporters' interests, such initiatives can be seen as efforts to maintain the standard of living of the average consumer as well as possible under difficult economic conditions.

As economic policy encountered difficulties in reaching desired goals, pressures to make adjustments often threatened the integrity of each political coalition. When the government could find no solutions to the joint politico-economic problems, it was apparently forced to sacrifice less critical coalition members so as to protect others deemed more important to the survival of both the government of the day and, indeed, of the regime itself. The identity of the core members corresponded to the nature of each regime: In the case of authoritarian coalition, the military and within that, the army, was the sine qua non; for the Radical party–led democratic alternative, the equivalent was the middle-class consumer.

Under Videla, relations with the industrialists as a whole had always been somewhat ambiguous. After all, hadn't many of them all too

TABLE 3.8
Index of Real Wages in Manufacturing (3rd Quarter 1970 to 4th Quarter 1972=100)

Regime Type	Government	Real Wages
Military	Levingston	98.3
	Lanusse	100.1
Civilian (Peronist)	Cámpora	109.2
	J.D. Perón	112.5
	M.E. Perón	109.3
Military	Videla	77.8
	Viola	79.7
	Galtieri	69.1
	Bignone	86.8
Civilian (Radical)	Alfonsín*	106.1

*Through 1986.

Sources: For all governments except Bignone and Alfonsín, these figures were calculated on the basis of the data in República Argentina, Salarios e inflación: Argentina 1970-1983 (Buenos Aires: Ministerio de Trabajo, 1984); data for the more recent governments were taken from CEPAL, Balance preliminar de la economía latinoamericana, 1986 (Santiago: Economic Commission for Latin America and the Caribbean, 1987), p. 17.

willingly participated in the programs of the now openly despised Peronists? As early as the three-month price "truce" of March–June 1977, the industrialists were forced to accept temporary limitations on their ability to maintain the profit margins threatened by inflation. The ideological preference of the Martínez de Hoz economic team—reinforced by the IMF agreement—for free trade based on Argentina's international comparative advantage in agriculture led to steady reductions in the external tariffs protecting the domestic market from foreign industrial goods. With the flood of foreign imports attracted by the increasingly overvalued peso, significant parts of the industrial sector of the economy was severely threatened by 1980.[21] The same deliberate slowdown in peso devaluation after mid-1978 in response to military pressures to deal with the stubbornly high rates of inflation eventually led to growing criticism from the important agricultural sector as well and to its gradual alienation.[22] After a series of earlier protest resignations by various officials close to the export sector in the Ministry of Agriculture, the minister himself left in April 1979. Relations between agriculture and the government were decidedly strained. Finally, by the time of the banking crisis of March–April 1980, even the core financial sector had been damaged by government policies.[23] Legally obliged to protect small deposits, the government went beyond its obligations to include those of the wealthy as well.[24] Nevertheless, by its end in March 1981, the Videla government was severely isolated and only parts of the army remained in the original political coalition. General Roberto Viola, Videla's successor in the presidency, attempted unsuccessfully to regain civilian support for his government through the placement of representative figures of the major interest groups in the new cabinet.[25]

Though less structured around interest groups, Alfonsín's political coalition has been subject to pressures as well, threatening the government with a loss of popularity. IMF calls to act against inflation led initially not only to cuts in government spending but also to significant increases in interest rates. Although the ensuing recession of late 1984 to mid-1985 produced higher unemployment and falling real wages, it failed to reduce inflationary expectations.[26] A subsequent response was the afore-mentioned Plan Austral of June 1985, which attempted to share the need for sacrifice among both business and labor. The good showing of Alfonsín's Radical party in the November 1985 legislative elections was as much a demonstration of the weakness of the Peronist opposition as it was an indication of the president's popularity.[27] Confronted by worsening inflation and deteriorating worker income in 1987, the government was not so lucky in the September congressional and guber-natorial elections, losing its majority in the Chamber of Deputies and several key governorships.[28]

Throughout his term, Alfonsín has made gestures to suggest that his administration is willing to listen to the complaints of organized labor and business raised at meetings held by the tripartite Economic and Social Conference. At the same time, however, he indicated that he and his ministers made policy.[29] In the face of the various threatened and actual general strikes called by the Peronist-affiliated trade union con-federation to protest low wages, the government has made periodic strategic concessions in the form of limited wage increases.[30] At other times, as with the *sinceramientos* of June and July 1986, it officially recognized earlier increases conceded by business under the table.[31] The pact with the accommodationist "Group of 15" unions, concluded in March 1987 by the naming of a Peronist as labor minister and by the promise of labor reforms, clearly was meant to divide the trade union opposition.[32] Until the military mutinies of April 1987 and the renewed economic difficulties reflected by rising inflation and deteriorating foreign trade that became visible in mid-year, Alfonsín managed to maintain a surprising amount of popular support by responding innovatively where necessary to the criticism of his opponents and thereby controlling the political initiative. The electoral defeat of September, however, suggested that this kind of political improvisation has its limits.

Conclusions

This chapter has sought to place Argentina's recent economic austerity policy in a political perspective. Quantitative data from the first two years of each program—encompassing Videla's military bureaucratic-authoritarian regime (1976–1977) and Alfonsín's populist democracy

(1984–1985)—demonstrate significant differences. Although each leader significantly cut government spending and raised taxes (as a necessary response to IMF requirements), those who paid the costs were from divergent parts of society. The principal losers under the more recent military experiment were the urban consumers of the middle and lower classes. Not only were social programs drastically cut, but the heavy reliance on production and consumption taxes meant that their payments were disproportionate to their incomes. The winners, however, were the military and the agricultural exporters who saw defense expenditures rise while export taxes were reduced to very low levels. Under democracy, the order of sacrifice and benefit has been reversed. Now proportionally more is spent on social programs such as welfare and social security (if not in constant currency), whereas the military budget has been slashed severely. Although production and consumption taxes are still the most important elements following the changes of 1985 associated with the Plan Austral, taxes on foreign trade (especially on exports) have been raised back to traditional levels. What remains somewhat puzzling are the low levels of income and wealth taxes under a populist government. These low figures may reflect, in part, the difficulty of collection in times of high inflation.

The differences between the two austerity programs, however, may be more particular to the specific regimes examined than to bureaucratic-authoritarian or populist regimes in general. The expenditure and taxation policies for the 1970–1972 military governments and for the Peronist administration of 1973–1975 present a different pattern: more social spending under the military of the early 1970s, and greater use of income and wealth taxes during the entire 1970–1975 period. Although such differences probably reflect easier economic conditions, other factors are likely to be involved as well.

These differences in spending and taxation can be explained by the idea of politics as reflective of particular social linkages. The divergence between the Videla and Alfonsín administrations reflects the dissimilarity of the two political coalitions, each of which expressed its policy preferences and, to the degree possible, pressured for favorable treatment. Such a notion of coalitional politics suggests that even under a military autocracy, policymakers never really enjoy total decisionmaking autonomy. Ties between export agriculture and financial groups on the one hand and key military personages such as Economics Minister Martínez de Hoz on the other influenced austerity policy in the 1976–1977 period. In a similar way, Alfonsín and his ministers were aware of reactions to official programs from the middle and skilled working-class voters who had given the Radical party government its electoral majority. The greater pressures felt by the democratic administration obviously reflected its need to face popular opinion—in a way clearly more direct and representative than reflected by the pressures that the military would encounter.

The notion of coalitional politics also helps explain the differences between regimes of a similar nature. O'Donnell[33] has suggested that industrialists as a group played a key role in the 1966–1973 military regime, in contrast to the situation under General Videla. The central role of organized labor in the 1973–1976 Peronist regime[34] presents similar insights when contrasted with the Alfonsín years, when labor became the major oppositional force.[35] In the present Radical party version of populism, middle-class support is deemed more important than that of industrial workers.

The linkages of state and society are critical for the identification of regimes. To the question raised in the introduction to this chapter as to whether regimes make a difference in the form austerity policy takes, the answer is clear. Where such regimes are alike politically in terms of their social ties, the resulting policies will likely mirror them to a considerable extent. The important caveat is to make sure that similar appearing regimes are, in fact, really alike in terms of their social composition.

Notes

1. For a discussion of the definitions of *regime*, see Karen Remmer, "Exclusionary Democracy," *Studies in International Comparative Development* (Winter 1985–1986), especially Note 2.

2. Guillermo O'Donnell, *Modernization and Bureaucratic-Authoritarianism* (Berkeley: Institute of International Studies, University of California, 1973).

3. See Torcuato Di Tella, "Populism and Reform in Latin America," in Claudio Veliz (ed.), *Obstacles to Change in Latin America* (London: Oxford University Press, 1965).

4. For various accounts of repressive IMF programs in Argentina, Peru, and Brazil, respectively, see Roberto Frenkel and Guillermo O'Donnell, *Los programas de estabilización convenidos con el FMI y sus impactos internos* (Buenos Aires: Estudios CEDES No. 1, 1978); Barbara Stallings, "Peru and the U.S. Banks: Privatization of Financial Relations," in Richard Fagen (ed.), *Capitalism and the State in U.S.-Latin American Relations* (Stanford, Calif.: Stanford University Press, 1979); and Reinaldo Gonçalves, "Brazil's Search for Stabilization," *Third World Quarterly* (April 1985).

5. Marcelo Diamant, *El péndulo argentino: ¿Hasta cúando?* (Buenos Aires: CERES, 1984).

6. See for example, William Riker, *The Theory of Political Coalitions* (New Haven, Conn.: Yale University Press, 1962); and Sven Groenings, E. W. Kelly, and Michael Leiserson (eds.), *The Study of Coalition Behavior* (New York: Holt, Rinehart & Winston, 1970).

7. Edward Epstein, "Legitimacy, Institutionalization, and Opposition in Exclusionary Bureaucratic-Authoritarian Regimes: The Situation of the 1980s," *Comparative Politics* (October 1984).

8. The Austral Plan included a price-wage freeze, a new currency unit (the austral) worth 1,000 pesos and pegged initially at 0.8 to the U.S. dollar (a devaluation of some 35 percent), and a pledge to rely on taxation rather than the printing of unbacked currency to cover the fiscal deficit. The wage freeze

was relaxed somewhat in January 1986. A "second stage" of the Austral Plan, announced in February 1986, allowed for prices to be "administered" upward; it also allowed for the reactivation of the economy through concessions to agriculture (including a series of periodic currency devaluations to stimulate export sales), new government housing, and the privatization of selected parts of the state sector of the economy. See Roberto Frenkel and José María Fanelli, *Argentina y el Fondo en la última década* (Buenos Aires: CEDES, 1985), and *Del ajuste caótico al Plan Austral, Las políticas de estabilización recientes en la Argentina* (Buenos Aires, CEDES, 1986); and Edward Epstein, "Recent Stabilization Programs in Argentina, 1973–1986," *World Development* (August 1987), pp. 1000–1003. What could be seen as a "third stage" was introduced as a response to escalating inflation rates at the end of February 1987. After a further wage increase on top of that already authorized for the first quarter of the year and higher public-service charges, wages and prices were frozen again until July. The existing policy of mini-devaluations of the austral was continued after a larger than normal "catch-up" (*Latin American Weekly Report*, March 12, 1987, p. 10). Subsequent developments included renewed government emphasis on privatizing parts of the state sector of the economy and further efforts to reduce the government deficit as inflationary pressures continued to increase (*Latin America Weekly Report*, July 2, 1987, p. 4; October 1, 1987, pp. 1–2).

9. As can be seen in Table 3.2, real spending rose between 1978 and 1981— a good reason for seeing these years as qualitatively different from the beginning years of the Videla government. The spending cuts of 1982–1983 represent the combined effects of two separate military governments and three finance ministers. Given the qualitative differences in policy, this 1982–1983 period cannot be said to represent any coherent single austerity program; hence it is not discussed here.

10. The financial advantages to export agriculture were in great part counteracted in the 1978–1980 period by an increasingly overvalued peso. See Juan Sourrouille, *Política económica y procesos de desarrollo: La experiencia argentina entre 1976 y 1981* (Santiago: Estudios de la CEPAL No. 27, 1983), pp. 145–157.

11. The key points of the 1976–1977 IMF agreements were cuts in the government fiscal deficit, limits on the money supply, promises to reduce restrictions on international payments and trade, and, for the 1977 part alone, minimum levels of international reserves. All of these elements were continued in the 1984 plan, which also included references both to the need to reach agreement on debt rescheduling with the private sector and to limits on the level of new debt. See Frenkel and Fanelli, *Argentina y el Fondo, op. cit.*, pp. 28–29, 61–62.

12. This is not to deny the importance of the ideological values held by key policymakers. The more important point is that the ideological commitments and political needs tended to converge.

13. Interview of December 10, 1984 with Jorge Bustamante Alsina, subsecretary of industrial development in the Videla government.

14. Jorge Schvarzer, *Martínez de Hoz: La lógica política de la política económica* (Buenos Aires: Ensayos y Tesis CISEA No. 4, 1983).

15. Edgardo Catterberg, "Las elecciones del 30 octubre de 1983: El surgimiento de una nueva convergencia electoral," *Desarrollo Económico* (July–September 1985), p. 265.

16. Alejandro Foxley, *Latin American Experiments in Neoconservative Economics* (Berkeley: University of California Press, 1983).

17. Schvarzer, *op. cit.,* pp. 43–54. Financial interests also benefited from the 1977 official guarantee of bank deposits at the time of the 1980 financial crisis (interview of December 18, 1984, with José Martínez de Hoz, minister of economics in the Videla government; Ernesto Feldman and Juan Sommer, *Crisis financiera y endeudamiento externo: Consecuencias de la política económica del período 1976-1981* [Buenos Aires: Centro de Economía Transnacional, 1984]).

18. *La Nación* (Buenos Aires), January 26, 1984, p. 1. The initial economic expansion of the Alfonsín government would be brought to a halt by the final quarter of 1984 by the need to reach agreement with the IMF on a stand-by.

19. See Russell Smith, *Labor Organizations, Wage Policy, and Economic Stabilization in Alfonsín's Argentina* (Topeka: School of Business, Washburn University, 1985), pp. 10–12.

20. *Clarín* (Buenos Aires), June 14, 1985, p. 2.

21. See Feldman and Sommer, *op. cit.* The highly critical Industry Day speech in 1980 of the prominent industrialist acting as government intervenor in the Argentine Industrial Union was indicative of opinion in some of the most important circles of heavy industry (Eduardo Oxenford, *2 de setiembre de 1980: Día de la Industria Argentina* [Buenos Aires: Unión Industrial Argentina, 1980]).

22. See, for example, *Dinámica Rural* (Buenos Aires), August 1979, pp. 16–22.

23. *Clarín* (Buenos Aires), March 29, 1980, p. 8; April 26, 1980, p. 6.

24. Schvarzer, *op. cit.,* p. 87.

25. Interview of January 8, 1985, with Lorenzo Sigaut, secretary of finance in the Viola government; interview of January 16, 1985, with Argentine political scientist Jorge Schvarzer.

26. Frenkel and Fanelli, *Del ajuste caótico, op. cit.,* p. 15.

27. *Latin America Weekly Report* (London), November 8, 1985, p. 3.

28. *Latin American Weekly Report* (London), September 17, 1987, p. 1; CEPAL, *Panorama Económico de América Latina 1987* (Santiago: Economic Commission for Latin America and the Caribbean, September 1987).

29. *Review of the River Plate* (Buenos Aires), May 21, 1986, pp. 389–390.

30. *Latin America Weekly Report* (London), January 3, 1986, p. 2; April 25, 1986, p. 1.

31. Interview of June 27, 1986, with Argentine economist José María Fanelli.

32. For details of the pact with part of organized labor, see "El pacto radical-sindical," *Somos* (Buenos Aires), April 1, 1987, pp. 4–10.

33. Guillermo O'Donnell, "State and Alliances in Argentina, 1956–1976," *Journal of Development Studies* (October 1978).

34. See Juan Carlos Torre, *Los sindicatos en el gobierno 1973-1976* (Buenos Aires: Centro Editor de América Latina, 1983).

35. The union pact of March 1987 would now appear to be defunct, reflecting not only the opposition of most of organized business but also the new cabinet resulting from the government's massive September electoral defeat (*Latin American Weekly Report,* July 2, 1987, p. 4; September 24, 1987, p. 4).

4

Austerity Programs Under Conditions of Political Instability and Economic Depression: The Case of Bolivia

Kenneth P. Jameson

Introduction

Poverty is a way of life for a large majority of Bolivians. In 1985 only Haiti among the countries in the Western Hemisphere had a per capita GNP lower than Bolivia's $470, according to World Bank statistics. In terms of social indicators, Bolivia is generally at the bottom of the list: It has the lowest life expectancy, the second highest infant mortality rate behind Haiti, the second lowest daily calorie supply behind Ecuador, the highest crude death rate, and the highest population-to-physician ratio.[1]

This low socioeconomic base combined with a decline of 23 percent in GDP between 1981 and 1986 (see Table 4.1, column 2), as a result of the Latin American depression, emphasize that the costs of a particular austerity program to many Bolivians are less than the costs of perennial poor macroeconomic performance. The first section of the chapter sketches both the macroeconomic context of Bolivia's relatively good economic and social performance through the 1970s and its continual decline in the 1980s.

A second factor that plays a central role in determining the nature and cost of austerity programs is Bolivia's political instability. There have been 193 governments in Bolivia's 163 years of independence, and during one recent four-year period (August 1978–October 1982), there were 11 different governments. The second section introduces the major political players since the nation's 1952 revolution. Their efforts to establish a stable political regime are rooted in a history that has strongly influenced the nature of Bolivia's austerity programs.

The remainder of the chapter deals directly with the question of political regime and the costs of austerity programs. The analysis begins

TABLE 4.1
The Macroeconomic Performance of Bolivia, 1971–1986

(1) Year	(2) Growth of GDP (Annual %)	(3) Growth of Manufacturing	(4) Growth of Agriculture	(5) Growth of Mining	(6) Growth of General Government	(7) Current Account Balance (million $)	(8) Net Factor Payments (million $) [a]
1971	4.9	1.3	5.9	0.3	10.4	-2.8	-17.2
1972	5.7	8.3	5.9	3.7	8.8	-2.9	-21.6
1973	6.8	4.3	4.6	22.2	6.1	0.9	-22.9
1974	6.1	12.1	3.7	-3.1	9.8	146.8	-40.5
1975	5.1	6.8	6.7	-14.0	7.3	-169.9	-36.9
1976	6.8	7.5	2.9	14.0	6.5	-72.8	-40.0
1977	3.4	6.0	-3.4	2.9	4.2	-81.5	-75.0
1978	3.1	4.2	2.7	-4.0	2.5	-308.7	-109.3
1979	2.0	2.6	2.0	-6.0	2.1	-383.4	-166.4
1980	0.8	-1.0	5.2	-2.0	1.3	-54.1	-295.0
1981	-0.7	-6.6	-0.9	-0.2	-4.5	-492.0	-395.3
1982	-5.6	-12.8	10.4	-3.9	8.9	-219.0	-459.1
1983	-7.3	-3.4	-27.6	-1.0	3.6	-204.1	-411.0
1984	-2.4	-15.2	15.8	-13.9	0.4	-194.5	-431.2
1985	-4.0	-11.6	2.5	-12.3	-2.0	-347.4	-410.4
1986	-2.9	-1.0	-1.9	-19.4	———	-324.9	-446.0
Sectoral Share in 1984		11.5	19.7	15.1	13.3		

Year	(9) Government Deficit as % of GDP	(10) Inflation Rate	(11) Money Supply (Million of Bolivian Pesos)	(12) Wage Index	(13) Open Unemployment Rate	(14) Cumulative Contracted Debt (million $)	(15) Debt Service Ratio
1971	16.5	3.7	—	104.3	9.0	782	15.5
1972	6.4	6.5	1	102.1	8.1	966	24.4
1973	7.1	31.5	1	109.1	7.1	1048	18.6
1974	1.1	62.8	1	87.5	6.1	1210	12.9
1975	9.8	8.0	2	81.4	5.2	1550	15.3
1976	9.2	4.5	3	97.9	5.5	1979	17.4
1977	11.3	8.1	5	101.0	5.3	2442	22.8
1978	10.7	10.4	6	101.4	5.5	3102	28.1
1979	7.5	19.7	6	100.0	5.6	3499	30.2
1980	9.0	47.2	8	94.5	5.8	3642	27.8
1981	7.8	32.1	12	86.3	9.7	4535	27.5
1982	14.7	123.5	39	84.9	10.5	4553	31.3
1983	19.1	275.6	88	93.9	14.2	4820	31.6
1984	27.4	1281.3	684	55.7[b]	15.1	4947[c]	37.8
1985	9.1	11749.6	88 trillion	25.3[b]	18.0	4977[c]	29.1
1986	2.2	276.0	161 trillion	18.0	——	5314[c]	34.3

[a] Includes deferred and arrears payments, which rose from $27.6 million in 1983 to $174 million in 1985.

[b] Highly unstable depending on inflation rate and permitted wage adjustments.

[c] Estimates.

Sources: Columns 1-10:
1971–1980: IBRD, "Bolivia: Structural Constraints and Development Prospects" (January 12, 1983).
1981–1985: IBRD, "Updating Memorandum on Bolivia" (December 15, 1986).
1986: IDB, Economic and Social Progress in Latin America, 1987 Report, "Statistical Profile of Bolivia," p. 238. The fact that these data are not from the same consistent data sets may affect their values.

Column 11: IMF, International Financial Statistics, 1986 Yearbook.
Column 13: ILO, Yearbook of Labor Statistics, Table 16 (various years).
Column 14: Banco Central de Bolivia, "Resumen Estadistico" (1985).
Column 15: IBRD, World Debt Tables (various issues).

with the government of General Hugo Banzer (1971–1978) and then moves to an examination of subsequent political and economic events. Separate treatment is given the two recent civilian governments. Hernán Siles Zuazo governed from August 1982 until August 1985, giving Bolivia its first extended civilian government since 1964. He was replaced by Victor Paz Estenssoro (1985–), who undertook Bolivia's most extensive and coherent austerity program. The final section summarizes the lessons from Bolivia.

A number of patterns appear in the Bolivian experience. The only meaningful austerity programs were proposed and/or implemented under civilian governments, largely because adoption of a stabilization program was a central step in overcoming the key economic bottleneck: access to foreign exchange. The international opprobrium toward Bolivia's military regimes because of their repressive policies and involvement in drug trafficking meant that only civilian governments could use austerity programs to gain access to the dollar resources of the IMF, the World Bank, and the U.S. government. Thus, the usual assumption that bureaucratic-authoritarian regimes are more able to impose austerity is reversed in Bolivia's case.

The incidence of the programs' costs was quite complex. The endemically poor—peasants and urban poor—bore their usual share of the costs. The only exception was the Siles period, when runaway inflation began and governmental control of the economy was so ineffective that peasants entered the drug traffic and urban poor came into the informal sector. With this exception, the trade-off between rich and poor was less clear than that between the state and the private sectors, and between the formal and informal segments of the private sector.

Let us turn now to an overview of Bolivian macroeconomic performance.

The Macroeconomic Context

The decade of the 1970s was a period of relatively good macroeconomic performance for Bolivia. The economy grew impressively until the late 1970s, then wavered through 1981 and finally collapsed in the 1980s. Table 4.1 presents the major macroeconomic series needed to understand this period.[2] Virtually all of the indicators in the 1970s were favorable: GNP growth was positive in every year from 1971 to 1980 and averaged a respectable 4.9 percent per year (column 2); inflation, by Latin American standards, was relatively moderate at an average of 17.2 percent, and the one period of rapid inflation in 1973–1974 was quickly stabilized to 4.5 percent by 1976 with no loss of growth (column 10); after a devaluation in 1972, the fixed-exchange rate remained stable, with free convertibility until 1979.

Just as the crisis of the 1980s would be closely linked to the external sector, this favorable performance was facilitated by the balance-of-payments situation. Terms of trade declined in 1971–1973 and then rose significantly, especially in 1979–1980. The current account was generally close to balance except in 1978 and 1979, when substantial deficits and a decline in international reserves occurred. Exports rose from $189 million in 1970 to $926 million in 1980.[3] Capital flows in the form of loans played a central role. Loans from private international banks rose from an annual average of $37.8 million in 1965–1969 to $41.5 million in 1970–1974 and then more than doubled to $85.5 million annually in 1975–1978. Transnational banks accounted for a mere 0.3 percent of new capital entering the country in 1970, but their share had risen to 61.8 percent by 1978. There was a parallel increase in their share of interest and amortization payments, from 2 percent to 74 percent. Almost 70 percent of these funds were provided to state enterprises producing for export, with the state petroleum company, Yacimientos Petrolíferos Fiscales Bolivianos (YPFB), and the state mining company, Corporación Minera de Bolivia (COMIBOL), the major recipients.[4]

The 1960s and 1970s also saw marked improvements in a number of social indicators, including an apparent decline in poverty levels, as the endemically poor were helped by this growth process. Information is relatively dispersed, though consistent, on these issues. Unemployment declined and then remained relatively stable (column 13); life expectancy, which was 43 years in 1960, rose to 51 by 1980; infant mortality fell from 167 per thousand to 129; and illiteracy of those over 15 fell from 61 percent to 37 percent. In addition, the primary school enrollment rate rose from 64 percent in 1960 to 84 percent in 1980; the secondary rate rose from 12 percent to 36 percent; and the population-physician ratio fell from 3,830 to 1,850.[5] The index of per capita food production rose from 100 in 1969–1971 to 115 by 1976, and between 1970 and 1975 the labor force covered by social security rose from 9 percent to 17.3 percent.[6]

Thus, economic and social performance was relatively positive in Bolivia through the 1970s. An escape from the poverty that the country had long suffered seemed possible.

Starting with the 1980s, however, economic performance deteriorated. A decline in international reserves and the devaluation of 1979 were the first signs of difficulty. There were international pressures from a variety of sources, many of them linked to Bolivia's political instability. By 1980, the disengagement of the transnational banks was underway. Their share of new capital fell by 50 percent, and their transactions resulted in a net outflow of capital. This was offset in large degree by inflows of foreign official capital in the form of project disbursements during 1979. After a military coup in 1980, this source of dollars also contracted by almost 50 percent. International reserves declined further, and net reserves became negative by 1980 and continued to decline.[7]

By 1982, international factors had completely reversed the progress of the 1970s. The debt service ratio increased to 37 percent of exports in 1984, as loans came due and exports declined (column 15). It would have been well over 50 percent had Bolivia not ceased payment on its private debt in March 1984. The terms of trade had turned against Bolivia, the international recession had lowered demand for Bolivian exports, and the scarcity of foreign exchange limited investment in all sectors, exports included.

The effects of this macroeconomic decline have been profound, especially among the urban poor and state employees. By 1984, real wages had fallen to 56 percent of their 1979 level (column 12); the open unemployment rate rose from 5.6 percent in 1979 to 10.5 percent in 1982 to 18 percent in 1985 (column 13). A 1985 survey in La Paz found that, in spite of high unemployment in the formal sector, 43 percent of families had two or more persons working, many of them in the informal sector. At the same time, however, 4 percent of families had no income aside from gifts and donations; family income declined by 8 percent from 1978–1980 to 1981–1983, saving became negative, and by 1983 family consumption had fallen to 82 percent of its 1980 level.[8]

Not surprisingly, continued economic decline had substantial effects on the marginal elements of the society. Malnutrition appears to have increased during the 1980s. The percentage of children entering the Cochabamba hospital with normal nutritional levels fell from 66 percent in 1977 to 44 percent in 1983, with a concomitant increase in severe malnutrition cases.[9] Broader surveys show consistent increases in malnutrition; only 55.5 percent of urban children exhibit normal nutritional levels.[10] Reductions in government resources dedicated to health and education will exacerbate these trends in the future.

So, during this period the major costs to the population have been the costs of the depression in Bolivia, and it is against this backdrop that the question of specific austerity programs must be viewed. In addition, the nature of the political structure must be taken into account, for that certainly affected the outlines of the austerity programs.

The Political Context

Although modern Bolivia has always been a relatively poor country, some have been better able to escape this poverty than others. The names Patiño, Aramayo, and Hochschild were synonymous with wealthy, extractive elites during the 1940s. Their wealth was based upon control of 80 percent of Bolivia's tin production, which returned the Patiños an average of 45 percent per year on their capital.[11] Their wealth and domination of political power were important factors in the Revolution of 1952, in which a mass insurrection, spearheaded by the miners, defeated the army of the Bolivian elite. It brought to power the Movimiento Nacionalista Revolucionario (MNR), a party founded in 1941. The MNR exhibited corporatist tendencies and had carefully infiltrated all areas of the government.[12] By 1952, it espoused strong nationalism, abolition of feudal relations in the countryside, alliance of the peasants with the workers and the middle class, and staunch anticommunism. In reality it had a limited base in rural areas, although rural agitation forced a land reform that gave peasants control over the land they had been cultivating. The militant working class was represented through the uneasy MNR alliance with the Confederación Obrera Boliviana (COB), a national confederation of all unions that was dominated by the miners.

Its role in the revolution has allowed the MNR to remain a dominant force in Bolivian politics, though more through the personalities of the early MNR leaders than through the party's vague and changeable program. The MNR provided Bolivia with most of the central political figures of today:

1. Victor Paz Estenssoro, a party founder and leading MNR intellectual, has been president of Bolivia three times (1952–1956, 1960–1964, and 1985–). He is a canny and pragmatic politician, willing to make alliances to gain power. He has collaborated with military governments and, more recently, has developed strong support among the domestic business sectors.

2. Hernán Siles Zuazo, also a founder of the MNR, was its second president (1956–1960). He implemented a stringent IMF austerity program and, in doing so, broke the concordat of the MNR and the unions represented by the COB. Siles broke with Paz in 1964 after Paz's attempt to extend his term of office. Siles took leadership of the left wing of the MNR, forming the MNR-Izquierda in the early 1970s, and again became president in October 1982 as the leader of a left-of-center coalition, Unión Democrática y Popular (UDP).

3. Juan Lechín Oquendo, who headed the miners' union (FSTMB) from its inception in 1944 and in that role dominated the COB, playing a key role in stabilizing or destabilizing governments. His backing of the MNR in 1952 was essential for the revolution's success, although he has generally been an opponent of whatever government was in power since that time.

The military, which was reconstituted during Siles' first term of office and which quickly returned to its accustomed role as a political player, provided the other important political leaders. Important military presidents were General René Barrientos Ortuño (1964–1969), who attempted to forge an alliance of the military with the peasants, and General Hugo Banzer Suárez (1971–1978), who replaced General Torres' progressive nationalist military government (1970–1971). After leaving office, Banzer formed the Acción Democrática Nacionalista (ADN) party and was the largest vote-getter in the 1985 elections. He acquiesced in Paz's accession to power and has grudgingly supported him in ruling the country.

This remarkable continuity of major political figures has not translated into regime or policy continuity. The last stable political regime before the Paz government of 1985 was that of Banzer, and the intervening ten governments, military and civilian, were too weak to develop and implement a coherent economic program. Thus the Banzer period, the "banzerato," can provide a good point of reference for the more recent events.

The Banzer Regime (1971–1978): Right-Wing Authoritarianism

Following a violent coup against the left-leaning government of General Torres in August 1971, General Hugo Banzer's regime became a precursor of the right-wing military governments that would dominate Uruguay, Argentina, and Chile during the decade. As with other rightist authoritarian regimes, the banzerato was marked by the repression of mass-based political mobilization in the miners' union and peasant groups.

Banzer's support came from the right wing of the military and of the political parties, the erstwhile reformist MNR and the Falange (FSB), which entered the government as junior partners providing technical and political support. The base of the two parties was the business community of La Paz and of Santa Cruz, the new agro-industry of the eastern lowlands allied with the private mining and service sectors. Soon the political parties began to demand full participation in decisions; at one point Paz declared that he, not Banzer, was the "caudillo of Bolivia."[13] So Banzer moved against the political parties, and Paz resigned his ceremonial cabinet post and went into exile in January 1974. After foiling an attempted coup, Banzer sought to stabilize his regime by outlawing political parties in November 1974, following the example of General Pinochet in Chile. However, the highly politicized nature of the Bolivian military ensured that it would reflect any tensions in the society and would eventually turn on Banzer.[14] This occurred when he was replaced by General Juan Pereda in 1978.

There were two critical economic resources to be controlled during this period: oil and the dollars generated by international loans. Table 4.1 (column 14) shows the rapid increase in foreign debt that occurred as the Banzer regime instituted a process of debt-led growth. Contracted debt increased fourfold, from $782 million in 1971 to $3.5 billion by 1979.[15] Control of this resource allowed Banzer to develop a clientelist system as the basis of his control. Among the groups supporting the regime, the gains were shared according to proximity to the state (Banzer) and to the oil revenues and loan dollars at his disposal. One indicator was the rapid increase in government employment between 1970 and 1974, from 66,000 to 141,000.[16] Patronage flowed through personalized patron-client relations to such an extent that Malloy and Gamarra characterized the system as "neo-patrimonial."[17] The primary gains in the private sector were made by the agro-export sector of Santa Cruz, Banzer's home department. Concessionary credit was the key mechanism, with an estimated 80 percent of all agricultural credit going to Santa Cruz.[18] At a macroeconomic level, the Banzer strategy was successful, as is apparent from the GDP growth figures (Table 4.1, column 2).

However, the peasants and miners were viewed as potential opponents of the regime and were repressed. Many of the mines were placed under virtual military occupation, and a massacre of peasants demonstrating against the removal of subsidies on basic food items such as cooking oil, pasta, and coffee served notice that peasant resistance would be met with violence.[19]

Dissatisfaction with the concentration of these benefits, with the repression and the strictures on the political system, and with Banzer's performance on highly charged nationalist issues (such as access to the sea) led to growing opposition. A hunger strike initiated by the wives of four exiled miners in December 1977 mushroomed into a mass hunger strike and a general strike in La Paz in January 1978. Banzer was forced to broaden participation in the July elections, which had been designed to install a puppet government.[20] Opposition within the military and absence of popular support forced Banzer out of power in August 1978, ushering in four years of rapidly changing governments and a generalized instability until 1985.

Bolivia After Banzer:
Many Governments and Little Stability

Banzer's fall underlines the weak point of his narrowly based clientelist political regime, in that it was caused by the mobilization of the sectors that had benefited little or had suffered repression. The limits of debt-led growth were also being reached, and the neopatrimonial government faced severe difficulties in a time of contracting resource availability.[21] Bolivia was entering an extended period of economic depression (see Table 4.1) and governmental instability (see Table 4.2).

The challenge facing each of the post-Banzer governments was twofold: to find some basis for political stability, be it military power or popular support, and to find resources that could turn around the deteriorating economy or at least buy support from the central political groups. Over much of the period this latter task was reduced to finding a means of obtaining dollars from official external sources, and a *sine qua non* was an austerity program that would free up an IMF stand-by loan.

Banzer's Economic Legacy

Banzer's departure in 1978 marked the beginning of a period of recession in Bolivia—an austerity enforced by deterioration in macroeconomic performance. The contraction of the oil sector, which had been the guarantor of international loans, was a key element. Bolivia's oil reserves were rapidly depleted during Banzer's period. By 1978 oil production had fallen 40 percent below its 1973 high, and it continued downward; priority was given to the domestic market, which accounted for 66 percent of production, up from 31 percent in 1973.[22] These changes reduced Bolivia's export income from oil, even when petroleum prices

TABLE 4.2
Political Scorecard (1971-1987)

President	Dates	Mode of Accession	Actions
Gen. Hugo Banzer Suárez	8/71-7/78	Military Coup	Repressed dissent; created stability built upon clientelism
Gen. Juan Pereda Asbún	8/78-11/78	Coup after fraudulent election in his favor	Ineffective
Gen. David Padilla Arancibia	11/78-8/79	Coup against Banzer group	Called new elections; resisted call for IMF austerity plan to fight inflation
Walter Guevara Arze (MNR)	8/79-11/79	Election deadlock; president of Senate headed interim government	Negotiated with IMF and tried to stabilize economy
Col. Alberto Natusch Busch	11/79	Coup by right-wing military	Popular opposition forced him out
Lidia Gueiler Tejada (MNR)	11/79-7/80	Head of lower house; appointed as interim president by Congress	Held June elections and implemented IMF stabilization program; got $150 million standby
Gen. Luís García Meza	7/80-7/81	Right-wing coup with drug support	Repression and drug involvement led to international isolation
Military Junta	7/81-9/81	Coup within the right-wing military	Tried to move against drugs to get international credibility
Gen. Celso Torrelio Villa	9/81-7/82	Consolidation	Same, but met popular opposition
Gen. Guido Vildoso Calderón	7/82-10/82	Internal military decision	Got military out of government
Hernám Siles Zuazo	10/82-8/85	Elected by Congress to resolve political impasse	Was an initial success; political weakness led to desperate economic policies and hyperstagflation
Victor Paz Estenssoro	10/85	Chosen by his Congress majority	Initiated stringent austerity program; reasserted state authority

Sources: This table relies heavily on James Dunkerley, Rebellion in the Veins: Political struggle in Bolivia, 1952-1982 (London: Verso, 1982), and on a chronology prepared by Dunkerly for a joint presentation on "Latin America's Fragile Democracies: Bolivia," at the Kellogg Institute, University of Notre Dame, on November 4, 1985.

rose dramatically after the Iran-Iraq War broke out. At the time Banzer left office, a gradual but accelerating decline in foreign resource inflows was under way—partly in response to Bolivia's extremely unstable political situation, partly because of a general slowing of international bank loans, and partly because of the Mexican default in 1982. So debt-led growth was over and the foreign exchange constraint on economic performance became acute.

The key to Bolivia's economic performance was thus access to the dollars necessary to maintain imports for consumption and investment and to repay creditors, allowing continued access to credit. Aside from normal economic activity such as the export of petroleum products and tin, there were three sources of dollars to which government policy could facilitate access: IMF stand-by loans, which were generally made conditional upon a stringent stabilization package; funds from multilateral institutions such as the World Bank or the Inter-American Development Bank, requiring project development and some level of international support; and public bilateral loans or aid, mostly from the United States, but at times made available by Brazil, Venezuela, and Argentina.[23]

Most of the governments during this period pronounced their dedication to stabilization/austerity, although only the civilian governments attempted coherent programs.

Military Interventionism and Instability (1978–1982)

Banzer's fall, the depletion of oil revenues, and the increase in inflation to 19.7 percent in 1979 (Table 4.1, column 10) should have generated pressure to seek an IMF stand-by loan; but it was not until November 1979, under the government of Lidia Gueiler, that the effort was made. Gueiler devalued the peso from P20 to P25 per U.S. dollar, removed many price controls, increased the domestic gasoline price by 73 percent, and pledged fiscal sobriety and resistance to all but minimal nominal wage increases.

Measured by its immediate objective, the program was a success. The IMF provided a $150 million stand-by loan, $111 million of which was to be disbursed by June 1980. A Structural Adjustment Loan from the World Bank was agreed upon, and the United States freed $50 million of aid plus $30 million of wheat.[24] At the same time, however, peasant and labor opposition quickly eroded any stabilization impact.[25] The campesinos quickly blockaded roads to demand reductions in the cost of transporting their products and to maintain controls on imported basic foodstuffs. The unions successfully used mobilizations and strikes to force the government to increase the wage adjustments. These government concessions, in turn, alienated the main business organization, the Confederación de Empresarios Privados de Bolivia (CEPB), which then began to oppose the government at all turns.

The experience corresponded with Kaldor's assessment of austerity programs, which center on devaluations: "It cannot be taken for granted that the internal distribution of income, which is the outcome of complex political forces, can be effectively changed by devaluation. It is more likely that a large-scale devaluation will cause an internal price upheaval . . . which will end up by reproducing much the same price relationships— between prices and wages and between internal and external prices— as prevailed before devaluation."[26] And to make matters worse, the dollars obtained were not sufficient to offset a movement toward general economic decline, so GDP stagnated during 1980.

Gueiler's successor, General García Meza, did not face the same external pressures for an austerity program, because a program had recently been installed. Moreover, his brutal repression muted economic demands. Nonetheless, the rhetoric of austerity was present in the government's self-description: "The combined political/economic program calls for immediate austerity measures, the rapid design of longer-term economic plans and continuation of military rule for at least three years."[27] García announced an economic program on January 9, 1981, which attempted to lower the fiscal deficit by squeezing the urban lower and middle classes. Wages were frozen, price subsidies were reduced, and social security coverage was narrowed; all were made feasible by the repression that had been implanted. Capital controls were established as an alternative to a "humiliating" devaluation of the currency and as a means of maintaining the flow of IMF dollars. In actual fact, this program and other military programs at best paid lip service to real stabilization. Imposing austerity would gain no additional dollars from international agencies because of the military's unsavory international reputation; consequently, the post-Banzer military maintained power through the use of force and repression because patrimonialism was not feasible.

Initially, García Meza benefited from the disbursements on international agreements reached by Gueiler. In addition, the Videla military regime in Argentina committed balance-of-payment support to its Bolivian client regime in the form of two loans totaling $325 million and with preferential sales of wheat and purchases of Bolivian natural gas. Also important was the greater government involvement in the country's rapidly growing cocaine traffic, which provided resources for García Meza and his apparatus, starting with an estimated $1 million to finance his rebellion.

But the dollar pipeline to the regime soon closed. Its repressive excesses and involvement in drugs soon led to a 15-month suspension of $135 million in U.S. aid, and Venezuela cut off $40 million in aid.[28] The scarcity of dollars was made more acute by García Meza's 1981 capital controls, which made access to dollars critical to economic actors seeking to protect themselves from the effects of the continuing economic decline. Capital flight grew to an estimated $370 million in 1980, and "dollarization" (the use of the dollar in all functions in the domestic economy) increased rapidly.[29]

García Meza's departure did renew the flow of dollars from the United States, but his neglect of stabilization left the Torrelio government with little choice but to float the peso, which fell from its fixed value of P24.5 per U.S. dollar when he took the presidency to P174 per U.S. dollar by August 1982. That maxi-devaluation contributed to an inflationary upsurge of 123 percent in 1982.[30]

The military's desire to return to the barracks is understandable, as were the difficulties that would confront any civilian administration taking power in the aftermath of such a poor performance. It is against this background that we should view Bolivia's most recent administrations of Hernán Siles Zuazo and Victor Paz Estenssoro, which followed the restoration of democracy in October 1982.

Democracy Restored: Hernán Siles
(1982–1985)

Siles' leftist UDP coalition had won a plurality in the 1980 elections. In order to get the military out of the government, the other parties agreed that he should take the presidency. His government was in a weakened position from the start, however; no more than a fragile coalition of six parties, it was soon disrupted by the departure of its moderate element, the Movimiento de la Izquierda Revolucionaria (MIR). Siles faced a hostile Congress controlled by the MNR and Banzer's right-wing ADN. Politics again focused on the personality of one of the founders of the MNR and his efforts to bring together enough support to govern the country.

The government's minority position in Congress prevented any effort to deal with inflation through an austerity program, and the leftist tinge of the president's coalition, which included the Communist party (PCB), made it unlikely that international institutions would come forth with significant dollar flows in any case. Thus Siles' economic policy was far from IMF orthodoxy. After an initial price liberalization, the economic technicians from the MIR and then from the PCB expanded price controls while attempting to restructure economic institutions. These policies represented a return to a Bolivian version of Latin American structuralism, the assumption being that if inflation in basic goods could be directly controlled and if supply would increase in response to changes in structure, price stability and growth could be attained. The actual result was hyperstagflation—that is, hyperinflation of 11,749 percent for the full year of 1985 and continued economic contraction.

Siles initially called for "one hundred days of sacrifice"—his version of a social pact of voluntary restraint on wage and price increases. The restoration of democratic political order gave him a short honeymoon of support, and his stabilization efforts were initially successful; monthly inflation fell from 41 percent to 13 percent for six months.

The underlying struggle over income shares soon reasserted itself, however, in the form of agitation for wage increases by the unions and evasion of price controls by business, making periodic price readjustments

unavoidable. These readjustments took form in six "paquetes," or economic packages, during Siles' three-year government; each consisted of
a devaluation of the official exchange rate, an increase in the minimum
wage and in the salary of public employees, and an increase in controlled
prices. The paquetes were not austerity programs in the traditional
sense—as seen most clearly in the behavior of the money supply, which
surged at an ever-increasing rate (Table 4.1, column 11), and in the
fiscal deficit, which increased from 7.8 percent of GDP in 1981 to 27.4
percent in 1984 (column 9). Rather, they were efforts to slow the decline
in GDP and to allocate the income losses.

It is now clear that the Siles regime attempted to impose these
economic costs on the private sector—especially the formal sector, which
could be controlled by the government. Government restrictions were
placed on most elements of economic activity. A "dedollarization" policy
in November 1982 gave the state formal control over all foreign exchange
proceeds by making dollar deposits illegal;[31] bank regulation was expanded and legal reserve ratios were gradually raised to limit any
independent monetary activity; and continual efforts were made to
monitor and enforce price controls as a first step in structural change.
Other steps were the expansion of state enterprises and the implementation
of cogestión, or workers' control in the state mining enterprise (COMIBOL)
in partial response to the demands of the COB. The expansion of the
state was financed by money creation.

There was drama in Siles' efforts to stabilize the economy, but the
script was repetitive and did not solve the underlying problems. Whenever
Siles announced a paquete, the unions raised immediate opposition
because the wage increases generally lagged behind both the devaluation
and the expected inflation.[32] There were six general strikes during the
Siles period—a tactic that forced the weakened government to grant
wage increases for miners and other public-sector employees, thus eroding
the effects of the program, increasing the fiscal deficit, ratcheting inflation
upward, and making another paquete necessary. At the same time, the
private sector through the CEPB opposed the expansion of government
activity and what were seen as concessions to the unions. Its leadership
took on an ever more active role in mobilizing opposition to Siles and
began to develop an alternative economic program in preparation for
his departure.[33]

To maintain a functioning government and to buy as much support
as possible, Siles expanded domestic credit to the government at whatever
rate was needed. This was an accelerating process, especially given that
government revenues were declining because of tax evasion and lags in
tax collections. It resulted in hyperinflation.

At the same time Siles was attempting to expand the state sector,
growth occurred in a whole new private sector—the informal sector—
where activities ranged from urban street vendors to drug dealings to
contraband imports and stolen ore from the mines. With the collapse

of the formal sector, the informal sector began to provide ever-increasing numbers of jobs in street commerce for those who could find no other source of income. According to estimates, informal employment accounted for 40 percent of total nonagricultural employment in 1984.[34] One of the ironies of the Siles policy is that it may have created a much more active private sector at the same time it tried to increase state control over the economy.

The expansion of the informal sector had a major impact on the incidence of the costs of austerity. Those engaged in drug or currency dealings at the top earned large incomes. The street vendors were also able to resist falling incomes at the lower end of the income distribution. Indeed, both of the most lucrative resources—dollars and coca-cocaine incomes—became accessible to broader segments of the population and were not entirely monopolized by the elite. Healy has documented how peasants and local elites were able to move up the processing ladder to obtain a greater share of the burgeoning incomes from cocaine.[35] And the existence of gray markets for dollars, ranging from curb markets to *financieras*, which paid high interest rates for dollar deposits, allowed a broader segment of the middle class to hold and use dollars. These adjustments were possible because the control of the state over the society was eroding rapidly.

Siles certainly succeeded in forcing the formal private sector to absorb the costs of the economic decline, although the reaction was often entry into the informal sector (e.g., speculation on dollars). The same flexibility aided large components of the urban informal sector. Peasant mobilizations, such as blockades of roads into urban areas, also prevented the imposition of full costs in that direction. And Siles' efforts to expand the state were ultimately unsuccessful, for real tax revenues fell from 15.3 percent of GDP in 1981 to 4.8 percent in 1984,[36] and the increasing inflation eroded the inflation tax from money creation.

As economic conditions deteriorated, popular and labor opposition, spearheaded by Juan Lechín, forced Siles to agree in November 1984 to call elections a year early and to step down in August 1985. Siles' one accomplishment may have been to unite so many disparate elements of the civilian opposition that an effective austerity program finally became possible once he bowed to pressure and in 1985 retired from the active political scene.

Paz and the New Economic Policy (1985–   )

The July 1985 election was a notable event, given Bolivia's military and political instability. When no candidate received an electoral majority in the national vote, the other representative of the 1950s, the MNR's Victor Paz, was elected by the Congress, although he had fewer votes than ADN's Banzer. Paz had run as a standard-bearer of the Revolution of 1952 (Bolivia's caudillo), but he had no coherent policy framework.

The popular discontent with hyperinflation and the continued economic decline made it possible, indeed essential, for the new government to undertake a rigorous austerity program.

After some initial attempts by his advisers to develop a coherent economic policy, Paz turned to the program that had been developed by Banzer and his technicians. The formal private sector was bent on reversing Siles' policies, which Paz found both politically and technically appealing.[37] The program adopted by his government came directly out of the CEPB, through a process of consultation at Harvard.[38] It called for the ascendency of the private over the state sector of the economy, for stringent austerity policies, for the reassertion of government as the rule-maker for markets, and for clear alignment with the United States.

Thus, both of the leaders of the MNR's 1952 revolution, Siles and Paz, reacted to the growing economic crisis of the 1980s by reversing policies they had implemented in the 1950s. Siles refused to repeat his 1956 stabilization program; Paz almost uniformly reversed the MNR program of 1952, thereby facilitating a coalition between the MNR and the ADN, which has governed Bolivia through 1988.[39] The past model of Bolivia had been state capitalism, with the state as a major entrepreneur, especially in mining and petroleum. The new model was the neoliberal "social market economy," where, as far as possible, the state's role would be confined to guaranteeing the operation of markets.

The economic program was incorporated in the Nueva Política Económica (NPE), Decree 21060 of August 29, 1985. Its detailed articles contained far-reaching steps to stop the hyperinflation, to stabilize the economy, and to restore the private sector to unquestioned dominance.[40]

There were a number of changes in the financial system. The government legalized dollar holdings and contracts denominated in dollars or indexed to inflation. It also devalued the official peso to the free market rate, from 67,000 to 1,075,000 pesos per U.S. dollar,[41] and established an auction mechanism that has maintained a close correspondence between the Central Bank official rate and the free market rate. Even more important was its ability to stabilize the exchange rate within several months of its accession. This stabilization removed the inflationary impulse of maxi-devaluations and signaled the government's intention to avoid using the inflation tax and to bear the exchange costs of inflation. Jeffrey Sachs, one of the prime architects of the program, cites its ability to stabilize the exchange rate as the key to stopping the hyperinflation abruptly.[42]

Another key weapon against hyperinflation was the government's control of the fiscal deficit and of the resultant money emission by limiting expenditures to the revenues available, while attempting to raise those revenues through a tax reform and changes in implementation. For example, the collection of the tariff duties was contracted to a private company, the Societe Generale de Surveillance.[43]

Economists generally agree that these are the steps necessary to stop a hyperinflation, and that they can succeed if a government has credibility.

Paz had credibility and thus inflation slowed, to zero in some months; in 1986 it was 276 percent, down from the 11,000 percent level of 1985.[44] The exchange rate stabilized at 1.9 million pesos per U.S. dollar and rose to 2.1 million by 1987, thus facilitating the currency reform in January 1987 that introduced a new currency, the boliviano (1 boliviano = 1 million pesos).

In economic theory, control of inflation (even hyperinflation) does not entail stagnation. Stabilization of an inflationary situation does not necessarily imply austerity, since other elements of the policy choices will determine whether the economy grows and who gains or loses in the process. Nonetheless, many of Paz's policies were quite recessionary, especially when combined with major declines in the prices of oil and tin during 1986. Prices were allowed to float freely—a process that, in other countries, had often led to overshooting, a reduction in effective demand, and resultant recession. These effects were intensified by the decisions to lower tariff rates and to remove many restrictions on imports, thereby adversely affecting domestic producers of competing goods, and by the increase in domestic prices of oil and many basic consumption goods.[45] Thus the 2.9 percent decline of GNP in 1986 should have come as no surprise.

It is impossible to assess the distributional effect of this recession with any accuracy. The price changes probably affected the urban poor most adversely. Wage earners were similarly affected by the rise in the unemployment rate, the freeze on wages through the end of 1985, and the subsequent restrictions on wages that caused real wages to erode.

The least ambiguous element of the Paz program has been its attack on the state sector and its employees, and on labor in general. Public-sector employment was to be reduced, or relocated, by 10 percent or roughly 30,000 workers. COMIBOL was dismantled into four entities, and worker involvement in decisions was canceled. Employment in mining was reduced by close to 75 percent during 1986, from 32,000 to 9,000. A number of state mines were sold. The reorganization of the mines gutted the miners' union and led to Juan Lechín's departure as the head of the COB, now headed by Simón Reyes, a Communist. Any legal restrictions on firing workers were removed throughout the entire economy, thus providing private-sector employers much greater latitude of action. All public enterprises were forced to "rationalize" in order to obtain credit, and several (such as the industrial holding company known as the Bolivian Development Corporation, or CBF) were closed immediately.

The formal private sector probably gained at the expense of the informal sector, as government has begun to regularize the functioning of markets.[46] As the government stabilizes and reorganizes the economy, the large business interests it represents should be able to use their position to force out the informal operators whose activities and importance had grown in the early 1980s. Steps have been taken against the illegal informal sector and drug trafficking. The most notable has been the joint operation of the U.S. military and Bolivian authorities against cocaine laboratories, although there is continual pressure to reduce coca acreage and to restrict peasant involvement at all levels.

President Paz was initially successful in establishing a viable political regime that built upon widespread discontent with Siles' policies and Paz's astute political alliance with Banzer.[47] He has imposed an IMF/Chicago-style austerity-stabilization program and had the political power to make it operate and to stop the hyperinflation. He has also been successful in generating inflows of dollars from outside the economy—a measure that is the key to success in any Bolivian austerity program. The IMF provided a $57 million stand-by loan.[48] The IDB doubled its disbursements to $116 million in 1986 and to more than $200 million by the end of 1987. An IMF compensatory financing package of $78.3 million and a Structural Adjustment Loan of $51.4 million were agreed upon in December 1986, which brought total financial inflows for the year to $306 million, more than offsetting the $234 million in debt service paid to non-private creditors—for Bolivia has yet to renew the servicing of loans from private banks suspended in May 1984.[49] The claims on the country from these loans have been dramatically reduced through the purchase of $300 million worth of private loans (and potentially as much as $600 million), at the going market price of 11 percent of their face value.

But Bolivia's austerity program has not been successful in reviving the moribund economy—a common occurrence, apparently, where such rigid orthodox programs are concerned. The official statistics show 2 percent GNP growth in 1987, (a figure that has been widely disputed); however, comparison with the heterodox program of Peru (whose economy grew 8.5 percent in 1986), Argentina, and Brazil highlights the lethargy of Bolivia's economic growth, although its inflation performance is certainly far better. Paz's economic package has not dealt in any fundamental way with the underlying underdevelopment, or poverty, of the country. Thus the government has been led to announce a $1.5 billion revitalization program for 1988–1990, financed largely with additional multilateral capital flows. The government program may be an admission of the limits to private-sector efforts, since 60 percent of the funds will go for public-sector infrastructure investment; subsidies will also be available for transportation and energy costs of "productive" enterprises.[50]

In any case, the Paz government represented a radical change from Siles, and its success in stopping the hyperinflation gave it the required legitimacy to undertake much broader austerity policies whose clear beneficiary has been the formal private sector. In the medium term, these steps will cause political tensions that could lead to the collapse of Paz's regime and to the reappearance of political instability. The government has been forced to impose two states of siege, and several general strikes—as well as frequent strikes of oil workers, teachers, and transportation workers—have occurred. The government reached "a temporary state of illiquidity" in July 1987, when Argentina's payment for natural gas supplies was not received.

Public opinion polls in 1987 showed a decline in the popularity of both government parties. The ADN has split, and Banzer's former second in command, Eudoro Galindo, has taken some of the party's forty deputies into his new Frente Democrática Nacionalista. The MNR has disintegrated into seven different factions, each with its own leader. The most prominent of these was Gonzalo Sánchez de Losada, who won the nomination for the presidency in the 1989 elections. Paz's uncertain health could remove the party's one unifying force, and rumors abound regarding Banzer's heart problem. The ADN split with the MNR and supported a vote of censure against the economic policy, although Paz and Banzer patched over the split. Several ministers were forced to resign because they were suspected of having ties to the drug industry; the ADN was rocked by videotapes showing its parliamentary leader associating with the Bolivian drug kingpin; and another minister is suspected of purchasing a state mine through a dummy corporation.

The best indicators of Paz's political problems were the municipal elections in December 1987, when the MIR, led by a new breed of politician, Jaime Paz Zamora, made a strong showing at the cost of the MNR. The ADN and the MIR each won three major cities, although the ADN lost its undisputed control of La Paz and has had to reach a power-sharing agreement with the MIR.

Instances of pervasive corruption and internal factional splits—as well as the continued sluggishness of the economy—have recapitulated the familiar Bolivian pattern. The implication is that Bolivia's long-term political instability and economic weakness have not been altered in any essential fashion by the neoconservative government of Paz Estenssoro. Such an alteration may remain the task of a second Bolivian revolution, sometime far in the future.

Conclusions

General poverty, governmental instability, political fragmentation around key political figures, and a limited set of options for economic gain form the warp across which the current economic crisis has been woven to yield the design that is Bolivia's. Economic deprivation has become more severe, and certain segments of the population have seen a dramatic deterioration in their standard of living; others have been able to maintain themselves and, in some cases, are prospering.

For the most part, the civilian governments attempted to deal with these difficulties by developing an economic policy of austerity. The key to their hopes, and perhaps to their success, has been the increased access to foreign exchange that such programs provided. When this was not possible, as in the case of Siles, austerity was resisted with disastrous results. After Banzer, the military governments were weak authoritarian regimes, unable to impose austerity on the country. Their problem was compounded by their restricted access to sources of foreign exchange, for the viability of any stabilization program depended heavily on increased dollar flows.

The costs of the civilian austerity programs were allocated in a very complex manner, and often in ways that policymakers would have difficulty anticipating. The clearest pattern has been the treatment of the state sector, which was favored by Banzer's patrimonial regime as well as by Siles and has been castigated by Paz. The other military regimes ruled by repressing labor and the peasantry, and in some cases by taking advantage of drug proceeds. Siles' policies, perhaps in spite of themselves, gave wide latitude to the informal sector while penalizing the formal private sector. Paz has returned the formal private sector to dominance while weakening labor. These trade-offs are the clearest indicators of who paid the costs of the austerity programs in Bolivia.

Bolivia's primary objective, however, is to recover from the depression of the 1980s. Finding some agreement on that process, and on sharing out the benefits it may bring, will determine the outline of Bolivia's future.

Notes

Acknowledgement of research travel support is made to the Jesse Jones Faculty Research Travel Fund of the University of Notre Dame. My thanks go to Penny Farley and Julio Prudencio for their help with the data in this chapter.

1. IBRD, *World Development Report, 1987* (New York: Oxford University Press, 1987), Tables 1, 28, 29, 30.

2. Unless other references are provided, the statistical argument in the text will be based upon the data in Table 4.1.

3. Rolando Morales, *Desarrollo y Pobreza en Bolivia* (La Paz: Mundy Color, 1984), Tables A25, A29.

4. Michael Mortimore, "El Estado y los Bancos Transnacionales," *Revista de la CEPAL* (August 1981), pp. 124–150.

5. IBRD, *World Development Report, 1983* (New York: Oxford University Press, 1983), Tables 23, 24, 25.

6. Morales, *Desarrollo*, Tables B7, B23.

7. Mortimore, "El Estado."

8. Julio Prudencio and Mónica Velasco, *La Defensa del Consumo* (La Paz: CERES, 1987): Prudencio and Velasco, "La Nueva Política Económica y la Situación Alimentaria," in *Seminario Sobre La Nueva Política Económica III* (La Paz: UNITAS, 1987), pp. 97–118.

9. Rolando Morales Anaya, *La Crisis Económica en Bolivia y Su Impacto en las Condiciones de Vida de los Niños* (La Paz: Papiro, 1985), p. 105.

10. Prudencio and Velasco, *La Defensa*, Ch. 7.

11. Rene Ruíz Gonzales, *El Drama de Bolivia: Una Economía Deformada* (La Paz: Juventud, 1986), pp. 131–182.

12. See James Dunkerley, *Rebellion in the Veins: Political Struggle in Bolivia, 1952–1982* (London: Verso, 1982), pp. 30–32.

13. Dunkerley, *Rebellion*, p. 204.

14. The introductory essay by J. S. Valenzuela and A. Valenzuela in *Military Rule in Chile: Dictatorship and Oppositions* (Baltimore: The Johns Hopkins University Press, 1986) documents the importance of the professionalization and nonpolitical nature of the Chilean military for the stability and continuity of the Pinochet regime, for Pinochet had only to ensure his control of the military in order to ensure his control of the country.

15. IBRD, *World Debt Tables, 1986–87* (Washington, D.C.: IBRD, 1987), assesses the total Bolivian debt in 1986 at $3.9 billion, compared with the $4.9 billion in Table 4.1. The higher figures from the Central Bank include very short-term debt such as trade credits as well as some contingent loans. Its series has the advantage of being consistent and continuous over the whole period. In any case, the rapid increase in debt during the 1970s is clear in all series.

16. Catherine M. Conaghan, "Capitalists, Technocrats, and Politicians: Economic Policy-Making and Democracy in the Central Andes," Kellogg Institute Working Paper No. 109 (May 1988), p. 22.

17. James Malloy and Eduardo Gamarra, "The Transition to Democracy in Bolivia," in James Malloy and Mitchell Seligson, eds., *Authoritarians and Democrats: Regime Transition in Latin America* (Pittsburgh: University of Pittsburgh Press, 1987), p. 98.

18. Jerry Ladman, ed., *Modern Day Bolivia: Legacy of Revolution and Prospects for the Future* (Tempe: Arizona State University, 1982), p. 331.

19. Ladman, *Modern Day Bolivia*, p. 330.

20. See Dunkerley, *Rebellion*, pp. 240–248, for a detailed account of the mobilization against Banzer and his resultant fall from power.

21. As Malloy and Gamarra put it in "The Transition": "A patrimonial lame duck is extremely lame indeed" (p. 109).

22. Ladman, *Modern Day Bolivia*, p. 324.

23. One other major source of dollars not tapped by the government was the burgeoning drug traffic. Bolivia has been the source of more than 50 percent of the world's raw material for cocaine. Accurate estimates of the illegal drug's importance are impossible, although one careful attempt estimated growth from 30 percent of legal GNP to 50 percent between 1980 and 1984, or close to $1 billion. See Unidad de Análisis de Políticas Económicas (UDAPE), "La Economía Informal en Bolivia: Una Visión Macroeconómica" (La Paz: UDAPE, September 1985), pp. 91–101. Only García Meza attempted to capture those proceeds, and mainly for his own benefit. Few credible efforts were made to attract flight capital back to Bolivia, which could have been another source of dollars.

24. Dunkerley, *Rebellion*, pp. 270–275; *Business Latin America*, December 5, 1979.

25. The case has often been made that such IMF-style austerity programs are inherently flawed and do not work under even ideal conditions. See, for example, Lance Taylor, "IS/LM in the Tropics: Diagrammatics of the New Structuralist Macro Critique," in William Cline and Sydney Weintraub, eds. *Economic Stabilization in Developing Countries* (Washington, D.C.: Brookings Institution, 1981).

26. N. Kaldor, "Devaluation and Adjustment in Developing Countries, *Finance and Development*, June 2, 1983, p. 35.

27. *Business Latin America*, October 8, 1980, p. 323.

28. Dunkerley, *Rebellion*, p. 305.

29. See Kenneth Jameson, "Macro Policy in a Dollarized Economy: The Experience of Bolivia," Kellogg Institute Working Paper No. 89 (December 1986).

30. The monthly exchange-rate figures are taken from Banco Central de Bolivia, *Boletín Estadístico*, No. 243 (1983), Table 3.2.

31. See Kenneth P. Jameson, "Macro Policy."

32. The effect of wage adjustments on real wages during a high inflation period can be dramatic, as can be seen from the data on nominal and real minimum daily wages during 1985–1986 (in Bolivian pesos):

Month	Nominal Wage	Real Wage (deflated to 12/84)
January, 1985	935,000	554,041
March, 1985	4,035,000	676,763
May, 1985	6,240,000	690,120
July, 1985	10,170,000	378,977
August, 1985	30,000,000	671,584
March, 1986	30,000,000	252,561

See UDAPE, "Monthly Statistical Series" (May 1986).

33. See Conaghan, "Technocrats," for an excellent treatment of this process, which was led by the core leadership (the so-called *grupo consultivo*) of the CEPB.

34. UDAPE, "La Economía Informal," Table 44.

35. Kevin Healy, "The Boom Within the Crisis: Some Recent Effects of Foreign Cocaine Markets on Bolivian Rural Society and Economy," in Deborah Pacini and Christine Franquemont, eds., *Coca and Cocaine: Effects on People and Policy in Latin America*, Cultural Survival Report No. 23 (June 1986), pp. 101–144.

36. IBRD, "Updating Memorandum on Bolivia," December 15, 1987, Table 1.2.

37. Conaghan's "Technocrats" provides a detailed treatment of the CEPB's activities, which led to the formulation of the economic plan.

38. Several of Banzer's advisers had Harvard degrees and maintained contacts there. One of them indicated to me that, when it had become clear that Siles would leave office through elections, it was natural to take a group to Harvard for a seminar with certain faculty friends to think about how to structure the post-Siles economic scene.

39. On October 16, 1985, a formal political pact was signed, guaranteeing ADN support for Paz in exchange for influence in a number of ministries and state agencies. See James Malloy, "Bolivia's Economic Crisis," *Current History* (January, 1987), pp. 9–12, 37–38.

40. See *Ultima Hora*, August 29, 1985, pp. 5–8. IBRD, "Updating," pp. 12–13, also provides an overview of the program and of further adjustments made during the following year, such as the adoption of a uniform 20 percent tariff.

41. Banco Central de Bolivia, "Estadísticas Monetarias y Financieras," No. 29 (February 1986), p. 38.

42. Jeffrey Sachs, "The Bolivian Hyperinflation and Stabilization," *American Economic Review*, Vol. 77, No. 2 (May 1987), pp. 279–283.

43. IBRD, "Updating," p. 14.

44. Initial government estimates placed the inflation rate at 92.5 percent in 1986. The higher figure was taken from a later and more complete publication: Interamerican Development Bank, *Economic and Social Progress in Latin America, 1987 Report* (Washington: IDB, 1987), p. 238. Inflation fell to 15 percent in 1987.

45. Joseph Ramos, in *Neoconservative Economics in the Southern Cone of Latin America, 1973–1983* (Baltimore: Johns Hopkins University Press, 1986), shows the effect of overshooting. Paz's plan did not seem to have learned the lessons of other Southern Cone stabilization experiences, as summarized in V. Canto and J. de Melo, "Lessons from Southern Cone Policy Reforms," *World Bank Research Observer* (July 1987), pp. 111–142.

46. For an assessment of the likely effects of the government policies and of the increase in discharged public employees entering the informal sector, see Roberto Casanovas, "El Sector Informal Urbano y la Nueva Política Económica," in *Seminario sobre la Neuva Política Económica III* (La Paz: UNITAS, 1987). One U.S. heavy equipment manufacturer indicated in an interview that its Bolivian distributor had had major problems since 1980 because it had to compete with ten informal-sector operations. Paz's regime should make their task easier.

47. Most of the information in this section is taken from various 1987–1988 issues of the *Latin American Weekly Report* and the *Andean Group Report*, both of which are published by Latin American Newsletters.

48. The IMF was much tougher in its stance than might have been expected. Instead of coming forth immediately with funds after Bolivia had undertaken its stringent program, it held up the money until June 1986, after a tax reform and value-added tax had been forced through the Congress. This toughness seems to signal the increasing role of "structural adjustment" thinking in the Fund.

49. *Latin American Weekly Report* (various issues, 1987–1988).

50. *Andean Group Report* (July 1987).

5

Austerity, External Debt, and Capital Formation in Peru

Paul Beckerman

Peru's Politics, Economy, and External Finance Since the Late 1960s

Overview: Politics, Economics, and Finance

Since 1963 Peru has had three constitutional governments and two military regimes. Fernando Belaúnde Terry, leader of the Acción Popular party, was first elected president in 1963. His liberal reformist government ended in an October 1968 army coup led by General Juan Velasco Alvarado. Velasco's "revolutionary" military government attempted a radical tranformation of Peru's economy and society—the controversial "Peruvian experiment." The military government's euphemistically named "second phase," following Velasco's replacement by General Francisco Morales Bermúdez in an August 1975 coup, was a lengthy transitional regime: It dealt with the profound external-payments crisis it inherited, and managed a restoration of civilian government. The elected government that took office under a new constitution on July 28, 1980, Fernando Belaúnde's second presidency, sought to reverse accumulating state power and to liberalize the economy, although after 1982 its energies were consumed by a new external-payments crisis. In 1985, disillusioned by Belaúnde's second presidency, Peru elected a young politician, Alan García Peréz of the Popular Revolutionary Alliance of the Americas (APRA) party. García promised a more pragmatic approach to managing the economy, even at the cost of external confrontation.

Whatever its regime type (elected-civilian or military) or regime ideology (populist, social democrat, "revolutionary," or centrist), Peruvian governments have constantly faced the problem of inadequate capital formation. The current external debt crisis, then, has both exacerbated the problem of capital formation and created additional barriers to renewed growth.

Peruvian politics in this period was dominated by six entities.

1. The military—particularly the army—has played a significant political role as a "moderating" power, as a combatant against left-wing guerrillas, and as a political force in its own right.

2. Although the traditional right-wing conservative parties virtually disappeared in the early 1970s (partly through confiscation of its property base, partly through obsolescence), urban professional and business interests came to support a laissez-faire party known as the Popular Christian Party (PPC), originally founded in 1967.

3. From the late 1950s into the 1960s, Fernando Belaúnde organized the reformist Popular Action (AP) party, which was supported by people who felt that Peru needed to change but who feared the more left-wing parties as well as the populist Peruvian APRA party.

4. The APRA party has played a central role in Peruvian politics since the 1920s. Under its founder, Victor Raúl Haya de la Torre, APRA developed an ideology of anti-imperialist, progressive pan-Latin Americanism, during its often violent struggle with the army and the traditional oligarchy. As it evolved, it made arrangements of convenience with right-wing adversaries, from which it acquired a damaging reputation for opportunism. It is often described as the only Peruvian political grouping with a genuine political organization and mass mobilization. In 1985 Alan García, a charismatic young leader with a "social democratic" orientation, assumed the presidency. He was the first Aprista to hold that office.

5. Peru's left-wing political parties currently form the largest legislative opposition bloc, since the Popular Action party suffered a deep loss of support after the failures of Belaúnde's second presidency. Peru's left is splintered ideologically and, to some degree, regionally. Consequently, the left-wing parties have never really succeeded in developing widespread electoral appeal. For years they focused their struggles on labor organization, often competing with the APRA.

6. Finally, there are the violent left-wing movements—notably the radical Maoist "Sendero Luminoso" ("Shining Path") guerrilla movement, which has engaged the security forces in an unusually brutal conflict since 1981.

Peru has had severe difficulties organizing itself politically and institutionally since 1963. The abruptness of its regime changes and the accompanying policy discontinuity have been severe problems.[1] Despite the energetic political and social reforms initiated throughout the period, Peru has failed to become an integrated, cohesive society. Class divisions in the urban areas, regional divisions, rural-urban divisions, and even ethnic and linguistic divisions remain sharp. Aside from the APRA, Peru's political parties remain organizationally weak, and public administration lacks continuity and effectiveness.

No government since 1963 has succeeded for long in dealing with the economy. All five governments have had to struggle with debilitating external-payments crises. The 1967 crisis was one of the traumatic episodes of Belaúnde's first government; the crisis that began in 1974 contributed to the demise of the revolutionary military regime; and the last three governments have spent much of their energy fighting balance-of-payments fires. The economy remained stubbornly dependent on external factors, managing occasional fitful growth when world commodity export prices were high and external finance was available, but declining again when it ran into balance-of-payments constraints.[2]

Table 5.1 indicates the degree of Peru's economic stagnation since 1975. From 1970 to 1974 annual real growth averaged 6.3 percent. Between 1976 and 1978, however, real GDP fell 2 percent and per capita real GDP fell 6.6 percent. GDP growth averaged 2.8 percent (about the same as population growth) through the modest 1978–1982 recovery, before declining a calamitous 12 percent in 1983. Real GDP recovered 4.7 percent in 1984 and 1.9 percent in 1985, then rose 8.5 percent in 1986. Even so, per capita real GDP remains 2.7 percent lower than it was in 1970.[3] GDP per employed worker, which followed a pattern similar to per capita real GDP over the 1970s, fell at an annual average rate of 4.9 percent between 1980 and 1985.

After rising at a respectable 3.4 percent average annual rate between 1970 and 1975, per capita private consumption fell at a 1 percent average annual rate between 1975 and 1980, then plunged at an average 3.3 percent annual rate between 1980 and 1985. Although it rose 13.1 percent between 1985 and 1986, it was still 0.6 percent lower than in 1970 (see Table 5.1). World Bank figures show that per capita caloric intake fell by a total of 6.6 percent between 1965 and 1985. Value added by Peruvian agriculture grew between 1970 and 1985 at a real annual rate of only 0.5 percent. Fertilizer use fell almost 25 percent between 1970 and 1984. Meanwhile, between 1970 and 1984 manufacturing value added grew at an average annual rate of only 1.1 percent. Manufacturing labor productivity fell nearly 40 percent between 1970 and 1985, and nearly 50 percent between 1980 and 1985.[4]

Table 5.2 shows some of the consequences of Peru's economic performance for its labor force. The proportion of the labor force adequately employed fell from nearly 55 percent to about 35 percent between 1973 and 1984. The proportion unemployed rose from 4.2 to 10.9 percent over the same period. Real remuneration levels fell precipitously: Real "salaries" were 42 percent lower and real wages 41 percent lower in 1986 than in 1973—despite having recovered 24 and 34 percent, respectively, in 1986 relative to 1985.

Peru's relationship with external creditors since the 1960s has ranged, over several cycles, from warm to frigid. The nature of the relationship has had remarkably little correlation with the political nature of Peru's governments. Belaúnde's first government significantly increased its borrowing from commercial banks. It needed bank funds in part because the confiscation measures it spoke of undertaking cost it bilateral U.S. support and discouraged inflows of foreign risk capital.[5] The 1968–1975

TABLE 5.1
Peru: Macroeconomic Performance Indicators, 1970-1986

	1970	1971	1972	1973	1974	1975	1976	1977	1978	1979	1980	1981	1982	1983	1984	1985	1986
Real GDP growth rates[a]																	
Total	7.3%	5.1%	5.8%	6.2%	6.9%	2.4%	3.3%	-0.3%	-1.8%	4.3%	2.9%	3.1%	0.9%	-12.0%	4.7%	1.9%	8.5%
Agriculture		3.0%	0.8%	2.4%	2.3%	-0.8%	2.9%	1.1%	-4.3%	3.3%	-4.2%	12.3%	3.4%	-7.9%	8.9%	2.3%	3.7%
Mining		-4.0%	7.1%	-0.6%	3.7%	-13.2%	7.8%	32.2%	15.2%	9.4%	-4.5%	-4.8%	8.3%	-7.4%	6.4%	6.1%	-2.5%
Manufacturing		8.6%	7.3%	7.4%	7.5%	4.7%	4.2%	-6.5%	-3.6%	3.9%	5.3%	-0.1%	-2.7%	-17.3%	2.8%	4.1%	17.8%
Real GDP[b]	71.2	74.9	79.2	84.1	89.9	92.1	95.1	94.9	93.2	97.2	100.0	103.1	104.0	91.5	95.9	97.7	106.1
Per capita real GDP[b]	93.3	95.4	98.2	101.4	105.4	105.0	105.6	102.6	98.2	99.8	100.0	100.4	98.7	84.6	86.4	85.8	90.8
Per capita real private consumption[b]	96.2	97.2	98.7	107.1	114.2	113.6	112.4	110.6	101.8	99.2	100.0	100.4	95.7	84.0	84.6	84.5	95.6
GDP per employed worker[b]	93.5	95.3	97.9	101.0	104.5	104.7	105.3	102.4	98.3	100.2	100.0	99.7	97.8	85.6	88.8	77.7	
Total manufacturing output				80.4	89.8	94.2	98.6	94.9	91.5	95.0	100.0	99.9	97.2	80.5	82.7	85.5	
consumer goods				92.2	99.9	103.3	106.3	97.3	92.9	96.1	100.0	99.7	97.7	85.7	83.5	85.7	
intermediate goods				67.1	78.5	80.1	87.8	91.8	93.0	98.1	100.0	98.7	98.9	81.8	89.9	92.8	
capital goods				87.3	95.3	113.1	111.0	97.9	81.3	80.5	100.0	104.8	89.8	58.2	55.0	59.9	

[a] in percentages per year
[b] 1980=100

Source: Banco Central de Reserva del Peru, Memoria (Lima, various annual issues).

TABLE 5.2
Peru: Employment and Wage Indicators, 1973-1986

	1973	1974	1975	1976	1977	1978	1979	1980	1981	1982	1983	1984	1985	1986
Labor force (millions)	4.5	4.7	4.8	5.0	5.1	5.3	5.4	5.6	5.8	6.0	6.1	6.3	6.6	
Percent adequately employed	54.5%	54.2%	52.7%	50.5%	46.0%	41.5%	41.5%	41.8%	45.3%	43.1%	37.5%	34.8%		
Percent inadequately employed	41.3%	41.8%	42.4%	44.3%	48.2%	52.0%	51.4%	51.2%	47.9%	49.9%	53.3%	54.2%		
Percent unemployed	4.2%	4.0%	4.9%	5.2%	5.8%	6.5%	7.1%	7.0%	6.8%	7.0%	9.2%	10.9%		
Labor earnings indicators (1980=100):														
Average real minimum wage	122.3	117.9	124.9	106.5	95.0	74.8	80.8	100.0	84.3	78.4	80.5	62.3		
Lima private sector:														
"Real salaries"	171.4	163.8	150.5	148.6	113.4	97.4	93.1	100.0	101.7	109.7	94.1	86.8	80.0	99.8
"Real wages"	136.7	137.1	113.0	131.9	100.9	91.9	94.6	100.0	97.9	99.3	82.2	70.1	60.5	81.1

Note: "Adequately employed" workers are those working 35 hours or more per week and earning income equal to or higher than the 1967 minimum wage reflated by the consumer price index. The labor force is defined as those persons employed or actively seeking employment.

Source: Banco Central de Reserva del Peru, Memoria (Lima, various annual issues); unpublished data compiled by the Ministry of Labor.

"revolutionary" military government also increased foreign borrowing from commercial banks, for similar reasons: Its nationalizations and other reforms involving confiscation or government intervention discouraged bilateral and multilateral credit flows. Risk-capital inflows were discouraged not only by the nationalizations but also by the industrial-ownership reforms undertaken by the military. Beginning in 1970, but especially after 1972, foreign commercial banks lent Peru significant sums in syndicated operations.[6] By 1975, however, Peru's external accounts had deteriorated sharply (see Table 5.3). From 1975 through 1978, the Morales Bermudez government and the commercial banks dealt with a stormy debt crisis. Initially Peru sought to avoid dealing with the IMF, and during 1976 the banks tried themselves to monitor a Peruvian stabilization program. The banks found that they had no leverage over government expenditure—particularly military expenditure. In 1977 the government negotiated an IMF arrangement, which worked badly at first and had to be renegotiated in 1978. In the middle of 1978, however, a terms-of-trade improvement turned Peru's external accounts around (see Tables 5.3 and 5.4) and eased the crisis.

The banks and international multilateral lending institutions perceived a brighter future for Peru at the outset of the 1980s, when the nation's external accounts and terms of trade had improved sharply and a new constitutional government committed to economic liberalization took over the government (see Tables 5.3 and 5.4). Accordingly, commercial-bank and official lending increased sharply during 1981 and 1982. The debt crisis struck in mid-1982, however. Commercial banks disbursed some funds in 1982 and 1983 under programs carried out in conjunction with an IMF program. Once interest arrears mounted after May 1984 and the government abandoned its stand-by agreement with the IMF, commercial banks, preoccupied with the problems of larger debtors, largely gave up their attempts to deal with Peru.

Fernando Belaúnde:
Civilian Reform (1963–1968)

In 1963, Fernando Belaúnde Terry took office as elected constitutional president after a brief military interregnum. He had founded the Popular Action party in the mid-1950s as a reformist alternative to the traditional oligarchy and to the APRA. Cultivating an image as an Alliance-for-Progress-generation leader, Belaúnde secured widespread electoral support, promising land reform, rural development, and housing for urban lower classes. Unfortunately for his objectives, the APRA joined with the National Odrista Union (UNO), the personalist party for the former military dictator Manuel Odría (1948–1956), in a legislative coalition that blocked most of Belaúnde's initiatives, particularly reform of the antiquated, largely indirect tax system and land reform.

The Belaúnde government was unable to raise taxes from the low level of 12–13 percent of GDP. At the same time, it had difficulty securing

TABLE 5.3
Peru: Balance-of-Payments Flows, 1971–1986

		1971	1972	1973	1974	1975	1976	1977	1978	1979	1980	1981	1982	1983	1984	1985	1986
Current account	*	-34	-32	-192	-807	-1535	-1072	-783	-164	953	-102	-1729	-1609	-871	-221	125	-1035
Trade surplus	*	159	133	79	-405	-1097	-675	-423	304	1722	826	-553	-426	293	1007	1161	-26
Merchandise exports	*	889	945	1112	1503	1330	1341	1726	1972	3676	3916	3249	3294	3015	3147	2967	2499
Merchandise imports	*	730	812	1033	1908	2427	2016	2148	1668	1954	3090	3802	3720	2722	2140	1806	2525
Net services	*	-232	-204	-313	-447	-515	-479	-465	-598	-921	-1075	-1337	-1347	-1383	-1386	-1181	-1135
Service payments	*																
Service receipts	*																
Pub.-Sec. interest payments	**	57	55	81	118	190	203	220	270	384	492	525	552	646	834	738	606
Capital account	*	-32	117	390	1203	1223	1161	1080	170	324	776	486	1687	613	928	206	712
Long-term capital	**	-28	115	383	895	1135	642	728	444	656	462	648	1200	1384	1189	691	603
Direct investment	**	-50	24	49	144	316	171	54	25	71	27	125	48	38	-89	1	22
Net public-sector borrowing	**	14	120	314	793	793	446	659	405	617	371	305	909	1431	1392	814	586
Bilateral, multilateral	**	34	58	65	198	269	188	270	240	333	202	101	170	386	530	499	331
Commercial banks	**	2	60	244	407	376	195	-121	116	525	335	157	497	724	984	422	609

	1971	1972	1973	1974	1975	1976	1977	1978	1979	1980	1981	1982	1983	1984	1985	1986
Net Priv.-sector borrowing	8	-29	21	-42	26	25	15	14	-32	64	218	243	-85	-114	-124	-5
Short-term and other capital	-28	-48	-178	194	-177	-438	-294	-204	-52	338	555	533	-552	-721	-349	22
Net errors and omissions *	16	-90	-41	-73	-191	-326	-112	52	112	-187	672	-162	225	-457	14	22
Balance of payments *	-51	-4	87	405	-509	-359	46	31	1165	652	-570	-84	-34	250	345	-295
Borrowing from the IMF *	16	67	0	0	0	219	12	107	229	144	0	331	176	129	0	0
Repayment to the IMF *	23	37	57	16	0	0	0	0	79	119	46	48	94	85	50	0
Gross foreign-exchange reserves *	381	443	526	925	426	289	357	390	1521	1980	1200	1350	1365	1630	1827	1430
Net foreign-exchange reserves **	346	398	411	693	116	-751	-1101	-1025	554	1276	791	896	896	1103	1383	924
Current account/GDP	-0.5%	-0.4%	-2.1%	-7.0%	-11.3%	-7.8%	-6.1%	-1.5%	6.8%	-0.6%	-8.6%	-7.9%	-5.4%	-1.3%	0.9%	-4.9%
Gross for.-exch. reserves, in months of total imports of goods and services	3.9	4.3	3.9	4.1	1.5	1.2	1.4	1.7	5.3	4.7	2.4	2.7	3.3	4.5	5.6	3.8

Note: 1984-1986 figures include no interest on accumulated interest arrears.

Sources: *International Monetary Fund, International Financial Statistics (Washington, various issues); **Banco Central de Reserva del Peru, Memoria (Lima, various annual issues).

TABLE 5.4
Peru: International Economic Conditions, 1971-1986

	1971	1972	1973	1974	1975	1976	1977	1978	1979	1980	1981	1982	1983	1984	1985	1986
Selected commodity exports																
Copper: value (US$ million)	180.0	193.0	333.0	316.0	183.0	236.0	385.0	425.0	693.0	752.0	529.0	460.0	443.0	442.0	464.3	436.2
Volume (1,000 metric tons)	195.0	209.0	194.0	184.0	156.0	182.0	321.0	349.0	377.0	350.0	324.0	335.0	292.0	337.0	353.9	341.0
Unit price (US cents/lb.)	41.9	42.1	78.0	78.2	53.2	58.8	54.4	55.3	83.5	97.4	74.1	62.3	68.8	59.4	59.5	58.0
Fishmeal: value (US$ million)	267.4	220.0	138.0	202.0	168.0	168.0	184.0	196.0	256.0	195.0	141.0	202.0	79.0	137.0	116.7	204.5
Volume (1,000 metric tons)	1759.7	1524.0	348.0	629.0	781.0	592.0	436.0	483.0	657.0	416.0	315.0	616.0	205.0	401.0	499.4	716.0
Unit price (US$/metric ton)	154.9	144.0	395.4	321.0	215.0	284.2	421.8	405.3	389.7	469.4	448.0	328.8	386.7	342.4	233.7	285.5
Petroleum: value (US$ million)	6.0	7.0	15.0	28.0	41.0	50.0	52.0	186.0	652.0	792.0	689.0	719.0	544.0	618.0	645.5	235.7
Volume (1,000 metric tons)	1.4	1.8	2.6	2.2	4.0	4.8	4.1	13.7	24.1	22.5	19.9	22.7	20.5	23.5	27.0	22.0
Unit price (US$/barrel)	3.9	3.6	5.8	12.8	10.1	10.5	12.6	13.6	27.1	35.2	34.7	31.6	26.6	26.3	23.9	10.7
"Non traditional" exports (US$ million)	31.0	52.0	114.0	151.0	96.0	137.0	224.0	353.0	810.0	845.0	701.0	762.0	555.0	726.0	718.9	648.9
Merchandise imports/GDP (percent)	10.7%	10.7%	11.1%	16.5%	17.8%	14.7%	16.9%	15.4%	14.0%	18.0%	18.8%	18.3%	16.9%	12.6%	12.5%	11.9%
Pub. sec., cap. goods (1980 GDP = 100)	1.2	1.3	1.8	3.1	2.9	2.7	2.0	2.1	1.8	2.5	2.6	2.7	2.6	2.3	1.1	0.8
Priv. sec., cap. goods (1980 GDP = 100)	0.9	0.7	1.1	1.7	2.5	1.9	1.9	1.7	2.6	3.8	4.8	4.6	2.5	2.1	2.6	2.7
Export prices index (percent change)	-8.8%	2.6%	54.6%	31.7%	-4.5%	-3.0%	-0.5%	-2.4%	49.1%	27.1%	-15.4%	-17.1%	9.8%	-7.8%	-12.2%	-14.8%
Import prices index (percent change)	7.1%	9.2%	15.0%	11.3%	10.3%	2.2%	7.8%	14.2%	0.0%	10.8%	12.0%	3.4%	0.7%	2.2%	0.8%	2.3%
Terms of trade (1970 = 100)	85.2	80.0	107.5	127.2	110.1	104.4	96.5	82.4	122.9	141.0	106.6	85.5	93.2	84.1	73.2	61.0
Public-sector interest/public-sector debt	9.6%	8.7%	11.3%	12.5%	13.8%	10.4%	9.7%	9.7%	11.3%	13.1%	13.3%	14.8%	16.1%	17.4%	13.2%	9.7%
Percent revaluation of average exch. rate (in terms of the U.S. dollar)	0.0%	0.0%	0.0%	0.0%	-4.1%	-27.6%	-33.8%	-46.1%	-30.4%	-22.2%	-31.6%	-39.5%	-57.2%	-53.0%	-68.4%	-21.3%
Real effective exch. rate (vis-a-vis U.S)	63.1	73.3	69.4	65.1	69.0	84.7	118.4	116.6	100.0	71.3	70.2	76.2	70.9	84.2		

Note: 1984-1986 figures include no interest on accumulated interest arrears.

Source: Banco Central de Reserva del Peru, Memoria (Lima, various annual issues).

credit from foreign official agencies, because the United states objected to Belaúnde's hints that he might nationalize the International Petroleum Company (IPC), a consortium owned mainly by large U.S. oil firms. The United States also objected to Peruvian purchases of French military aircraft. The Belaúnde government therefore resorted to deficit financing and borrowing from foreign banks. In 1964 it secured a $40 million syndicated bank loan, Peru's first significant foreign bank loan since 1931. Government expenditure rose from 17.5 to 20 percent of GDP between 1965 and 1967 as the government undertook a public-investment program. The deficit rose to about 4 percent of GDP by 1967, thereby stimulating the economy and, hence, imports. With exports stagnating, the external accounts deteriorated sharply in the second half of 1966 and the first half of 1967, and reserve loss obliged the government to seek IMF assistance.

In June 1967 an IMF mission arrived to negotiate a "stand-by" accord. Its "conditionality" was essentially a government commitment to reduce its deficit to zero. Aware that the IMF would take this position, the government had already used decrees to enact various tax increases and expenditures cuts in advance of the mission's arrival. Largely on the basis of these measures, the government negotiated an IMF agreement, which opened the way to credit from commercial-bank and multilateral sources totaling nearly $100 million. The congress, however, refused to ratify the tax increases and expenditure cuts, although the IMF program was allowed to proceed. Still, on September 1, with the balance of payments worsening sharply, the Central Bank had no choice but "to suspend its participation in the foreign-exchange market," precipitating a 30.7 percent devaluation of the Peruvian *sol.*[7]

The following year, after the devaluation trauma, the government persuaded the parliamentary opposition to raise taxes, pointedly noting the military's restiveness in the face of the economic instability. In July 1968 the government negotiated an accord with external creditors, rescheduling amortization due in 1968 and 1969 into 1970 and 1971. Presidential elections were scheduled for 1969, and, to the Army's growing consternation, the APRA seemed likely to win them. A political scandal broke out over alleged secret provisions in a draft settlement with the IPC.[8] In the wake of this crisis, the armed forces led by the army's commander, General Juan Velasco Alvarado, seized power on October 3, 1968.

Juan Velasco:
Military "Revolution" (1968–1957)

Peru's "experiment from 1968 to 1980 in militarily directed change" is the subject of a vast and still-growing social science literature.[9] A few weeks after taking power, the new government nationalized the IPC and declared that it intended to lead a revolutionary transformation of Peru. In July 1969 the government announced an ambitious agrarian reform, which not only seized the large highland *haciendas* and the commercial sugar and cotton enterprises of the northern coastal area, but also invented a variety of institutional forms under which workers could hold the land cooperatively. In 1970 it introduced the "industrial-community" system, under which workers gradually came to participate in the ownership of private-sector industrial enterprises. In the same year the government announced a substantial educational reform.[10] It nationalized large foreign-owned mining properties, forming them into the state-owned companies known as MineroPeru and Centromín. It also nationalized three large commercial banks (allowing them to operate as autonomous state-owned enterprises) and the nation's fishing fleet. Throughout the Velasco presidency the government carried out a massive program of public infrastructure investments. It proclaimed a determination to forge a more integrated society, to improve living standards, and to relieve Peru's singularly poor income distribution. It also declared its intention to reduce Peru's external economic dependence and proclaimed a vigorously nonaligned foreign policy.

The "experiment" was so ambitious that it may be meaningless to generalize about whether it left Peru better or worse off. As some writers have emphasized, by dismantling the traditional oligarchy, the revolution opened the way to modernization. But it certainly did not accomplish what the military had hoped for. The agrarian reform seized properties and organized them into cooperative units, but it did not succeed in raising agricultural productivity or rural incomes. The industrial-owned reform withered away after 1975. The nationalized enterprises never proved sufficiently dynamic or efficient. By the late 1970s, Peruvian society remained as divided as ever. Its income distribution was no better, its living standards had scarcely improved, and external dependence was as severe as ever.

The reasons for which the revolution fell short are still a matter of controversy.[11] By 1974 the investment program and growing national income had begun to collide with Peru's balance-of-payments constraint; but the regime's own contradictions had tangled it up well before then. In some measure, the Army was defeated by the very problems it had intended to overcome. The regime's instinct apparently was to unite and mobilize the society by commanding it to do so; but it never figured out how to persuade a disunified society to unify itself. Some observers pointed out in the mid-1970s that the regime's characteristic approach to reform involved giving people property shares in the economic entities in which they worked, undoubtedly in the hope tht they would attain a stake in their society.[12] Unfortunately, however, this measure divided the society and rigidified the income distribution, since the different economic entities had different productivity characteristics. At least until the world sugar price tumbled and several years of drought occurred, sugar cooperative members in northern Peru, for example, were better off than highland subsistence farmers. The regime was especially sensitive to this criticism. In any case, although it had a program to redistribute income claims, it was unsure how to augment productivity, capital formation, or saving.

Politically, the regime was caught in a dilemma: Although it wanted to mobilize the nation, it was also determined to decide on and to enact changes through military-style command. The regime retained decision-making power entirely within the military command: Beginning in 1972, when it sought to organize mass support through a national institution called the National System of Support for Social Mobilization (SINA-MOS), it characteristically made certain that the organization could only follow, not initiate, policy directives.[13] Moreover, the regime's purposes, or ideology, confused people and seemed peculiarly negative. The government said often that it was "neither capitalist nor socialist," but it never conveyed a clear sense of what it was. Velasco's embittered personality and the army's secretive style complicated efforts to win the nation's trust. In part, the government's approach reflected deep ideological divisions among the army's leading officers.[14] The Peruvian populace therefore maintained its political distance from the government.

Because of the nationalizations, as well as the lingering differences over arms purchases and a dispute over Peru's claim to a 200-mile territorial waters limit, the United States renewed pressure on Peru, applying punitive clauses of legislation that governed foreign aid and lending. Again, Peru's access to credit from official U.S. and multilateral lending sources was limited. And again, more or less to compensate for the limitation on "soft" official credit available to it, the government turned to commercial banks for term credit. In 1970, when it nationalized the Banco Continental, it indemnified the bank's principal foreign shareholder, the Chase Manhattan Bank, in cash. This move actually improved relations between the government and the international banking community.[15] In 1971 and 1972 commercial banks provided $110 million in new credit. Then, in 1973, 1974, and 1975 the new-credit flow rose to $450 million a year, mostly in syndicated operations (see Table 5.3).

Bankers' preoccupations, resulting from the 1967 balance-of-payments crisis, were probably dispelled by the rapidity with which Peru's balance of payments recovered in 1968 and 1969. The devaluation discouraged imports; higher world commodity prices improved export performance; and the agreements with banks and the IMF enabled Peru to refinance amortization. The commerical bankers were impressed by the military's apparent financial conservatism, and they believed that the various export investment projects—notably the investment in an oil pipeline from the rain forest over the Andes to the port of Talara in the northern part of the country—would ensure future balance-of-payments solidity. The U.S. government relaxed its pressure in the early 1970s after reaching an understanding with the Peruvian government regarding indemnification for confiscated property. Bilateral lending by the United States and other foreign governments picked up along with bank lending, reaching $139,

$270, and $359 million, respectively, in 1973, 1974, and 1975. Total external debt rose at a rate of about $1 billion a year in these years, and the debt-GDP ratio began to increase as well (see Table 5.5). By contrast, multilateral lending remained relatively small—on the order of $35 million a year.

As early as 1973, however, a new round of balance-of-payments pressures became evident. In 1974 and 1975 they intensified, as the current-account deficit soared first to $800 million and then to $1.5 billion (about 7 and 12 percent of GDP, respectively). The failure of the anchovy catch in 1973, a disappointingly low level of oil production, declining sugar prices, and relatively low prices for Peru's traditional mining products all contributed to the deepening crisis. At the same time, domestic growth induced import growth (see Tables 5.3 and 5.4). The government resisted devaluation and imposed severe foreign exchange rationing measures. The inflation rate drifted to a higher level (see Table 5.5) as the public-sector deficit—pressured by heavy public investments— rose toward 10 percent of GDP (see Table 5.6). Political difficulties intensified at the same time. In July 1974 the government responded to press criticism by confiscating the principal newspapers and turning them over to national entities supposedly representing different social groups. This action generated protests by Lima's middle class, which at last felt that the government was threatening its interests. The crises deepened through 1974 and 1975 as President Velasco's health declined. In July 1975 the government was compelled to devalue and to introduce recessive austerity measures. In what became characteristic components of "austerity packages," it reduced subsidy, raised expenditures and raised controlled prices in order to improve public-sector finances and derive increased sales-tax revenue. These measures were intended to increase public-sector saving (or to decrease public-sector dissaving), to reduce private-sector consumption demand, and thus, in turn, to force a reduction in the demand for external saving.

Francisco Morales Bermúdez:
The First Debt Crisis (1975–1980)

On August 29, 1975, General Francisco Morales Bermúdez, a respected officer who had served briefly as finance minister during the foreign-exchange crisis of 1967 and was already Velasco's prime minister, deposed Velasco in a bloodless coup. Upon assuming power, he announced that the new government would introduce the revolution's "second phase," implying that it would "consolidate" rather than attempt further reforms. He promised to maintain the Velasco reforms, but it was widely assumed that Morales Bermúdez style would be far more conservative. In any case, over the first year of his government, the balance-of-payments crisis intensified. Economic performance leveled off as a result of the fiscal measures taken to control the external accounts (see Tables 5.1 and 5.2). The price adjustments lifted the inflation rate from the (repressed)

TABLE 5.5
Peru: External Debt (in US$ million), 1971-1986

	1971	1972	1973	1974	1975	1976	1977	1978	1979	1980	1981	1982	1983	1984	1985	1986
Total external debt:*	3,692	3,832	4,133	5,238	6,257	7,384	8,567	9,325	9,334	9,595	9,606	11,465	12,445	13,338	13,721	14,466
Public external term debt	997	1,121	1,491	2,182	3,066	3,554	4,311	5,135	5,764	6,043	6,127	6,825	8,256	9,648	10,462	11,048
Bilateral	269	315	390	565	825	991	1,259	1,671	1,737	1,849	1,346	1,195	1,321	1,508	1,793	1,938
Multilateral (excl. IMF)	191	211	220	243	259	268	330	408	485	610	784	949	1,106	1,305	1,426	1,529
Commercial banks	138	198	455	861	1,320	1,514	1,239	1,208	1,563	1,536	1,524	1,986	2,406	2,972	3,110	3,262
COMECON	0	14	42	138	263	361	743	916	935	985	930	925	1,076	1,070	1,026	986
Suppliers	399	383	384	375	399	420	740	932	1,044	1,063	1,543	1,770	2,347	2,793	3,107	3,333
Central-bank term debt	34	67	17	0	0	385	626	751	869	710	455	707	1,089	862	825	788
IMF	34	67	17	0	0	220	232	347	520	538	445	707	698	699	727	755
Private-term debt	1,211	1,182	1,202	1,260	1,286	1,311	1,326	1,340	1,308	1,373	1,508	1,665	1,580	1,466	1,342	1,337
Short-term debt	1,450	1,462	1,423	1,796	1,905	2,134	2,304	2,099	1,393	1,469	1,516	2,268	1,520	1,362	1,092	1,293
Real growth rate of external debt	-6.4%	-5.0%	-6.2%	13.9%	8.3%	15.4%	7.7%	-4.6%	0.1%	-7.2%	-10.6%	15.4%	7.8%	4.9%	3.4%	1.7%
Pub.-sec. interest/incr. in pub.sec. debt	109.6%	44.4%	21.9%	17.1%	21.5%	41.6%	29.1%	32.8%	61.0%	176.3%	625.0%	79.1%	45.1%	59.9%	90.7%	103.4%
Pub.-sec. interest/GDP	0.8%	0.7%	0.9%	1.0%	1.4%	1.5%	1.7%	2.5%	2.7%	2.9%	2.6%	2.7%	4.0%	4.9%	5.1%	2.9%
Pub.-sec. interest/total exports	5.2%	4.7%	5.9%	6.3%	10.7%	11.7%	10.4%	11.2%	9.0%	10.2%	12.4%	13.2%	16.8%	21.0%	18.9%	17.9%
External debt/GDP	54.0%	50.3%	44.5%	45.3%	45.9%	53.9%	67.3%	86.1%	66.8%	55.7%	47.6%	56.5%	77.2%	78.8%	94.6%	68.2%
External debt/total exports	339.3%	328.6%	301.2%	280.9%	352.5%	427.3%	405.5%	385.2%	219.3%	198.6%	227.4%	273.8%	324.0%	335.6%	350.6%	426.9%

*External debt does not include interest, interest arrears beginning in 1984.

Source: Banco Central de Reserva del Peru, Memoria (Lima, various annual issues).

TABLE 5.6
Peru: Prices and Monetary Aggregates, 1972-1986

	1972	1973	1974	1975	1976	1977	1978	1979	1980	1981	1982	1983	1984	1985	1986
Percentage increase in GDP deflator	5.6%	14.7%	16.3%	20.2%	34.5%	40.7%	60.7%	77.7%	54.0%	66.3%	64.6%	110.7%	113.6%	166.1%	71.2%
Percentage increase in consumer prices	7.9%	9.8%	16.7%	23.8%	33.1%	38.2%	57.7%	66.6%	59.2%	75.4%	64.4%	111.2%	110.2%	163.4%	77.9%
Year-end central bank discount rate (percent)	9.5%	9.5%	9.5%	9.5%	12.5%	14.5%	28.5%	29.5%	29.5%	44.5%	44.5%	60.0%	60.0%		
Banking system assets (end of year; 1980 broad money supply = 100)															
Net foreign assets	1.2	1.3	2.1	0.4	-3.9	-9.6	-15.3	9.9	32.2	24.1	73.6	153.9	451.2	1552.5	1004.5
Domestic credit:	5.5	7.2	9.1	12.8	19.7	27.2	41.8	48.5	81.2	157.3	260.1	693.0	1337.9	2458.0	4344.3
Claims on public sector	2.6	3.8	5.2	7.8	13.4	19.5	31.4	29.7	42.5	70.8	117.3	384.0	741.8	1147.9	2259.3
Claims on private sector	2.9	3.4	3.8	5.0	6.3	7.6	10.4	18.7	38.7	86.5	142.8	309.0	596.1	1310.1	2085.0
Narrow money supply	4.6	5.8	8.2	9.5	12.0	14.5	21.0	35.9	56.6	83.0	111.8	219.5	473.9	1827.0	3392.6
Broad money supply	6.0	7.3	9.8	11.4	14.1	17.6	28.4	54.6	100.0	168.5	285.9	581.7	1350.7	3476.3	3121.0
Percentage increase in narrow money supply	28.9%	25.9%	41.1%	16.5%	25.8%	20.5%	45.6%	70.6%	57.7%	46.6%	34.7%	96.2%	116.0%	285.5%	85.7%
Percentage increase in broad money supply	23.0%	22.7%	34.8%	15.3%	24.5%	24.7%	60.8%	92.4%	83.3%	68.5%	69.6%	103.5%	132.2%	157.4%	-10.2%
Increase in net foreign assets/ previous year's broad money supply (per cent)	1.6%	1.3%	12.0%	-17.7%	-37.8%	-40.4%	-32.4%	89.1%	40.8%	-8.0%	29.3%	28.1%	51.1%	81.5%	-15.8%
Increase in public-sector claims/ previous year's broad money supply (per cent)	13.1%	20.0%	19.6%	25.8%	49.7%	43.3%	67.1%	-5.9%	23.4%	28.4%	27.6%	93.3%	61.5%	30.1%	32.0%
Increase in private-sector claims/ previous year's broad money supply (per cent)	9.8%	9.3%	5.4%	12.1%	11.2%	9.6%	15.8%	29.4%	36.5%	47.8%	33.4%	58.1%	49.4%	52.9%	22.3%

Source: International Monetary Fund, International Financial Statistics (Washington, various issues).

10–20 percent range that characterized the Velasco years toward 20–30 percent (see Table 5.5).

The economic problems of 1976–1978 were in many ways an early version of the 1980s debt crisis. With the current account still in an unsustainable deficit and international reserves falling sharply (see Table 5.6), the new government undertook multiple discussions with commercial banks, the IMF, and foreign governments—particularly the U.S. government. In June 1976, to lend credibility to its request for $400 million in new commercial-bank credit, the government announced another austerity package, including a 44.4 percent devaluation as well as tax increases and subsidy cuts that sharply raised the prices of foodstuffs.[16] The austerity program led to widespread demonstrations and a wave of strikes. Peru's left-wing parties achieved a new public prominence as they led the demonstrations. The government had to impose a state of national emergency. At this point, the president announced that the government would carry out a transition to civilian government.[17]

The government's measures persuaded a consortium of U.S. and European commercial banks to provide nearly $400 million in new credits. The demonstrations dissuaded the government from carrying out an IMF program. Instead, the government agreed that the bank loan would carry a kind of conditionality: The banks themselves would monitor the performance of the government budget (see Table 5.7) and the balance of payments. In September 1976, the central bank began a crawling-peg devaluation of the exchange rate. This stablization program failed, however, mainly because, the military government in late 1976 made a large arms purchase from the Soviet Union and approved a budget with a high deficit, including military pay raises.[18] As a result, the banks suspended disbursements to Peru, resolving not to deal with the country without an IMF agreement. The government was forced to return to the IMF in order to close its 1977 external financing gap.

To set the stage for the IMF negotiations, the government enacted yet another "stabilization package" in January 1977, involving expenditure and subsidy cuts partly offset by wage increases. Difficult negotiations ensued: The Fund pressed the government to cut all subsidies, cut public-sector investment and other (particularly military) expenditure items, raise taxes, eliminate import restrictions, devalue heavily, and limit wage increases. After a further round of austerity measures in June, the government reached agreement on an IMF stand-by program in October 1977. Tables 5.1 and 5.2 indicate the extent to which the austerity measures raised unemployment and reduced real GDP, real consumption, and real wages during 1977; Table 5.3, however, shows that they reduced the current-account deficit. The program, which was to run through 1979, aimed at reducing the public-sector deficit from 8.3 percent in 1977 to 3.5 and 2.9 percent in 1978 and 1979, through higher taxes, expenditure cuts, and higher public-sector prices—particularly the gasoline price. The government also promised to resume crawling-peg devaluation, which it had interrupted in August.

Peru was to receive $110 million from the IMF over eighteen months, but the main point was that the agreement allowed negotiations to begin for new credit of about $260 million and for refinancing of amortization due in 1978. In March 1978, however, an IMF mission found Peru in serious violation of the IMF program conditionality. Not only had Peru missed year-end performance criteria, including the public-sector deficit and international-reserve criteria, but the government introduced a two-tier exchange rate. Most serious, the government was alleged to have fiddled the reserve figures. The IMF program and bank discussions broke off in an acrimonious atmosphere.

In May 1978 Javier Silva Ruete and Manuel Moreyra were appointed finance minister and central-bank president, respectively—Morales Bermúdez' fourth economy team. They were under intense pressure from the outset, because some banks had already acted to declare Peru in default. Just before they took office, the government announced another round of austerity measures, including yet another return to crawling-peg devaluation. A new round of strikes and demonstrations resulted. The new ministerial team asked the IMF to renegotiate the program. An agreement was concluded in August, and the government was able to reschedule maturities due in 1978 and 1979 soon afterward.[19] The previous agreement was made less severe: The 1978 public-sector deficit was to be reduced to 4 percent and the 1979 deficit to 2 percent of GDP. The Fund acceded to less ambitious revenue measures, and to a crawling rather than a sudden "real-effective" devaluation. For the second year running, however, real economic activity fell in 1978, and real wages diminished sharply (see Tables 5.1 and 5.2).

Fortunately, this turned out to be the turning point of the external crisis. In the second half of 1978, Peru's balance of payments turned around quite suddenly, mainly because of a striking terms-of-trade improvement (see Table 5.4). Mineral prices rose sharply, dramatically improving the current account: The current account/GDP ratio rose from 1.5 percent in 1978 to +6.8 percent in 1979. The trade account benefited from a remarkable increase in so-called nontraditional (mainly manufacturing) exports, as a consequence of devaluation and special export incentives granted by the government to help out in the emergency. In late 1978 the government reached an agreement with the commercial banks to reschedule amortization due; but the balance of payments remained so strong that in early 1980 Peru paid some amortization ahead of schedule in order to reduce its interest bill. After two years of negative growth, real GDP grew 4.3 percent in 1979. But the inflation rate, which had risen to 60 percent in 1978, remained stubbornly at this level. The primary reason for the inflation appears to have been the monetization of the country's growing international-reserve position. (See Tables 5.3 and 5.6.) In 1979 banking-system external assets rose by 89.1 percent of the increase in the broad money supply.

In 1980, following the military's decision to relinquish power, Fernando Belaúnde, whom the military had deposed in October 1968, defeated an APRA party candidate in elections for a new constitutional president. The economic crisis had helped to undermine Morales Bermúdez politically. The fact that Belaúnde and his Popular Action party had consistently opposed the military all the while making no deals with the "de facto" regime, made him particularly appealing to the electorate. He took office in July 1980.

The Second Belaúnde Presidency: Renewed Crisis (1980–1985)

The economic authorities appointed by Belaúnde—notably Manuel Ulloa as economy minister and Richard Webb as central-bank president—committed themselves to a program of economic liberalization, following the approach advocated by the World Bank and other international agencies. Under the military governments, Peru had developed a system of fiscal subsidies for exports (the CERTEX program) and had restricted imports through tariffs and other means. Within its first months in office, the government decreed a sweeping liberalization of the trade system. Following neoliberal financial doctrine, it sharply increased banking-system interest rates, reduced required-reserve ratios, and removed taxes on credit operations, with the aim of encouraging saving and rationalizing credit allocation. It also clearly stated that, although it was reducing the special incentives for nontraditional (mostly industrial) exports enacted in 1978, it would maintain the crawling-peg devaluations.

When the government took office, inflation was running at about 60 percent a year; but because it expected to carry out corrective adjustments of controlled prices and some deregulation, inflation control tended to be a secondary priority. The government hoped that over time it would gradually improve public-sector performance, and that this would slowly reverse the inflationary pressure: The essential thing was not to allow prices to become or remain distorted. The labor minister made an effort to piece together a "social pact" among the government, business, and labor intended to control prices and wages, but he never succeeded in getting past disputes between business and labor over the rehiring of workers dismissed under the military governments. Because the government did not make an urgent effort to control public-sector expenditure, the deficit soon reemerged as a problem. And because domestic financial resources remained scarce, the deficit could not be financed without causing inflation or external difficulties.

This liberalizing approach—"getting prices (presumably) right," but without really controlling public expenditure—was criticized as early as 1981. Various economists pointed out that the trade liberalization posed dangers to the newly rebuilt reserve position. The shock of having prices, interest rates, tariff protection, and export support suddenly adjusted might bee too much for the industrial sector, which was still precariously recovering.[20] The basic neoliberal response was that by "getting prices (including the exchange rate, wages, and interest rates) right," the economic system would come to operate at full potential. Even those who accepted this view recognized that the distorted economy might need time to carry out the requisite "structural changes," in response to the new price array, and that during the adjustment process the economy might function badly: Resources might move out of inappropriate sectors before they could be taken on by appropriate sectors. In any case, the liberalizing measures undertaken in 1980 and 1981 must have thrust Peruvian industry into an "adjustment" period, since real manufacturing fell in 1981 and 1982 (see Table 5.1).

The Belaúnde government restored what it hoped would henceforth be normal relations with commercial banks. Bankers generally found the new authorities' neoliberalism congenial, since by the early 1980s neoliberalism had influenced banks as much as official lending institutions. In addition, helpful personal relationships had formed between bankers and some of the new government's personalities. In 1981 the banks provided more than $850 million (about 4 per cent of GDP) in new syndicated credit. The World Bank and the Inter-American Development Bank significantly increased credit operations with Peru in this period, providing new loans at a rate of about $200 million a year after 1980.[21] The balance of payments—particularly the current account—deteriorated severely in 1981 and 1982, however, largely because of plummeting minerals prices and soaring world interest rates (see Table 5.4), but also because of sharply higher imports resulting from trade liberalization (see Table 5.3). Private-sector consumption imports increased sharply. The government concluded that Peru needed IMF support for a longer-term program of liberalizing reforms and, accordingly, sought an Extended Fund Facility (EFF) agreement with the IMF in 1981 and early 1982.

The IMF approved a three-year EFF in June 1982, along with a SDR 200 million Compensatory Financing Facility (CFF) loan to assist the country through a period of declining export prices. The total value of the EFF was SDR 650 million (on the order of US$720 million), to be disbursed every quarter if Peru met economic-performance conditions. In 1982 these criteria included a reduction in the public-sector deficit to 4.2 percent from 8.4 percent of GDP in 1981; virtually no direct central-bank financing of the deficit; a ceiling of $1.1 billion in new external long-term borrowing; and a loss of no more than $100 million in net international reserves (net, that is, of the increase in the central bank's obligations to the IMF). The government promised to use a crawling-peg devaluation policy to keep the effective real exchange rate from appreciating (there had been some upward drift over 1981), to cut real liquidity, and to liberalize interest rates further. Also in June, on the strength of the IMF agreement (negotiated in March), Peru secured two large commercial bank loans: a $200-million loan from the Arab-Latin American Bank and a $350-million loan managed by Wells Fargo Bank of San Francisco (a bank that had made a specialty of leading lending operations to Peru). Throughout 1982 as a whole, Peru secured a total of $840 million in new bank credit.

In August 1982, however, Mexico declared that it could not make amortization and short-term credit payments due, and Argentina, Brazil, and Chile encountered severe payments difficulties. Chile's crisis raised questions in Peru about the liberalization approach. Despite falling commodity-export prices (see Table 5.4), Peru's balance of payments managed to perform remarkably close to the IMF program targets over 1982. The public-sector deficit was 9.2 percent of GDP, however—far above the performance criterion. Part of the problem was the need to maintain a higher devaluation pace to meet the external-accounts targets, thus pressuring domestic prices, which rose at a 77 percent annual rate over the second part of the year. The devaluation and the inflation in turn pressured the government accounts. At the same time, the adjustment program affected economic performance: Per capita real GDP and consumption declined, and real manufacturing suffered a second year of real decline (see Table 5.1), while unemployment crept upward (see Table 5.2). Yet real labor earnings in Lima were still higher than in 1981.

The following year was singularly disastrous for Peru. In early 1983 the climatic phenomenon known as "el Niño" kept Peru's offshore waters too warm to permit adequate spawning of anchovies; it also caused heavy rain and flooding in the northern and central parts of the country and drought in the southern part. These disasters and the austerity imposed under the IMF program caused aggregate demand to drop precipitously (see Table 5.1). The inflation rate leaped into the three-digit range under the force of the crawling-peg devaluation.

Like other Latin American nations, Peru attempted to negotiate "involuntary" loans with its commercial-bank creditors in order to meet its international obligations. The fact that Peru was already working within an EFF arrangement with the IMF was helpful for negotiations with the Bank Advisory Committee that was set up for Peru. Nevertheless, the public-sector deficit persisted above the performance target. The nation's economic authorities struggled on several fronts, searching for ways to prevent the missed performance criteria from wrecking the EFF, negotiating with the commercial banks, and coping with the domestic disaster. In January 1983 Carlos Rodriguez-Pastor, who had worked on Peruvian loans for the Wells Fargo Bank, took over as economy minister from Manuel Ulloa. He immediately cut public-sector investment expenditure heavily (see Tables 5.7 and 5.8). As the extent of the natural disasters became clear, Peru declared a temporary debt-service moratorium for the period from March to May. Difficult negotiations with the IMF and commerical banks continued throughout the year. By the end of the year, Peru had secured an agreement to lock in some $2 billion in vital short-term bank credit lines and a concerted new money-rescheduling agreement. This agreement hinged on continuation of the EFF, however, and it was clear that the deficit was running far above the 4.1 percent of GDP originally agreed for 1983.[22]

In September 1984 the central bank announced that it would henceforth
pre-announce the devaluation rate several weeks in advance, as a means
of reducing the uncertainty created by the crawling peg. Toward the end
of the year, however, the government secured a package of sharp tax
increases. The IMF disapproved of the exchange-rate policy. This and
other disagreements between Peru and the IMF could not be bridged,
and at the beginning of 1984 they ended the EFF. In April 1984 the
IMF and the government negotiated a new one-year, $250 million stand-
by program that permitted Peru to begin a rescheduling-refinancing
agreement negotiated with the commerical banks. The public-sector
deficit target was set at 4.1 percent of GDP (compared with 12.3 percent
in 1983). Peru committed itself to not losing net international reserves
over the year and promised to raise taxes, to cut public investment to
6.5 percent of GDP (from more than 10 percent), to maintain high
interest rates, and to end the pre-announcement of devaluations. These
commitments permitted the commercial-bank rescheduling and some
disbursements to proceed, but the program failed after Peru missed the
first set of quarterly performance targets in August 1984.

As early as May 1984, the failure of the stand-by program seemed
inevitable, and the government stopped making regular interest payments
to commercial banks. Although they maintained contacts with commercial
banks and occasionally made irregular interest payments, Peru's authorities became increasingly convinced that there was little point in
servicing debt to creditors who were unlikely to provide additional credit
in the foreseeable future. Once the APRA candidate won the elections
in early 1985, the government essentially ended its efforts to reach
agreement with its creditors. During its last seven months in power, the
Belaúnde government took some measures to control public-sector finances, with relatively better results: Increases in gasoline prices and
in other controlled prices carrying heavy taxes increased indirect-tax
revenue substantially. These measures dampened economic activity, however; for 1985 as a whole, real-output growth was well below population
growth (see Table 5.1).

By this time, the Belaúnde government was plainly a lame-duck
administration. The economic events of the previous two years had badly
discredited the Popular Action party. Since the rightist Popular Christian
party had participated in the government, it too was discredited. Accordingly, the 1985 election shaped up as a contest between the APRA
and a left-wing coalition. Having lost the previous election under a
candidate associated with the APRA's "old guard," the party came under
the sway of Alan García, a young, charismatic politician with a marked
social-democratic bent and personal ties to European socialists. He secured
the APRA nomination and won the April 1985 election on the first
round, defeating the left-wing parties and trouncing the PPC and AP.

The two following sections deal with the relationship among capital
formation, austerity, and external debt—first in theory and then with
respect to Peru up to the time that García took office.

Capital Formation and
External Debt in Macroeconomic Theory

The constraint on capital formation has been one of the debt crisis's most troubling consequences for developing nations.[23] To understand the issue, first imagine an economy that receives no external saving. In such an economy, capital formation determines the physical productive capacity: Higher capital formation enables higher output and national income flows. In turn, national income sets the saving capacity. The amount saved is what is then available for new capital formation.[24]

With external saving, a nation can augment the domestic saving available for capital formation. A nation receives external saving to the extent that imports of merchandise and *final* (nonfactor) services exceed exports of merchandise and *final* services—that is, to the extent that the national-income accounts'[25] net-exports flow is in deficit.[26] A net-exports deficit must be financed: Over the period in question, the nation must either draw down external-asset holdings or receive financing from the rest of the world. This financing may come either as new "risk capital" or as additional interest-bearing debt.

From the viewpoint of neoclassical economic theory, it makes sense that poorer nations receive and wealthier nations provide saving flows. Physical capital and accumulated-saving stocks are, almost by definition, relatively scarce in poorer nations and abundant in richer nations. According to this logic, all other things being equal, savings should command a higher price in poorer nations, where they are more scarce and where the marginal productivity of capital is presumably higher; the higher price should attract savings to poorer nations. In reality, of course, part of the reason why developing nations pay high financial charges is that they are riskier places.

Until 1982 this theory apparently reflected reality, in the sense that finance flowed from wealthier to poorer nations. Finance tended to flow, however, as debt with floating interest rates, rather than as risk capital. As a result, nations' interest bills not only rose with the growing debt stock but also jumped when real world interest rates rose in the early 1980s. Interest payments are not a "final import" in the national-income accounts sense; that is, they are not part of a nation's external saving inflows. Rather, they are part of a nation's external financing requirement. A nation must effectively finance both its external-saving inflow *and* its net interest bill with its net external-finance inflow. Suppose a given amount of external financing is available to a nation; the larger the nation's interest bill, the smaller will be the amount of external saving available for capital formation.

When the real world interest rates rose, developing nations such as Peru lost external-saving flows: Not only did external financing become harder to obtain, but larger proportions of external-financing flows had to go to pay interest bills. After 1982, of course, financing flows to many nations had to be secured from "involuntary" lenders—that is, banks that reluctantly had to raise their exposure to avoid risking their existing exposure. To the extent that capital formation depends on external saving, and growing interest bills and limited availablity of external finance limit external-saving availability, the debt crisis threatens developing nations' long-term growth rates.

The Technical Appendix at the end of this chapter outlines the analytical relationship among an economy's capital formation, its real growth rate, and its external-debt accumulation, on the basis of a simple extension of the well-known Harrod-Domar growth analysis. The remainder of this section discusses this issue in analytical terms; the noneconomist may wish to skip it. The basic point is that Peru's heavy interest burden severely limits its capital formation. Unless Peru can secure adequate finance to cover its interest bill, its growth prospects will be significantly compromised.

Let s represent an economy's domestic saving as a proportion of gross domestic product (GDP), z its net-export surplus as a proportion of GDP, v its incremental capital-output ratio (ICOR), which is the additional real capital required per additional unit of real GDP, and a the rate at which its existing real capital stock depreciates. The "warranted" growth rate g—the rate at which the economy could grow if unconstrained by any factor of production besides capital—is given by

$$g = [(s - z)/v] - a. \tag{1}$$

For real economies, the depreciation and capital-output ratio can only be guessed within ranges, and the long-term values are subject to various measurement controversies. Nevertheless, for Peru, the domestic-saving ratio has not exceeded 20 percent. If Peru's capital-output ratio is 3.5 and its annual capital-depreciation rate is 4 percent, net exports would have to be -8 percent of GDP to allow long-term annual growth of 4 percent. With GDP now around \$21 billion, net exports would have to be equivalent to $-\$1.7$ billion—a deficit that Peru could not feasibly finance in present circumstances. This suggests that, whatever Peru does with regard to its external debt, it must make every effort to increase its domestic-saving flow: If the domestic saving ratio were 25 percent, net exports could be $-\$630$ million.

The balance of payments' current-account deficit measures the rate at which a nation accumulates "net financing"—that is, risk capital plus external liabilities less external assets (including international reserves). Suppose risk-capital inflows are negligible. A nation's next external debt— that is, external liabilities less assets (including international reserves)— would then accumulate at a rate equal to the current-account deficit. Again, if profit remittances on risk capital (and unrequited transfer payments) are negligible, the current-account deficit approximately equals external saving plus the net interest bill. Let d represent the ratio of net external debt to GDP, and r the real interest rate on external debt. The Technical Appendix indicates that the ratio of the outstanding debt stock to GDP grows at an annual rate h (approximately) equal to

$$h = -z + rd. \tag{2}$$

Formulas (1) and (2) together indicate what external-debt growth rate in a given year ought to be consistent with a given long-term growth rate, for given current values of r and d. Continuing with the stylized Peruvian figures given above, since Peru's 1986 external debt is on the order of $15 billion, we find that its GDP is on the order of $21 billion, and it real external interest rate is on the order of 3 percent; therefore, if real growth is to be 4 percent a year and external saving is to be 8 percent of GDP, external debt would have to grow at a rate equal to 10 percent a year and the debt-GDP ratio would have to grow about 6 percent a year.

Formula (2) alone reveals two of the fundamental dilemmas of external debt. The first, already noted, is that if external creditors limit the rate at which their exposure in a nation rises, the higher is the interest bill and the smaller is the proportion of the increase in exposure that goes to external saving. Second, what really matters to a developing nation is its external-saving inflow, the z part of the preceding formula. A nation might accept a period of external dissaving (i.e., allow z to be positive) if it believed this would persuade the rest of the world to provide external saving subsequently. If not, it might be inclined to suspend interest payments—that is, to finance interest payments by accumulating arrears. In this way, even though external debt mounts with arrears, at least the external saving inflow rises from something negative toward zero. This is presumably the rationale behind both Peru's limitation of interest payments and its preferential servicing of debt to creditors who provide new loans exceeding principal and interest.[27]

The algebra of Harrod-Domar formulas (1) and (2) indicates possible policy approaches for indebted developing nations along the lines of "structural adjustment." Formula (1) shows that by raising domestic saving s and reducing the ICOR v and depreciation a, a nation can maintain a given real growth rate with a lower external-saving flow. Economists recommend both diminished public-sector deficits and higher domestic interest rates in order to raise the domestic saving rate. The view that poorer nations should raise domestic saving rates by all civilized means available is unobjectionable, although there is plenty of scope for disagreement about the best ways to do so.

What matters in this context is not cutting the public-sector deficit but increasing public-sector saving (or reducing public-sector dissaving). The point is to cut public-sector consumption expenditure rather than capital formation, at least insofar as the latter is genuinely efficient. Moreover, there is no assurance that raising domestic interest rates or public-sector saving will induce a net increase in domestic saving. Raising domestic interest rates may discourage production and capital formation, thus reducing real income and saving. By reducing aggregate demand, a decrease in public expenditure may lower aggregate income, thus possibly reducing private-sector saving. Finally, while it is true that policymakers should do everything possible to increase domestic saving, there still ought to be a role for external finance.

Reducing v—the additional capital required per additional unit of output—amounts to improving the efficiency of new capital—an unobjectionable policy purpose. Economic theory suggests that the value of v tends to rise as a nation develops, on the view that the "best" (most productive) investment projects will be completed first. Technical progress operates to reduce the value of v over time: An advantage of maintaining steady capital formation is that it enables nations to "embody" such progress as it occurs. Economists frequently advise nations to improve the efficiency of their capital by subjecting more of their investment to "market discipline"—that is, by making resources available, providing scope to the private sector to carry out investment, and avoiding the "monumental" sorts of projects in which so many poorer nations (including Peru) have indulged. Schydlowsky and Wicht (1980) have pointed out the possibilities of using multiple labor shifts to take maximum advantage of existing capital. (One point that needs to be made about efforts to increase capital utilization is that in reality they may require a certain amount of investment—in such matters as additional transport facilities for evening hours, housing for additional workers, additional small machinery to expand assembly lines, and so on.) Finally, although the physical depreciation rate may seem difficult to reduce, even here there are possiblities: Better maintenance, imaginative use of second-hand equipment, and so on can lengthen the life of physical capital

Saving and Capital Formation in Peru

Peru's national-income accounts and related macroeconomic aggregate statistics indicate the extent to which capital formation has lagged in recent years. To be sure, Peruvian national-accounts data are problematic, since a large part of Peru's economy is "underground" and, hence, is not captured by the national-accounts estimates.[28] If they can be believed in rough terms, however, the data suggest that Peruvian capital formation has been deficient, and that it has been seriously affected by the fluctuating availability of external saving.

Table 5.8 gives estimates of saving and capital formation, first as proportions of GDP and then in "real" terms (deflated so that 1980 GDP is 100).[29] National capital-depreciation rates are unknown and probably unknowable; nevertheless, analysts often take it as a rule of thumb that a 14 to 15 percent annual gross capital formation rate of GDP may be insufficient to do more than replace physically depreciating capital.[30] By this standard, Peru's gross capital formation has been low, averaging 15.1 percent in the 15 years from 1972 through 1986.[31]

IMF data (not given) suggest that Peru's capital-formation rate was as high as 20 percent in the 1960s, and was relatively high in the early years of the military government (1968–1972). It slipped to about 13 percent in 1972 and 1973, then rose to the 16–18 percent range from 1974 through 1976. In these years Peru had a severe balance-of-payments crisis. The trade deficits implied, however, that these were years of high, if unsustainable, external-saving inflows: Peru's external-saving rate rose from a negative 1972 value and a slightly positive 1973 value to average 7 percent from 1974 through 1976. In the external-payments crisis years of 1977–1979, total capital formation fell to around 13 percent of GDP; external saving fell to 2.4 percent in 1977 and turned negative in the following three years. Total real capital formation was 22 percent lower in the three years from 1977 to 1979 than in the three years from 1974 to 1976; if total real external saving inflows were 100 in the earlier period, they were −37.6 over the later period (see Table 5.8).

The capital-formation rate rose at the beginning of the second Belaúnde government to 19 percent in the 1981 and 1982, but then slipped in the external-payments crisis from 1983 through 1985. In real terms, capital formation was 51 percent higher in 1980–1982 than in 1977–1979, and 25 percent higher than in 1974–1976. External saving was positive in 1980–1982, though considerably lower (both as a proportion of real GDP and in real terms) than it had been in 1974–1976. Domestic saving was markedly higher in 1980–1982 than it had been in 1974–1976, partly because the new government significantly raised interest rates to savers upon taking office in July 1980. With the sharp recession and balance-of-payments crisis of 1983, however, capital formation plunged again, along with external and domestic saving: capital formation averaged 26 percent lower in real terms in 1983–1985 compared with 1980–1982, while external dissaving reached 5.6 percent of GDP in 1984 and 7.1 percent in 1985. There was a striking 41 percent decline in real private capital formation from 1980–1982 to 1983–1985. One of the causes, apart from the reversal of business optimism, was "corporate distress": Peruvian enterprises were decapitalized by excessive debt and high interest rates.

The correlation of capital formation with external saving flows is well short of one (in fact, the correlation coefficient of the real capital-formation and real external-saving flows in Table 5.8 is 0.503),[32] but it is high enough to lend credence to the view that the availability of external saving is significantly related to Peru's capital formation. Private saving was relatively high as a proportion of GDP from 1981 through 1984. It fell in 1985, probably because of the recessionary measures taken by the government in the early part of the year and the elimination of dollar deposit accounts after Alan García took office, At the same time, the reversal of public saving performance from 1983 through 1985 was relatively impressive.

External saving flows turned increasingly negative beginning in 1983, although external debt continued to grow, rising 8.5 and 7.2 percent in 1983 and 1984, respectively (see Table 5.5). A large part of the reason for this was the external interest bill. After hovering between 2 and 3 percent of GDP from 1978 through 1982, the public-sector interest bill soared to more than 4 percent of GDP in 1983 and to more than 5 percent in 1984. The ratio of public-sector interest to total exports exceeded 20 percent in 1984 (see Table 5.5). In the 1980s, Peru's increasing debt was taken up largely by the interest bill, leaving little of the debt increase available for external saving. This point is made in a different form in Table 5.5, in terms of the ratio of each year's interest bill to the increase in the outstanding debt stock. The debt stock changed in part from valuation changes resulting from shifts in the dollar's exchange rate vis-à-vis other currencies in which Peruvian assets and liabilities are denominated; nevertheless, it is clear that a large part of the rising debt went to finance the interest bill.

Private- and public-sector capital formation behaved in quite similar ways over most of the period. Private-sector capital formation was nearly 13 percent lower in 1977–1979 than in 1974–1976; it was 43 percent higher in 1980–1982 than in 1977–1979, then 41 percent lower in 1983–1985 than in 1980–1982. Public-sector capital formation was 33 percent lower in 1977–1979 than in 1974–1976; it was 64 percent higher in 1980–1982. Public-sector capital formation did not decline as sharply in 1983 as private-sector capital formation: Table 5.9 shows gradual real declines in public-sector capital formation in 1983 and 1984.

In sum, Peruvian capital formation appears to have been affected by the varying availability of external saving. With external-saving flows alternately available and unavailable over the past fifteen years, Peru's capital formation has been subject to substantial variation. The growth rate of the nation's capital stock, while uncertain in magnitude, has undoubtedly been low—and this likely accounts in large measure for the country's declining real per capita growth since 1975.

Developments Since 1985

Upon his inauguration as president on July 28, 1985, Alan García announced that, for at least a year, Peru would limit interest payments on public-sector external debt to 10 percent of export proceeds. In subsequent months, the government set a general policy of paying interest only to creditor institutions that provided new financing in excess of debt service (a positive resource flow). Given Peru's uncertainties and the government's confrontational stance, overseas creditors were understandably reluctant to provide new resources. During 1986 arrears to the IMF mounted to the point that Peru became ineligible for further drawings. In the first half of 1987 the World Bank and the Inter-American Development Bank also interrupted new credit flows because of Peru's

TABLE 5.9
Peru: Estimated Real Capital Stock, 1971-1986

	1971	1972	1973	1974	1975	1976	1977	1978	1979	1980	1981	1982	1983	1984	1985	1986
Real GDP (1970 =100)	105.1	111.3	118.2	126.3	129.3	133.6	133.2	130.9	136.5	140.4	144.7	146.0	128.5	134.6	137.2	148.9
Gross capital formation (1970 GDP = 100)	13.7	14.6	15.4	20.1	24.2	22.4	18.1	15.7	18.0	22.9	27.8	27.9	20.9	20.0	16.9	17.3
Assumed capital depreciation rate	4.0%	4.0%	4.0%	4.0%	4.0%	4.0%	4.0%	4.0%	4.0%	4.0%	4.0%	4.0%	4.0%	4.0%	4.0%	4.0%
Capital-output ratio	3.3	3.1	3.0	2.8	2.8	2.7	2.8	2.9	2.8	2.7	2.7	2.7	3.2	3.1	3.1	2.8
Real capital stock	348.4	348.1	348.8	350.3	356.4	366.3	374.1	377.2	377.8	380.6	388.3	400.6	412.4	416.8	420.1	420.2
Growth rate of real capital stock	-0.5%	-0.1%	0.2%	0.4%	1.7%	2.8%	2.1%	0.8%	0.2%	0.8%	2.0%	3.2%	3.0%	1.1%	0.8%	
Estimated labor force (millions)	4.3	4.4	4.5	4.7	4.8	5.0	5.1	5.3	5.4	5.6	5.8	6.0	6.1	6.3	6.6	
Capital-labor ratio (1970 = 100)	96.9	94.2	91.6	89.2	88.1	87.8	86.9	85.0	82.7	80.9	80.0	80.0	80.0	78.5	76.3	

Source: Estimated from data published by the Banco Central de Reserva del Peru, _Memoria_ (Lima, various annual issues).

debt-service interruptions. In August the World Bank took the serious step of placing its Peruvian assets on nonaccrual status—that is, recognizing for accounting purposes that they were yielding no income. Arrears on interest and principal to commercial banks, which had been accumulating for more than a year before Garcia took office, were simply allowed to mount. Although there have been some deals involving the use of commodity exports to service commercial-bank debt, serious approaches to normalizing relations appear unlikely in the foreseeable future. Peru's Soviet-bloc creditors have also accepted arrangements involving the use of commodity exports as debt service; but, even so, Peru indicated in July 1987 that it might service to these nations because they were providing no new resources.

At the end of 1985, interest arrears were about $850–900 million (of which $350 million went to commercial banks, $450 million to multilateral and bilateral creditors, and the rest to other private creditors). By the end of 1986 interest arrears had risen to about $1.7 billion (including $700 million to commercial banks and $600 million to multilateral and bilateral creditors). Peru appears to have paid somewhat more than 10 percent of its export proceeds during 1986 in interest, mainly for trade financing, import suppliers, and multilateral credits. Some debt service was paid in the form of merchandise exports to service COMECON nations' debt.

In August 1985 and in the months following, the new government took steps to reactivate the economy. The new policy approach was inevitably unorthodox, in large measure improvised. The rationale for expansion was clear: Peru had still barely recovered from its 1983 real-GDP plunge, particularly in real per capita terms (see Table 5.1). Government indicators suggested that industrial capacity utilization was remarkably low whereas de facto unemployment was high. Efficiency considerations suggested that capacity utilization needed to be increased. Accordingly, the government instituted a variety of tax cuts and subsidies, often remarkably specific in nature, to stimulate demand and production. Against orthodox economic thinking, a system of multiple exchange rates was established to promote exports and encourage specific kinds of investment. A credit program for agriculture was also established. Resources effectively freed from external-debt service were directed to public works. The government authorized significant real wage increases and; to control inflation, instituted an intricate program of selective price controls. The exchange rate was initially fixed, although it has been readjusted several times since then. Interest rates were reduced, both to encourage production and to *reduce* inflationary pressures (on the "supply-side" reasoning that lower credit rates would encourage output and reduce pressure on prices.) Comparing it with the June 1985 Argentine "Austral Plan," the Lima press dubbed the process Peru's "Inti Plan," although it included no stabilizing stock.

As a result of this stimulus, Peru's economy grew 8.5 percent in real terms in 1986, a strong performance that went a long way toward making up the 12 percent decline of 1983. Manufacturing output, which had recovered 2.8 and 4.1 percent in 1984 and 1985, respectively, from its 17.3-percent 1983 decline, expanded 17.8 percent. Agricultural output grew 3.7 percent. These increases offset a 2.5 percent decline in mining and petroleum output, which was affected by strikes and depletion. The growth was strongly consumption based: Per capita consumption rose 13.1 percent (see Table 5.1). Contrary to the widespread impression that captital formation fell in 1986, real capital formation was 2.5 percent higher than in 1985 and private capital formation was 18 percent higher: Public capital formation fell 11 percent (see Table 5.8). Nevertheless, capital formation did fall as a proportion of GDP to a record low level. Real 1986 capital formation was 23.7 percent lower than the average over the 1980–1985 period; real 1986 private capital formation was about 15 percent lower. Price controls, the continuing struggle against left-wing guerrillas, and tense relations with external creditors discouraged private-sector confidence. Price controls repressed the inflation rate, which fell from a year-over-year rate of 163 percent in 1985 to 78 percent in 1986.

The current account reverted from the slight surplus in 1985 to a $1.1-billion deficit, entirely as a consequence of a decline in the trade surplus. Foreign-exchange reserves declined approximately $400 million. Table 5.8 shows that real external dissaving was 30 percent lower in 1986 than in 1984 and 1985, although it was still 4 percent of GDP. A sharp decline in public-sector saving was partly offset by increased private-sector saving.

The economic reactivation was carried out through deliberate measures designed to increase consumption and to improve the utilization of existing capacity. The government's economic authorities and advisers were forthright about their approach: They followed the logic that an economy as underdeveloped and beset by unemployment as Peru's must make the most efficient possible use of existing capital. At the same time, they never lost sight of the point that growth through higher capacity utilization and consumption stimulation was relatively "easy" growth; long-term growth based on capital formation would be much harder. In mid-1986, the government set up a National Private Investment Board in an effort to secure private capital formation. The private sector was invited to sign "letters of intent" to invest, negotiated on the basis of understandings with the government regarding particular policy settings. Unfortunately, this interesting policy approach was insufficient to offset all the other factors in the economy and in economic policy that discouraged capital formation.

In the political realm, while 1986 was hardly a smooth year, the García government at least maintained its legitimacy and its fundamental control. Its conflicts with guerrilla movements and drug dealers have been particularly vicious, and several sharp political crises arose over the security forces' conduct of the war with Sendero Luminoso. The guerrillas are far from taking power, but they may hope to provoke a military coup against which they would then be the focus of resistance.

As many observers expected, 1987 turned out to be a more difficult year for the government. At least until the middle of the year, economic growth ran even stronger than in the previous year. But the balance-of-payments pressures began to mount. Although, at $1.4 billion, the central bank's foreign-reserve position was about $200 million higher than at the end of 1986, and importers seemed to be making do with a smaller level of trade credit, there were signs of external-accounts problems. The exchange rate has lagged significantly behind the differential between domestic and international inflation, and the parallel-market premium has become significant (indeed, this was an issue recently disputed within the government).

The government's own political infighting was a problem in the first half of 1987. The cabinet was reshuffled, and top economic positions passed to different personalities. In July the president made what is widely regarded to have been a political and economic error: He introduced legislation to nationalize Peru's banks. A wave of middle-class protest resulted, followed by several anguishing months in which the banks battled the government in the legislature and in the courts. Up to this point, Lima's middle classes had been broadly tolerant of García's government; they may now give the opposition a more sympathetic hearing. From an economic viewpoint, of course, the measure seems hard to justify. Although the president promised that the government would direct the banks to provide more socially useful and productive credit operations, the confiscation can hardly have encouraged private investment and may have intensified the diposition to capital flight.

Conclusion

Latin American public opinion has come to associate "austerity" with the efforts of right-wing governments—in particular, those of doubtful legitimacy—to appease international financiers by wringing saving from their economies for transfer overseas. Peru's experience suggests that the matter is more subtle. Since the late 1960s, Peru's domestic saving has been relatively limited. Consequently, the nation's capital-formation capacity has become restricted, except to the extent that the nation has been able to secure external saving. External saving has alternated between positive and negative, however. When it was positive, Peru increased its capital formation. When it could not secure external saving and was called upon to carry out external dissaving, Peru's capital formation has diminished.

At this writing Peru's dilemma is that of the more generalized Latin American "debt crisis": Nations are being called upon to increase domestic saving and to carry out external dissaving in order to secure renewed external saving some time in the future. Foreign bankers regard the nations that do so as "cooperative" and the nations that do not as "confrontational." Through it all, however, the ultimate purpose of national policies must be adequate capital formation to permit increasing employment and higher productivity. Anything regarded as "solution" to the debt crisis must, explicitly or implicitly, ensure an adequate, stable flow of efficient capital formation. The issue is not only austerity per se but the purpose of austerity.

TECHNICAL APPENDIX: CAPITAL FORMATION AND EXTERNAL DEBT ACCUMULATION

This appendix outlines the extended Harrod-Domar analysis used in the second and third sections of this chapter. The basic Harrod-Domar analysis assumes that the economy has no external trade or financial relationships (see Jones 1975). Let Y represent the physical production flow per unit time, or real gross domestic product; K the physical capital stock; and I the addition to K per unit time. Suppose that each unit of capital added to K permits Y to rise by the fraction $1/v$. If the saving rate is the constant s, then the addition to the capital stock per unit time is

$$I = sY.$$

Since this addition to the capital stock permits production to rise by an increment of $(1/v)\ I$, or $(1/v)\ sY$, it enables production to grow at a rate of

$$\begin{aligned} g &= [(1/v)\ sY]\ /\ Y \\ &= s/v. \end{aligned} \tag{1}$$

In the theory of economic growth, this ratio is known as the "warranted" growth rate. As long as growth is not limited by a shortage of factor of production aside from physical capital, such as labor, the warranted growth rate would be the maximum possible growth rate.

To simplify its exposition, the Harrod-Domar analysis took v to be a "technical constant," known in growth theory as the "incremental capital-output ratio," or "ICOR." Subsequent theoretical analysis, the "neoclassical" theory set out by Solow in 1956 (see Solow 1970), allowed v to be a variable responsive to the relative scarcities of capital and labor, representing the possibility of substituting labor for capital in the production process.[33]

For simplicity, the original Harrod-Domar analysis neglected capital depreciation. If the capital stock depreciates at a periodic rate of a, then the net addition to the capital stock over any time interval is

$sY - aK,$

and the warranted growth rate with capital depreciation is then

$$g = [(1/v) (sY - aK)] / Y$$
$$= (s/v) - a. \tag{2}$$

To incorporate external debt, "external saving" must first be introduced into the Harrod-Domar analysis. In the national-income accounts, the inflow of external saving to an economy over any time interval is defined as the difference between imports and exports of merchandise and "nonfactor" services (plus the net outflow of "unrequited transfer payments," taken here to be negligible). Intuitively, an economy receives external saving if the value of the goods it recieves exceeds the value of the goods it sends abroad. In the national-income accounting identity, if C represents private consumption, I *total* capital formation, S total private saving, T public-sector revenue, G total public-sector expenditure, J *public* capital formation, M imports, X exports of goods and nonfactor services, and R net unrequited transfer payments to foreigners,

$$C + I + (G - J) + (X - M) \equiv C + S + T + R.$$

Substracting C from both sides and transposing,

$$I \equiv S + [T - (G - J)] + [M - X + R].$$

That is, total capital formation (incuding public-sector capital formation) equals the sum of private, public, and external saving.

Net unrequited transfer payments are neglibile for most Latin American nations. Net exports—less imports of goods and non-factor services—equal the negative of external saving. Suppose net exports are a proportion z of GDP. Total saving would then equal the sum of domestic and external saving:

$$sY - zY.$$

Capital formation is then given by

$$I = sY - zY - aK,$$

and the Harrod-Domar warranted growth rate with capital depreciation in an open economy becomes

$$g = [(s - z)/v] - a. \tag{3}$$

This extended version of the Harrod-Domar formula shows that, all other things being equal, the long-term warranted growth rate should be *higher*, as the national-income accounts' net-export surplus becomes lower (or the net-export deficit becomes higher) as a proportion of total production.

A balance-of-payments account describes the relationship of net external-debt accumulation and external saving. To simplifiy, assume that the stock of foreign investment within the economy, profit remittances from it, and inflows of new risk captial are relatively small—reasonable assumptions for most Latin American economies. Define an economy's "net external debt" as external debt less external asset holdings, particularly central bank international reserves. The balance-of-payments "current account" then equals net exports less net interest payments on net external debt (i.e., interest payments on the debt less interest receipts on the assests). Let D represent net external debt, r the international real interest rate on it, and B the current-account surplus. Then, by definition,

$$B = (X - M) - rD.$$

When risk-capital flows are negligible, net external debt increases by the current-account *deficit*; that is, $-B$ gives the addition to D over any time interval. Since

$$-B = (M - X) + rD \tag{4}$$

and $(M - X)$ is the external-saving flow, the addition to external debt equals the external-saving flow plus the interest bill. Let d represent the ratio of net external debt to GDP. The growth rate of the debt stock, h is the previous formula divided by D:

$$\begin{aligned} h = B/D &= (M - X)/D + rD/D \\ &= -z/d + r. \end{aligned} \tag{5}$$

Notes

The views expressed in this chapter are not necessarily those of the World Bank or any other institution with which the writer is or has recently been associated. The writer is grateful to Azucena Beckerman, Shane Hunt, Martha Rodriguez, Monica Rodreiguez, Eduardo Valdivia, and Milton Vega for their assistance with the data and their valuable discussion of the conceptual issues at an early stage, and to Werner Baer and Howard Handelman for their work on this chapter. The conclusions expressed here reflect neither these persons' views nor those of the institutions with which they are associated. The writer alone remains responsible for all remaining errors of fact or judgment.

1. Colombia provides an instructive contrast. Despite continuing violence and deep economic problems, thirty years of orderly, well-managed constitutional transitions have enabled Colombia to maintain administrative policy continuity.

2. Although Peru has diversified its primary commodity exports, it maintains high external dependence. Peru's diversified commodity export structure helps little when world commodity prices decline across the board.

3. For comparison, Brazil's 1986 per capita income was 82.5 percent higher than it was in 1975; Colombia's was 36 percent higher in 1985 than in 1970.

4. World Bank, *World Development Report*, various issues.

5. Oscar Ugarteche, *El Estado deudor: Economia politica de la deuda: Peru y Bolivia 1968-1984* (Lima: Instituto de Estudios Peruanos, 1986), pp. 192-201.

6. Ibid., pp. 208-213.

7. See Pedro Pablo Kuczynski, *Peruvian Democracy Under Economic Stress: An Account of the Belaunde Administration, 1963-1968* (Princeton, N.J.: Princeton University Press, 1977), for a detailed account of this period; see also Ugarteche, *op. cit.*, pp. 192-206.

8. Kuczynski, *op. cit*, pp. 218-294.

9. Jane S. Jaquette and Abraham Lowenthal, "The Peruvian Experiment in Retrospect," *World Politics* (January 1987), pp. 280-296. The quote is theirs.

10. Norman Gall, "Peru's Educational Reform," *American University Field Staff Reports*, Vol. 21, Nos. 3-5. (1974).

11. See Cynthia McClintock and Abraham Lowenthal (eds.), *The Peruvian Experiment Reconsidered* (Princeton, N.J.-Princeton University Press, 1983), for an evaluation of this "experiment"; see also Jaquette and Lowenthal, *op. cit.*

12. Adolfo Figueroa, "The Impact of Current Reforms on Income Distribution in Peru," in Alejandro Foxley (ed.), *Income Distribution in Latin America* (Cambridge: Cambridge University Press, 1975).

13. Cynthia McClintock, "Velasco: Officers and Citizens: The Politics of Stealth," in McClintock and Lowenthal, (eds.), *The Peruvian Experiment.*

14. Liisa North, "Ideological Orientations of Peru's Military Rulers"; McClintock, *op. cit.*, and Luis Pasara, "When the Military Dreams," all in McClintock and Lowenthal (eds.), *The Peruvian Experiment.*

15. Ugarteche, *op. cit.*, p. 212.

16. These measures were intended to improve the current account and to reduce the budget deficit. While it was clear that they would cause a once-and-for-all price-level increase, and that this would have a recessionary effect on real income, it was not properly appreciated that the once-and-for-all price-level rise would itself be an inflationary shock.

17. See Howard Handelman, "Peru: The March to Civilian Rule," in Howard Handelman and Thomas Sanders (eds.), *Military Rule and the Road to Democratic Government in South America* (Bloomington: Indiana University Press, 1981); Thomas Scheetz, *Peru and the International Monetary Fund* (Pittsburgh: University of Pittsburgh Press, 1986).

18. Scheetz, *op. cit.*, pp. 132-135. The banks insisted on having access to government accounts. They also insisted that Peru resolve certain nationalization issues involving their clients.

19. Ibid., pp. 142-145.

20. Daniel Schydlowsky made this argument during a number of public appearances in Peru.

21. See the World Bank's *World Debt Tables.*

22. The performance targets were set in *soles*. The sharp fall in GDP made the percentage-of-GDP figures higher.

23. The discussion in this section draws heavily on Paulo Nogueira Batista, Jr., *"Formacao de capital e transferencias externas de recursos, Revista de Economia Politica* (Rio de Janeiro, 1987). It has much in common with Marcelo Selowsky and Herman G. van der Tak, "Economic Growth and External Debt," *World Development* (September 1986), pp. 1107–1124.

24. Capital formation includes residential construction as well as construction of plant and installation of equipment. Increases in a nation's residential housing stock may contribute to production if they enable workers to live closer to their workplaces.

25. The "national-income-accounts net exports" flow is not customarily given in balance-of-payments accounts. The "trade account" includes only merchandise exports and imports, whereas the "current account" includes *factor* as well as final services. Factor services are those that go into the production of final goods and services—labor and financial charges, among others. The national-income accounts include only final goods and services.

26. External-saving outflows also include "net unrequited-transfer" outflows, which are negligible for Peru and most other Latin American nations. Unrequited transfer payments are cross-border payments made without compensation for goods, services, or claims.

27. Two points should be clarified here. First, the view that developing nations ought to receive external saving (i.e., run net-export deficits) does not contradict the view that they should promote exports and efficient import substitution. Even if imports exceed exports, they should both be relatively large as proportions of GDP, according to the view that international trade enables nations to produce and consume efficiently.

Second, the Harrod-Domar approach effectively presumes that capital formation is set by the available saving flow. Although the national-income accounting identity implies that capital formation must identically equal the overall saving flow, an economy's aggregate "desired" capital formation need not equal the saving flow: *Actual* capital formation and *actual* total saving must both equal the smaller of *desired* capital formation and *desired* total saving. No one can say for certain that any given saving-capital formation outcome is desired capital formation or desired total saving. Strictly speaking, even if the overall saving rate is low, it may be that desired capital formation is low.

In some degree one must appeal to common sense on this point. The third section of this chapter notes that Peru's capital formation declined in periods during which external-saving inflows declined. There is no reason to suppose that the fundamental need for investable resources declined in periods of balance-of-payments crises; in contrast, there are well-known reasons why the supply of external saving declined, particularly in the world debt crisis after 1982. Moreover, even if desired capital formation did decline during the balance-of-payments crises, the reason was largely that would-be investors perceived that less external saving was available.

28. See Mario Vargas Llosa, "In Defense of the Black Market," *New York Times Magazine,* February 22, 1987.

29. Total saving identically equals the sum of total capital formation and increases in inventory stocks; external saving is then taken to be imports less exports of goods and final services plus net unrequited transfer payments; domestic saving, then is the difference of total and external saving. Public saving

is the public sector's revenue (net of transfers and interest payments) less noncapital expenditures, and private saving is the difference of domestic and public saving.

30. Suppose capital lasts twenty-five years on average; then 4 percent of the capital stock depreciates every year. If the capital-output ratio is 3.5, 4 percent of the capital stock amounts to 14 percent of GDP.

31. This figure is lower than that for most developing nations for the same period and though approximately of the same order of magnitude as that for Chile and higher than that for Bolivia, it is well below that of Brazil. From 1975 through 1984 Brazil's capital formation averaged 21 percent of GDP (although it declined from 25 to about 16 percent); Chile's capital formation, which was relatively low, averaged 15 percent.

32. This correlation coefficient is significant at the 5 percent significance level, but it is just short of being significant at the 2.5 percent signficance level.

33. In the Solow analysis, with v varying, the warranted growth rate would tend toward an equilibrium equal to the labor-force growth rate, regardless of the saving rate. (Presumably this adjustment would occur only over the long run. Indeed, one problem of neoclassical theory is that it says nothing about how long it would take the warranted growth rate to move into equilibrium with the labor-force growth rate. It is possible that in reality the warranted growth rate is always tending slowly toward some equilibrium value, but that this equilibrium is constantly shifting and never attained.) Unemployment would therefore always tend to diminish in Solow's analysis, even if the saving rate were low. Even so, however, real wage rates would have to diminish to maintain employment and to reduce the incremental capital-output ratio if the saving rate were low. The Solow analysis therefore reaffirms the Harrod-Domar insight regarding the importance of the saving rate.

34. One important objection to the Harrod-Domar model and related approaches is the argument that a nation's capital stock is conceptually unmeasurable. See Joan Robinson, "The Production Function and the Theory of Capital," *Review of Economic Studies* (1953–1954), pp. 88–106, and Hywel G. Jones, *An Introduction to Modern Theories of Economic Growth* (New York: McGraw-Hill, 1976). This argument is an aspect of the "Cambridge, England" position in the celebrated "Cambridge capital controversy" of the 1950s and 1960s. This writer's view is that the "Cambridge, England" position is logically correct: The current physical capital stock of a nation cannot meaningfully be totaled in physical units; and although it might be conceptually possible to assign each kind of capital a value based on various considerations, the use of a value as a measure of the capital stock leads to circularity in any analysis where the implicit or explicit point is to *determine* the value of the capital stock. Nevertheless, I also take the view that the Harrod-Domar and Solow analyses are useful approximations that can be applied meaningfully to derive broad conclusions—as long as both writer and reader clearly understand the assumptions underlying the two models.

6

The Social and Economic Consequences of the National Austerity Program in Mexico

Miguel D. Ramírez

Introduction

In October 1986, after eighteen months of tense negotiations, Mexico and its creditor banks agreed in principle to participate in a $12 billion rescue package engineered by the IMF to finance Mexico through the remainder of that year and 1987. The accord came at a time when the collapse of oil prices (form $25 per barrel to $12.50 per barrel) caused oil revenues in 1986 to fall about 50 percent from 1985. To make matters worse, the Mexican economy contracted by at least 4 percent during 1986, whereas inflation accelerated to an annual rate of 105.7 percent.[1] This economic and financial debacle has sparked widespread debate about the causes, consequences, and costs of the debt and the nature of the IMF austerity program imposed during the 1983–1986 period. Supporters of the new austerity agreement see it as a victory for the Baker initiative since it recognizes the need for financial concessions so that Mexico can implement programs of economic reform to achieve sustained and balanced growth. However, critics of the "rescue package" argue that it merely increases the country's long-term debt service obligations while doing little to reverse the negative net transfers of capital from Mexico to the advanced nations (particularly the United States).[2] More important, they point out that the concessions in this latest accord are contingent upon further reductions in the already indadequate provision of collective consumption goods (such as subsidized transportation and housing) as well as upon increases in the prices of basic food products. The majority of the Mexican people—who already have endured drastic delines in their standard of living—should not, in their opinion, have to suffer needlessly through more years of austerity.

This chapter addresses these and other issues by placing them within a framework of analysis that emphasizes the structural factors underlying the economic and social crisis that has afflicted the Mexican people since 1982. In so doing it seeks answers to the following questions: How can a country with more than 72 billion barrels of proven oil and gas reserves be in such dire economic straits? What is the magnitude and nature of the present economic crisis? Should Mexico have to face more years of harsh austerity just to satisfy the major center banks and the IMF? If not, what options are available to Mexico, short of default, in its pursuit of a lasting solution to the crisis?

This chapter first briefly reviews the economic and social situation of Mexico during the 1950s and 1960s. It indicates that the rapid economic growth of this period was achieved at the high cost of imbalances in the allocation of resources, distribution of income, and generation of employment. It then analyzes the severe difficulties encountered by the administrations of Luis Echeverría and José López Portillo in dealing effectively with the socioeconomic imbalances generated by an industrialization strategy based on import substitutions. The third section of the chapter examines the austerity measures implemented during the Miguel de la Madrid administration (1982–1988). The point being emphasized here is that long-term goals such as political reforms and distributive economic growth cannot be achieved in the absence of a fundamental resolution of the debt problem. The chapter concludes with a discussion of economic and financial policies designed to restore real economic growth along with authentic development.

The Origins of the Crisis (1950–1972)

Beginning in 1940, and especially during the 1950–1972 period, Mexico's economy experienced a sustained expansion that was rivaled by that of only a few highly successful developed and developing nations. The nation's gross domestic product (GDP) averaged more than 6 percent real growth from 1952 to 1970, whereas per capita product growth hovered around 3 percent. More importantly, industrial production grew continuously throughout the period, reaching an unprecedented rate of almost 8 percent toward the end of the 1960s.[3] Even agricultural production experienced respectable growth rates of more than 4 percent per year during the 1950s and early 1960s, although by the end of that decade they would plummet to rates well below that of population growth (less than 1 percent per year).[4]

With the expansion in production came substantial sectoral shifts in both output and employment. For example, the agricultural sector employed 58 percent of the economically active population and constituted approximately 19 percent of GDP in 1950; by 1972 it employed no more than 37 percent of the labor force, and its output share had fallen to less than 10 percent. In contrast, the industrial sector made substantial gains during this period, especially in manufacturing, construction, and energy. As of 1972 it employed 24 percent of the economically active population and accounted for close to 35 percent of GDP. These figures represented an increase of 50 and 32 percent respectively over those levels prevailing during 1950.[5]

The rapid growth rate and structural transformation of the Mexican economy was based on the pursuit of "inward-looking" policies, which culminated with the implementation of a variety of protective measures designed to entice domestic producers into establishing enterprises that would produce what had formerly been imported. For example, the currency was fixed at 12.5 pesos per dollar beginning in April 1954 and ending in August 1976.[6] After the exchange rate was fixed, the peso became increasingly overvalued (especially during the late 1960s and early 1970s) and thus implicitly subsidized the importation of capital inputs and sophisticated technology by the newly created enterprises. More important, the administrations of Adolfo Ruíz Cortínez (1952–1958) and Adolfo López Mateos (1958–1964) effected important changes in the general tariffs for imports in order to better protect the newly emerging industries. It has been estimated that, by 1960, a protective barrier had been errected in which the manufacturing sector received nominal protection (for the final product) of 35 percent and effective protection (for the factors of production) of 74 percent. By contrast, the agricultural sector received nominal and effective levels of protection of 3.9 and 6.7 percent, respectively.[7]

The late 1950s and early 1960s would see the "easy" phase of import-substitution industrialization (ISI) come rapidly to a close as the high-yield, short-payout projects were no longer so numerous as in the earlier years.[8] It soon became apparent that as a result of the higher capital-output ratios of the new projects, a limit to the compression of the import coefficient (the ratio of imports to GDP) had been reached; in other words, the growing industrial sector necessitated imports of sophisticated machinery and equipment that could not be produced domestically. The protectionist policies referred to earlier, as well as a number of subsidies in the form of partial or total exemption from various taxes when importing capital goods, biased Mexican businesses toward "state of the art" machinery and equipment. It has been estimated that by the late 1960s, the import-substitution index for capital and durable consumer goods (the ratio of capital and durable consumer imports to the sum of the same *plus* the domestic value added by these goods) had reached a rigidly determined level of .53.[9]

Not suprisingly, foreign sources of funds became the most important adjustment mechanism for financing the growing current-account imbalances and public-sector deficits. It is evident from Table 6.1 that the rate of growth of long-term net foreign capital inflow accelerated considerably during the 1960s, especially between 1970 and 1975. The greater part of the debt contracted throughout these years was of a public nature;

TABLE 6.1
Mexico: Major External Indicators (in millions of U.S. dollars), 1950-1975

	1950	1960	1970	1975
Exports of Goods and Services	826.7	1371.8	2933.1	6305.5
Imports of Goods and Services	768.0	1672.3	3879.0	9998.4
Balance on Current Account	58.7	-300.5	-945.9	-3692.9
Net Capital Inflow (long-term)	51.2	109.5	503.9	4318.0
Net Capital Inflow (short-term)	62.1	182.4	498.7	-460.0
Reserves of the Bank of Mexico	172.0	-8.6	102.1	165.1

Mexico: Growth Rates of Major External Indicators (Average Annual Rates, %)

	1950-1960	1960-1970	1970-1975
Exports of Goods and Services	4.5	6.7	12.7
Imports of Goods and Services	6.0	8.7	15.9
Net Capital Inflow (long-term)	10.4	32.7	126.2

Source: Computed from "La Economía Mexicana en Cifras," (Mexico, D.F.: NAFIN, 1978).

that is, it was contracted directly by public agencies or by private institutions with the guarantee of the government and public development banks such as Nacional Financiera, S.A. (NAFIN).[10] Between 1960 and 1975 Mexico's external public debt as a percentage of gross domestic product rose from 9.7 to 24.4 percent. By comparison, the public debt-product ratio of Latin America as a whole increased from 11 percent in 1960 to about 21 percent in 1975.[11] More important, Mexico's external financial solvency—as measured by the public debt-service ratio (debt service as a percentage of total exports of goods and services)—deteriorated considerably during this period. From an average of 21.5 percent between 1960 and 1970, it increased to a level of 26 percent by the end of 1975.[12] The latter was well above the figure for Latin America as a whole, which stood at 14.8 percent.[13]

At this juncture, it is worth mentioning that, beginning in 1966, external private sources of funds became especially prevalent. Thus, of the total authorized public debt of $4,524 million between 1965 and 1970, 67 percent originated from private sources. Moreover, of the total private debt contracted during this period, 50 percent came from banks (a great number of them in the United States).[14] Thus, the privatization of the debt was under way long before the "recycling" of petrodollars in the 1970s.

During the late 1950s and 1960s Mexico experienced economic growth and financial diversification without inflation. The economic stability that the country enjoyed during this period, known as "stabilizing development," was often referred to as the "Mexican-Economic Miracle." However, the economic and financial policies pursued by the state, although they contributed to the rapid accumulation of capital, also exacerbated the maldistribution of income and wealth. In 1968 the poorest 40 percent of the country's families received only 10.7 percent of the national income, whereas the upper 20 percent received 58.1 percent of the national income. By 1975 the distribution of income had worsened significantly: The share of the bottom 40 percent of the families had fallen to 7.5 percent, whereas the upper 20 percent's share had risen to 62.2 percent. Thus, the Gini coefficient rose from .526 in 1968 to .57 in 1975, placing Mexico alongside Brazil and Ecuador as the Latin American countries with the worst concentrations of income.[15] These developments lend credibility to cross-sectional and cross-national studies which argue that ISI policies, by subsidizing the use of capital-intensive projects in highly protected oligopolistic markets, have inherently increased the concentration of income.[16]

On the employment front, Mexico's persistent annual population growth rates of more than 3 percent during the 1950s and 1960s accentuated the already serious problem of unemployment and underemployment. For example, Rene Villarreal reports that, by 1970, census estimates indicated that 3.5 million people, or 26.8 percent of the economically active population, were unemployed.[17] The growing pool of job seekers could have been better served if the industrialization process had been accompanied by the increasing use of labor-intensive technologies. As we have seen, however, the policy of import substitution has been characterized throughout Latin America by a decline in the relative cost of capital. Ann D. Witte (1971) demonstrates that in Mexico the price of capital relative to that of labor was reduced at an average annual rate of 5 percent from 1945 to 1965. This relative price effect made itself felt in the manufacturing sector, where the man-years required to produce 100,000 real pesos of value added per year decreased from 9.6 in 1945 to only 2.8 by 1968.[18] Finally, the overvalued exchange rate—maintained at 12.5 pesos per dollar until September 1976—implicitly subsidized the importation of capital-intensive technologies at the expense of domestic labor and capital.

Politically, Mexico experienced relative stability during most of the 1950s and 1960s. The dominant official party, the Institutional Revolutionary party (PRI), through its skillful co-optation of the leadership of the major labor confederations that came to form the Congress of Labor (CT), was able to neutralize any genuine opposition while, at the same time, keeping the demands of the popular sectors in check.[19] This strategy worked effectively until the late 1950s, when the level of strike activity increased sharply. At that time, the López Mateos administration (1958–1964) used federal troops to put down a major railroad strike that threatened to paralyze the country.[20] Although the López Mateos *sexenio* got off to a bad start on the labor front, the last four years of the administration would witness a significant dimunition in registered strikes and labor-management disputes. In no small measure this was the result of the government's implementation of an almost forgotten article of the Constitution of 1917 that called for labor to share in the profits with management. Meyer and Sherman observe that "by 1964 many Mexican laborers were earning an extra 5 to 10 percent a year under the profit-sharing law."[21]

The López Mateos administration proved to be the lull before the storm, however, for the presidency of Gustavo Díaz Ordaz (1964–1970) was rocked by demonstrations and protests by students, intellectuals, and workers who demanded sweeping economic and social reforms in order to deal with the country's growing distributional inequities. Beginning in the spring of 1966, campus after campus throughout the country exploded with strikes and violence. Students and many faculty members were particularly incensed at what they considered to be the exorbitant costs that went into the preparation of the 1968 Olympic games—scarce resources that they felt should be used to meet the country's pressing social problems. At any rate, the confrontations between the government and the students would reach a climax on the evening of October 2, 1968, with the tragic Tlatelolco student massacre—a few days before the start of the Olympic games. Although what happened at the Plaza de las Tres Culturas will never be completely clarified, what is certain is that the bankruptcy of "stabilizing development" was laid bare for the whole world to see, and confidence in the PRI and the legitimacy of the Mexican state was severely shaken.

Echeverría: The Origins of the Debt Crisis (1970–1976)

In view of these unfavorable social and economic developments, the Echeverría administration (1970–1976) decided to abandon the stabilization process of the previous decade. Instead, it embarked upon an ambitious program designed (1) to raise the state's provision of collective consumption goods such as subsidized health and housing,[22] and (2) to accelerate the process of import substitution in the capital goods sector.[23] The first action was obviously designed to alleviate some of the pressing social problems generated by the skewed distribution of income, whereas the second was counted on to reduce the country's ever-growing current-account deficits. To accomplish these goals, the administration greatly increased the rate of public spending. Since the private financial system was in no position to finance the requirements of the plan, the Bank of Mexico had no recourse but to turn to the printing press in order to cover the growing public-sector deficits. These deficits reached a level of 10 percent of GDP by the end of 1975, compared to only 2.5 percent in 1971.[24]

The increase in the annual rate of growth of the money supply from 7.5 percent in 1971 to almost 25 percent by the end of 1974 had a telling impact on the consumer price index. Inflation soared to 22.5 percent by 1975, compared to a rate of only 3.7 percent in 1971.[25] Not surprisingly, real yields on financial bonds and deposits became negative, thus, in turn, discouraging domestic private saving and encouraging capital flight.[26] Still, as the Echeverría administration was neither willing nor able to reduce the rate of public spending, it had no other recourse but to increase the public sector's external indebtedness. The latter rose on a net basis from $2,444 million in 1973 to an unprecedented figure of $4,462 million in 1976—an accretion of nearly 83 percent.[27]

By 1976 the economic situation had worsened considerably in terms of the growing debt-service ratio, which had reached an all-time high of 38.6 percent, and the failure of export revenues to rise as anticipated during the first half of the year.[28] As a result, the Bank of Mexico's reserves deteriorated beyond the capacity of the nation to acquire short-term debt. This situation led to a growing uncertainty among private investors as to whether the exchange rate—fixed at 12.5 pesos to the dollar since 1954—could be maintained, and thence to a flight of capital from the country, which, according to Leopoldo Solís, reached a level of approximately $4 billion during 1976.[29]

López Portillo:
Short-Lived Austerity and
the Petrolization of the Economy (1976–1982)

Faced with these unfortunate economic events, the government had no choice but to devalue the peso from 12.5 to 19.7 pesos per dollar at the end of 1976. In addition, the newly inaugurated administration of José López Portillo (1976–1982) agreed to implement an economic package prescribed by the IMF that called for the contraction of state expenditures and the liberalization of commerce. The plan dictated that the public-sector deficit be reduced by 6 percent of GDP; employment in the public sector not increase more than 2 percent during 1977; the rate of exchange vary so as to maintain equilibrium in the foreign exchange market; and prices and tariffs of the goods and services produced by public enterprises reflect their real costs of production.

These measures were implemented in varying degrees during 1977 with the expected results—namely, a reduction in the rate of GDP growth to 3.4 percent; a decline in the public-sector deficit from 7.5 to 5.2 percent of GDP; a deceleration of the rate of increase in prices; an increase in the reserves of the Bank of Mexico to $504.2 million from negative $320.9 million the previous year; and an increase of 28 percent

TABLE 6.2
Mexican Economic Indicators (Annual Growth Rates), 1976-1982

Item	1976	1977	1978	1979	1980	1981	1982
Gross Domestic Product	4.2	3.4	8.2	9.2	8.3	7.9	-0.5
Population	3.2	3.2	3.1	3.0	3.0	2.9	2.8
Per Capita Product	1.0	0.2	5.1	6.2	5.3	5.0	-3.3
Industrial Output	5.0	3.5	9.8	10.8	7.2	7.0	-2.9
Agricultural Output	-1.0	10.3	8.1	-5.9	10.0	8.0	-2.9
Public Sector Deficit (% of GDP)	9.9	5.2	6.7	7.4	7.9	14.7	17.9
Rate of Inflation[a]	19.6	30.4	16.7	20.3	28.7	26.7	98.2
Employment	2.0	3.9	3.7	5.4	6.2	6.4	-1.0
Real Minimum Wage	-8.7	-3.5	2.0	-4.0	2.9	1.6	-9.6

[a]GDP deflator with 1970=100

Sources: Computed from La Economía Mexicana en Cifras (México, D.F.: NAFIN,
1984); and Inter-American Development Bank (IDB), Economic and Social Progress in
Latin America, 1985 Report (Washington D.C.: IDB, 1986).

in the voluntary savings of the public.[30] More important from the
standpoint of Mexican workers, real minimum wages—which had grown
steadily during the early 1970s—experienced a sharp cumulative fall of
12.2 percent from 1976 through 1977 (see Table 6.2). In addition, the
urban unemployment rate (a twelve-month average for the metropolitan
areas of Mexico City, Guadalajara, and Monterrey) jumped from 6.7
percent in 1976 to 8.3 percent by the end of 1977.[31]

  The three-year austerity program recommended by the IMF was
destined to be short-lived—if not "de jure," then certainly "de facto";
for by 1978 it was discovered that Mexico had 40,194 million barrels
of proven oil and gas reserves, as compared to 6,338 million barrels in
1976. By 1981 its proven reserves stood at an impressive 72 billion
barrels, which at existing annual production levels would last well into
the twenty-first century.[32] Thus, the country was transformed into an
energy colossus capable not only of meeting its own internal needs but
also of developing its export capacity during a period of rising petroleum
prices. It appeared to policymakers in the government at the time that
the development and exploitation of oi and gas reserves would provide
a painless solution for Mexico's economic and social problems. Anticipating
a steady flow of income from future oil sales, the López Portillo
administration thus abandoned austerity and in 1978 embarked upon a
path of "free-spending" policies that would last through 1981.

The results, in terms of certain macroeconomic variables, were impressive. As Table 6.2 reveals, real GDP grew better than 8 percent annually between 1978 and 1981, whereas manufacturing output rose at an unprecedented rate of 11 percent during 1979. Also, employment growth averaged close to 6 percent per year for the period 1979–1981; and, more significantly, the government's effort at reducing the country's stubbornly high population growth rates seemed to be taking effect.

Other variables clearly pointed in another direction, but, in the optimism of the moment, they were overlooked or given "lip service" by policymakers in the government. One such variable was the increasing dependence of the country on revenues derived from oil exports, particularly from 1979 onward. Between 1979 and 1981 the value of oil exports rose from $3.9 billion to $14.5 billion, whereas their share in total exports increased from 43.9 to approximately 75 percent.[33] The irony is that Mexican officials had repeatedly emphasized Mexico's need to avoid the types of distortions that oil-rich countries such as Venezuela and Nigeria had experienced in their industrial and financial sectors. The Mexicans, by imposing a high rate of taxation on the earnings of the state petroleum corporation (PEMEX), created a revenue structure that would become heavily vulnerable to world market prices for one commodity. The increasing dependence of the federal government on the export revenues of PEMEX during this period is revealed by the fact that, of the total revenues generated by state enterprises, PEMEX contributed 30 percent in 1977 and 50 percent in 1981. More important, of the total tax revenues raised by the federal government during the 1977–1981 period, the portion contributed by PEMEX averaged close to 25 percent.[34]

Another discouraging trend, which had been rectified somewhat during 1977, was the country's ever-increasing public-sector deficits. As shown in Table 6.2, they rose from a low of 5.2 percent of GDP in 1977 to an all-time high of 17.9 percent by the end of 1982 (with the sharpest jump in 1981 and 1982). As in the past they were financed by the monetization of the government debt and by heavy borrowing from both private and public foreign sources. Thus, the Central Bank's claims on the government increased from 134 billion pesos in 1976 to 2.1 trillion pesos in 1982, whereas the total public foreign debt rose from $18 billion to about $55 billion over the same period.[35] Not surprisingly, the rate of inflation accelerated from 16.7 percent in 1978 to 98.2 percent by the end of 1982. Despite the government's award of emergency adjustment increases in minimum wages during March and October of 1982, many of the country's 22.8 million workers experienced sharp declines in their real wages during that year (again, see Table 6.2).[36]

Developments in the nation's external indicators during this period also clearly revealed the growing structural problems of the economy. For example, although the value of Mexico's merchandise exports increased from $9.3 billion in 1979 to $19.8 billion in 1981 (largely as a result of growing oil exports), its imports rose at an even faster rate. As can be seen from Table 6.3, the result was that the trade deficit in the balance of payments rose from $2.3 billion in 1980 to $4.2 billion in 1981. The disequilibrium in the current account was even more pronounced, primarily owing to interest payments on an increasing external debt. Table 6.3 reveals that total public and private indebtedness (disbursed debt) rose from $49.3 billion at the end of 1980 to $85.8 billion at the end of 1982. More troubling still, the debt service (interest and amortization) as a percentage of exports of goods and nonfactor services registered as an alarming figure of 65.4 percent by the end of 1982, compared to 44.7 percent the year before. By February 1982, the events of 1976 started to repeat themselves with a vengeance when, as a result of the worldwide recession combined with falling oil prices, rising interest rates[37] and a weak international reserve position (see Table 6.3), the peso was devalued by 67 percent.

The devaluation proved to be inadequate in halting the flight of capital from the country. In fact, it made matters worse inasmuch as López Portillo had postponed devaluation, arguing that "when a president devalues, he devalues himself." This was an obvious reference to the experience of his predecessor, Echeverría; and in light of his own actions, devaluation did nothing but further erode confidence in the government's ability to manage the crisis. The economic situation continued to deteriorate as a result of the government's inability to raise sufficient funds in international capital markets to meets its service on the external debt. By August of that year, the crisis had reached unmanageable proportions, so the López Portillo administration took the unprecedented move of closing foreign exchange markets and declaring a temporary moratorium on external debt payments.

When foreign exchange markets opened several days later, the announcement was made that an international financial assistance package was being negotiated. The rescue package consisted of a $1 billion advance payment for exports to the United States Strategic Petroleum reserve. $1 billion of U.S. government guarantees for purchase of U.S. agricultural goods, and a $1.85 billion loan from the Bank for International Settlements.[38] In addition, the Mexican government stated that it had begun negotiations with the IMF for a structural adjustment loan that would allow Mexico to draw on IMF lines of credit totaling $3.9 billion in 1983–1985. Finally, a two-tiered exchange-rate system consisting of a Free Rate and a Controlled Rate was implemented. The Free Rate that would be set daily to reflect underlying forces of supply and demand was to be used for "nonessential" transactions such as tourist expenditures. The Controlled Rate, on the other hand, would be applied to government-approved transactions such as debt-service payments on foreign debt contracted before August 1982, and to imports of essential capital and raw material inputs. Government officials estimated that about 85 percent of Mexico's international transactions would be financed by the Controlled Rate.[39]

TABLE 6.3
México: Major External Indicators (in Billions of U.S. Dollars), 1980-1985

Item	1980	1981	1982	1983	1984	1985[*]
Merchandise Exports	16.3	19.8	20.0	22.3	24.6	21.9
Merchandise Imports	18.6	24.0	13.5	8.6	11.3	13.5
Trade Balance	-2.3	-4.2	6.5	13.7	13.3	8.4
Net Services	-5.2	-9.8	-12.2	-8.4	-8.9	-7.9
Current Account Balance	-7.5	-14.0	-5.7	5.3	4.4	0.5
Capital Account Balance	10.5	23.4	7.5	-2.4	-1.5	-1.3
Net Change in Reserves[**]	-0.9	-1.1	1.8	-2.0	-2.1	2.3
Disbursed Debt	49.3	77.9	85.8	93.7	97.3	98.9
Interest payments	n.a.	8.4	12.2	10.2	11.7	9.9
Debt service	10.0	13.2	16.3	13.6	13.4	11.9
Debt service ratio (%)	42.2	44.7	65.4	40.7	n.a.	n.a.
Official exchange Rate (pesos/dollar)	22.95	24.51	56.40	120.09	167.83	257.00
Real Effective Exchange Rate (1980=100)	n.a.	89.10	133.80	179.30	124.00	132.30

[*] Preliminary estimate
[**] Net increases in Mexican international reserves are catalogued as a debit (with a negative sign) because they are defined as imports by balance-of-payments statisticians.

Source: Inter-American Development Bank, Economic and Social Progress in Latin America: 1984 and 1985 Reports (Washington, D.C.: IDB, 1984, 1985).

Despite these efforts to manage the crisis, capital flight continued unabated. In virtual desperation, the outgoing López Portillo administration decided to nationalize the banking system (on September 10, 1982), to suspend the convertiblity of the peso, and to impose strict foreign exchange controls. The nationalization decision was taken under the leadership of Carlos Tello Macías, then director of the Central Bank. A strong advocate of state intervention in the economy, he, and other members of the nationalist sector within the government, blamed the banking community for acting irresponsibly, thus contributing to a capital outflow exceeding $9 billion in 1982.[40] An investigation into Mexican bank accounts and real estate in the United States revealed that Mexican citizens had $14 billion in more than 1 million bank accounts in the United States and owned $30 billion in real estate, in addition to $12 billion in dollar accounts in Mexican banks.[41] Moreover, it was disclosed that the "Banco Hipotecario de Crédito had sent $300 million out of the country in a single day."[42] These disclosures led López Portillo to declare "that in recent years a group of Mexicans, led, counseled and supported by private banks, have taken more money out of the country than all the empires that have exploited us since the beginning of our history."[43] Ironically, after he flew off to self-imposed exile in Europe, it was soon revealed that López Portillo himself had defrauded the country during his tenure in office.[44]

Nationalization of the banking system and the imposition of exchange controls were designed to place the state firmly in control of the banking sector. In this way it could implement needed financial reforms without invoking monetarist measures of fiscal austerity. Carlos Tello objected to traditional IMF stabilization programs that placed the burden of adjustment on those individuals within society who could least afford it. However, during his brief tenure as director of the Bank of Mexico, many of his financial policies were rendered ineffective as result of the extreme conditions under which they had been instituted.[45]

The IMF Austerity Program: Miguel de la Madrid's Legacy (1983–1986)

Upon taking office in December 1982, President Miguel de la Madrid Hurtado replaced the controversial Carlos Tello with Miguel Mancera. The new administration—with its strong belief in market forces—set out to reverse many of Tello's nationalist policies. For example, it dismantled the exchange controls and reestablished the dual exchange-rate system. More significant, by the end of 1982, de la Madrid signed a bill authorizing the government to sell 34 percent of the nationalized banks' assets to the public. As a result, former bank owners could participate once again, in a minority status, in the ownership of the nationalized banks.[46] Hamilton indicates that, by the spring of 1984, "the government offered the shares of many of the nationalized banks' holdings in Mexican companies and foreign subsidiaries for sale, with preference given to former bank shareholders. . . . Since the stocks are being offered in large, indivisible portfolios, only the wealthiest Mexican owners will be able to purchase them."[47]

Perhaps the clearest indication of the shift in policy under de la Madrid's administration was the president's adoption of an IMF austerity program (EL Programa Immediato de Reordenación Económica) whose central tenet was fiscal austerity. In addition to the implementation of a dual exchange-rate system, the essential features of the new economic program included (1) a reduction in the public-sector deficit to 8.5 percent of GDP in 1983, 5.5 percent in 1984, and 3.5 percent in 1985;[48] (2) an increase in the prices charged for a wide range of goods and services provided by the public sector; (3) a move toward the elimination of import licensing requirements; and (4) a concerted effort by both the public and private sectors to promote nonpetroleum exports.

As Table 6.4 indicates, the IMF austerity measures put in place during 1983 initially produced some encouraging results. For example, the country's inflation rate was reduced from 98.2 percent in 1982 to 80.8 percent in 1983, and to 65.5 percent the following year. Still, this latter figure was double what the government had projected. Another achievement of the economic adjustment program was the reduction in the fiscal deficit from 17.6 percent of GDP in 1982 to 8.7 percent in 1984. However, as indicated in Table 6.4, it rose to 10 percent of GDP in 1985 as a result of the expansionary fiscal and credit policies put in place during the middle of 1984. A more accurate measure of the draconian reductions in real credit demand by the public sector is given by the operational deficit (public-sector deficit less total interest payments), since it excludes the distorting effect of inflation on the servicing of domestic debt. Table 6.4 reveals that, in 1983 and 1984 respectively, the operational budget registered surpluses of 2.4 and 0.3 percent of GDP, whereas 1985 showed a slight negative balance of 0.6 percent.

During 1983, Mexico also recorded a $5.3 billion surplus in its current account (see Table 6.3), which won the government high praise from the international financial community. In large measure, this was the result of a large drop in the value of imports: to $8.6 billion, rather than the $15.2 billion that had been anticipated. Meanwhile, Mexico's exports experienced a slight accretion due to the systematic devaluation of the peso and the global recovery that began in 1983. As can be seen from Table 6.3, the current account swing, along with the rescheduling of public foreign debt and the $5 billion commerical bank loan arranged in 1983, enabled the country's international reserves to increase by $2 billion by 1984. But by 1985 the merchandise balance had dropped to $8.4 billion, the current-account balance had plunged to only $541 million, and there was a net increase in the holdings of Mexican assets by foreigners of $2.3 billion (see Table 6.3). In part, these outcomes were the result of an increase in imports associated with the slight

TABLE 6.4
Mexican Economic Indicators (Annual Growth Rates and Percentages), 1982-1985

Item	1982	1983	1984	1985
Gross Domestic Product	-0.5	-5.3	3.7	2.7
Population	2.8	2.7	3.0	3.0
Per Capita Product	-3.3	-8.0	0.7	-0.3
Agricultural Sector	-2.9	2.9	2.5	2.2
Mining Sector (includes oil)	9.2	-2.7	1.8	1.0
Manufacturing Sector	-2.9	-7.3	4.8	5.0
Construction Sector	-5.0	-18.0	3.4	2.5
Money Supply (M1)	62.1	41.2	63.1	54.8
Rate of Inflation	98.2	80.8	65.5	57.7
Public-Sector Deficit (% of GDP)	17.6	9.0	8.7	10.0
Operational Deficit (% of GDP)[*]	7.3	-2.4	-0.3	0.6
Open Urban Unemployment Rate	4.2	6.9	6.3	5.0
Real Minimum Wage	-9.6	-18.0	-7.4	-1.3

[*]Defined as the public-sector deficit less total interest payments.

Sources: Inter-American Development Bank (IDB), Economic and Social Progress in Latin America, 1985 Report (Washington, D.C.: IDB, 1985); BANAMEX, Review of the Economic Situation in Mexico, Vol. 625, No. 729, August 1986 (México, D.F.: Banco Nacional de México); La Economía Mexicana en Cifras (México, D.F.: NAFIN); and Banco de México, Informe Anual (May 1986).

economic recovery experienced by the country during the second half of 1984 (see Table 6.4).

The downside of these austerity measures, however, however, has been soaring unemployment and a drastic deterioration in Mexico's standard of living. Table 6.4 reveals that Mexico's real GDP per inhabitant experienced an unprecedented cumulative drop of about 11 percent during the 1982–1985 period. Also, despite the government's minimum wage adjustments on the order of 50 percent during 1983, real minimum wages experienced an alarming drop of 18 percent during 1983—their sharpest fall in the post–World War II period. On a sectoral basis, the World Bank (1986) reports that during the 1981–1983 period, the decline in the real minimum wage was greatest in agriculture (31.3 percent) and community, social, and personal services (30.8 percent); and smallest

TABLE 6.5
Average Monthly Wages in the Manufacturing Sector (in U.S. Dollars), 1977-1983

Year	Mexico(1)	U.S.(2)	Difference (2)-(1)
1977	248.5	915.6	667.1
1978	283.9	997.1	713.2
1979	330.3	1075.8	745.5
1980	398.9	1163.2	764.3
1981	489.9	1278.4	788.5
1982	335.0	1360.0	1025.0
1983	354.2	1416.5	1062.3

Source: Computed from Secretaría de Programación y Presupuesto, Estadística Industrial Anual 1984 (México, D.F.: SSP, 1984).

in electric power (12.5 percent), transport and communications (22.6 percent), and construction (24.4 percent).[49] In like manner, Table 6.5 shows that average wages in 1,300 manufacturing enterprises surveyed by the Secretaría de Programación y Presupuesto (SPP) fell significantly— from their high of $490 per month in 1981 after steadily climbing during the previous four years. Moreover, the gap between average wages in the manufacturing sector in Mexico and the United States has sharply risen since 1981. The deterioration in both average and real minimum wages has continued in recent years. Moreover, in view of the fact that approximately 67 percent of Mexico's 25 million workers earn the minimum wage (about 536.6 pesos per day in 1983 [U.S. $3.20]), the possibility of a rupture of the "labor-state pact" in the near future is not unthinkable. In this connection Barry Carr (1983) reports that

> [t]he union leadership has been showing growing signs of frustration over its diminishing margin of maneuver as a result. This mood is manifested in ever more frequent displays of verbal radicalism. For example, the Confederation of Mexican Workers (CTM) has adopted a number of demands that traditionally have been the property of the Mexican left and of the independent labor unions. These include demands for the nationalization of the food processing and pharmaceutical industries, and a demand for the introduction of a system of wage adjustments based on price movements (salario remunerador).[50]

Returning to Table 6.4, we should note that the production cuts in the mining, manufacturing, and construction sectors (as a result of the sharp fall in imports) sent the open unemployment rate in the urban areas soaring in 1982–1983. In Mexico City, for example, the open unemployment rate was almost 8 percent during 1983, whereas it exceeded 13 percent in northern industrial cities like Monterrey and Guadalajara. Although unemployment figures resulting from the economic crisis are difficult to establish, it is estimated that more than 2 million workers lost their jobs during the 1982–1984 period.[51] The young have been particularly hard hit by the depression. The World Bank reports that in Monterrey, "twenty-six percent of those who were twelve to nineteen years old and in the labor force and 14 percent of those aged twenty to twenty-four were unemployed during 1983."[52] Unemployment also hit Mexico's 5.3 million unionized workers, as the following figures indicate: 25,000 unemployed in automobile manufacture, 21,000 in the metal industry, 25,000 in clothing and textiles, and 40,000 workers at PEMEX.[53] A similar fate befell government bureaucrats who, as a result of the public sector's cutback in expenditures, saw more than 110,000 of their jobs disappear from 1983 to 1985.[54]

Beyond the measures of "open urban unemployment," it is even more important to have measures of the "underemployed" and "disguised unemployed." These figures are extremely difficult to come by, however, and the estimates are nothing but educated guesses. For example, Peter Gregory (1980) calculates that underemployment in Mexico ranges between 16 to 50 percent, whereas Marvin Alisky's (1983) calculations yield an underemployment rate of 20 percent. If we couple the latter estimate with Mexico's overall (urban and rural) unemployment rate— reported to range from 26 to 28 percent—we can venture to say that Mexico in 1985 suffered from an unemployment and underemployment rate of 46 percent.[55] In other words, during 1985 approximately 11.04 million of Mexico's 24 million workers were either unemployed or underemployed![56] Is it any wonder, then, that many Mexicans are asking themselves whether the country's sacrifice will result in long-term economic growth and stability, or waste human and physical capital that had been acquired with much hardship?

If recent events are any indication, the answer is perhaps best given by Miguel Mancera, Mexico's president of the Central Bank, who concluded that more money flowed out of the country during 1985 than in either of the previous two years. As can be seen from Table 6.3, net capital flows were negative during the years from 1983 to 1985 as a result of reduced foreign loans, amortization payments, and capital flight. In fact, some international economists estimate that as much as $5 billion had escaped the country during 1985 alone.[57] Many economists blamed this turn of events on the government's handling of its two-tiered exchange-rate system. Faced with elections in July, the government failed to maintain its devaluation of the peso relative to the dollar, in line with the country's accelerating inflation rate, for fear of reducing the international purchasing power of the Mexican consumer even further. As Table 6.3 shows, the result was that the rate of devaluation of the real effective exchange rate slowed considerably, thus, in turn, driving a wedge between the official exchange rate and the black market rate, and ultimately stepping up the outflow of capital.

Mexico's problems were further compounded in 1985 by the devastating earthquake that hit the country in late September.[58] The collapse of shoddy government construction in the center of Mexico City and de la Madrid's inept handling of the crisis led to numerous charges of corruption and indecisiveness against government officials involved in the reconstruction effort. Perhaps the single most damaging blow to the administration's public image was the discovery of at least eight bodies of tortured victims in the ruins of the basement of the Judicial Police building. Needless to say, the government's call for moral rejuvenation (renovación moral) was dealt a severe blow in the eyes of the Mexican people.[59]

As things stood in 1986, Mexico was reeling from a drop in oil prices that caused oil revenues to fall off about 50 percent from 1985 (oil income represents nearly 45 percent of total government revenue).[60] In addition, the economy was expected to contract at least 4 percent by the end of 1986, and the Bank of Mexico projected that inflation would spurt to an annual rate of more than 100 percent—the worst one-year inflation rate in Mexico's history. More important, labor leaders such as Fidel Velazquez, head of the Confederation of Mexican Workers (CTM), have complained bitterly that the traditional wage increases granted in January and June of each year (33.1 and 25.1, respectively, in 1986) had become nothing but an excuse for a new escalation in prices rather than a necessary adjustment to maintain the purchasing power of the working class (real minimum wages were expected to fall between 14 and 15 percent during 1986). Many of these hikes reflected the government's policy of boosting prices controlled by the public sector and slashing subsidies on basic goods and services such as transportation and health care to make up for revenues lost from falling oil prices. The sharpest increases in controlled prices have been seen in those items that affect the working poor most directly: transportation by 117.4 percent; food, beverages, and tobacco by 108.7 percent; and health and personal care by 113.7 percent.[61]

Not surprisingly, the working poor have had to alter the composition and size of their basic consumption-basket either by substituting cheaper items for more expensive ones or, when this is not feasible, by reducing altogether their consumption of certain goods and services. Fuentes and Arroio (1986) cite a 1984 study of low-income families by the Instituto Nacional del Consumidor (INCO) that revealed a marked deterioration in the daily diet. That is, 11.4 percent of these families eliminated meat products, 7.5 percent milk, 6.7 percent fish, and 4.4 percent soft drinks; and 3.3 percent did without fruits and vegetables.[62] More significant, the authors maintain that the consumption of calories and proteins by the Mexican people fell by 20 percent between 1983 and 1985, thus the nutritional requirements of the population are below those that prevailed ten years ago.[63] Finally, whereas in 1982 47 percent of a typical family's minimum salary was spent on food, by 1985 that figure had risen to 64 percent.[64]

//

Alternatives to Austerity

The limited progress made by Mexico's stabilization program throughout 1986 carried the cost of aggravating the social and political climate
of the country. Moreover, that progress is predicated upon the country's
continued ability to generate export surpluses so that it can service its
outstanding external debt. As can be seen from Table 6.3 (net services
row), Mexico's total net payments to foreign capital during the 1982–
1985 period amounted to a staggering $37.4 billion—a figure that exceeds
the amounts called for by the Baker Plan (roughly $30 billion)! Clearly,
the negative financial flows from Mexico and other Latin American
countries to the industrialized nations are unsustainable. On the one
hand, negative financial flows require the unlikely prospect that the
United States (Mexico's largest trading partner)[65] and other industrialized
nations will willingly accept persistent and growing trade deficits in the
face of protectionist sentiments at home. Even if they could expand
demand to accommodate debtor's exports, some industries would still
unavoidably experience an increase in structural unemployment as a
result of debtor competition. Equally implausible, the negative financial
flows require that Mexico continue indefinitely servicing its debt by
generating trade surpluses and reverse transfers, which also represent
very real forgone opportunities for higher growth and living standards.

Not surprisingly, Mexico's stabilization program has been linkened to
a "ratcheted wheel that tightens the nation's social fabric one more notch
at each swing; inevitably a breaking point will be reached, with possibly
far-reaching social and political consequences."[66] To forestall such a
consequence would require (1) a significant reduction and eventual
elimination of the debt burden, and (2) a set of consistent policies
designed to change the country's prevailing pattern of economic growth.
Before looking into the nature of these policies, let us first examine some
recent and bold proposals for dealing with the debt problem, since it
is upon the resolution of this problem that the success of the reforms
outlined below rests.

A first step toward a viable solution of the debt crisis has been
offered by Harold Lever and Christopher Huhne (1986). They argue
that

> [t]he key to achieving new bank lending would be a form of insurance
> akin to the export credit guarantee schemes operating in most advanced
> countries. Under these schemes exporters are insured so that they are paid
> even if they are unable to collect debt for exports. But it is not their
> practice to insure the foreign-currency lending needed to make debt
> payments.[67]

For this reason it is necessary, in their opinion, to establish a Western
Hemisphere Development Institution (or an expanded World Bank),
financed by the industrialized nations, that would guarantee the necessary

flow of lending. The annual ceilings of guaranteed "new money" would be set by the IMF on a case-by-case basis for each of the debtor nations. Moreover, the secured loans would be given on the condition that the banks write down each year, according to circumstances, that part of their debt judged to be nonperforming. They would also be required to agree to long-term rescheduling of the interest on that part of the debt judged to be bad.

More important, the IMF would be required to radically change its present philosphy and orientation. Instead of imposing austerity measures designed to extract transfers from countries such as Mexico, it would estimate the latter's reverse net transfers and, on that basis, insure new lending so that the nation can resume growth and improve its living standards. Debt relief for Mexico could be in the form of (1) new voluntary commercial bank lending (guaranteed by the advanced nations); (2) reductions in interest payments to commercial lenders; and (3) proposals to convert parts of official and private debt into grants.[68] Of course, these measures would be in vain if wealthy Mexicans continue to shift vast sums of money across the border as illustrated by Morgan Guarantee Trust Company's estimate that about $16 billion fled Mexico between 1983 and 1985.

David Felix (1985) has cogently argued that in order to prevent the further recycling of "debt-dollars" to the advanced nations, Latin American governments would do well to draw on the experience of these nations in times of crisis. He points out that, during World War I,

> Britain and France, the two leading international lenders of the Laissez-faire era, compelled their nationals to register their foreign securities with the Treasury, which liquidated them as needed, paying the owners in local currency bonds, the foreign exchange being used to help cover current account deficits. As the Chancellor of the Exchequer put it to parliament, "The government wanted to get these securities, as far as possible, into one hand, so that they might be controlled and used for the purpose of paying our debts in the United States. They believed that these securities would afford us a very great resource which would be fully sufficient to meet our Obligations." With the World War experience in mind, the Tory government on the eve of World War II took the precaution of requiring registration of all foreign securities, which could sell them as needed, and did.[69]

In view of the fact that there has been no letup of capital flight from Mexico to the United States, it is high time for the Mexican state to recapture these assets in order to service its external debt. But many skeptics would argue that it is highly unlikely that Mexico will do so because the dominant upper classes in the country derive substantial economic and financial benefits from the debt-expansion/debt-service cycle.[70] This is undoubtedly true, but it is equally true that in times of crisis the Mexican state has taken unprecedented steps that have revealed the extent of its autonomy vis-à-vis the private domestic sector. A case in point was the nationalization of the banking system, which, according to Hamilton (1984), took many powerful economic groups such as the Chihuahua Group (a major supporter of the National Action party [PAN]) completely by surprise.[71] With no resolution to the economic quagmire in sight, the PRI will be searching for novel ways to institutionalize populism so as to preserve the legitimacy of the state.

Toward Renewed Growth

If Mexico is to have any hope of growth and improvement in its social conditions, its external constraint must be removed through debt relief. Hence a solution to Mexico's long-term social and economic problems will require both short-term and structural changes in its external and domestic economic policies. One hopes that the reforms outlined below, some of which have been instituted or are being considered by the Mexican government, will move the country's economy toward the renewed growth needed to escape the current austerity. First and foremost, future growth ought to be based upon labor-intensive activities in order to provide employment for those currently unemployed or underemployed, as well as for the projected 800,000 people who will enter the job market every year.[72] Investment should be redirected toward labor-absorptive activities such as roads, bridges, agriculture, and urban infrastructure. The government has made limited progress in this direction by generating 155,000 jobs through implementation of projects to install drinking water and sewage systems and to improve housing under the Program for Employment in Critical Urban Zones. Moreover, under the Program for Job Creation in Rural Areas, 235,000 jobs are being created throughout the country via projects whose mix of capital and labor reflects the country's factor endowment.[73] Yet much remains to be done, since the jobs being created through these various programs are barely sufficient to offset even half the number of projected entrants into the labor force each year.

Another area that has been neglected in the past, but which ought to form part of any employment program in the future, is the promotion of small- and medium-sized industries, which tend to be more labor intensive than the largest enterprises. Many firms in the country's metal-working and electrical machinery industries are small. But they play an important role by bringing technology into rural areas, by providing employment, and by supplying implements that make full use of locally available resources. The Mexican government, through the Fund for Promoting Small- and Medium-Scale Industry (FOGAIN), has moved in the right direction by significantly increasing the amount of resources to these institutions since 1983.[74] In addition to these measures, the government should continue to eliminate factor-price distortions such as interest ceilings, high rates of effective protection, and overvalued exchange rates that lower the relative price of capital and thus promote capital-intensive projects.

•

In a related area of reform, the Mexican government should renew promotion of those export manufactures that emphasize labor-intensive technologies. In other words, a strategy of export substitution should be encouraged, whenever feasible, in such areas as clothing, footwear, electrical machinery, construction services, tourism, and financial services. On the other hand, import-competing industries should be *gradually* dismantled or reorganized where it is clear that excessive protection and a protracted divorce of production decisions from market conditions (if applicable) have led to inefficiency and corruption. In turn, those import-substituting industries that have proved to be relatively efficient should be encouraged to develop an export capacity. This could be accomplished by liberalizing trade on a *gradual* basis; that is, tariffs on imports, including capital goods, would be reduced and equalized, thus eliminating the distortion of prices alluded to earlier in the chapter. Also, it would be necessary to subsidize exports since cost competitiveness and quality standards are higher there than in the domestic market. Finally, the country should undertake periodic devaluations so that the exchange rate is maintained in line with rising domestic prices and costs. These measures would improve the efficiency of resource allocation within the industrial sector while at the same time enhancing the relative attractiveness of production for the external market.

Mexico's present pace of minidevaluations, its formal admission into GATT on July 25, 1986,[75] and its promotion of frontier regions as export platforms for manufactured goods (*maquiladoras*) are encouraging signs.[76] The importance of *maquiladoras* is worth emphasizing because they have surpassed tourism in providing the country with badly needed foreign currency. For example, on a net basis, they brought in about $1.3 billion during 1984—second only to petroleum, which was estimated to have earned $16.5 billion.[77] More important, they provide employment to individuals with little formal education at approximately the Mexican minimum wage (U.S. $3.32 per day in 1983).[78] However, given their predominant location along the U.S.-Mexican border, they have established few links with the rest of the economy. As of 1983, their total value added—though significantly higher than in 1981—stood at only 0.57 percent of the nation's GDP,[79] compared to a share of 1.7 percent for the electricity industry.[80] Thus, unless the Mexican government establishes these enterprises in the interior of the country, they will continue to remain "enclaves" with only a marginal contribution to employment and income.[81]

Clearly, a successful strategy of export substitution, no less than one of import substitution, will requre the government to assume a strong interventionist role. This means that the Mexican government should be able to provide (1) market information, by establishing trade offices in potential markets, and (2) communications and transport infrastructure, such as port facilities, transport networks, power supplies, and marketing assistance. Both commercial banks and development banks (as in South

Korea) should be encouraged to favor exporters in their lending operations, as well as to assist them in resolving the operational and managerial difficulties that are likely to arise in the early stages of export entry. Unless the government is determined to promote export growth and diversification, the call for export substitution will become an empty slogan.[82]

Third, the public sector should create incentives to ensure adequate utilization of authorized public expenditure. Basic guidelines should be established for the allocation of public resources to high-priority activities, as well as for the modernization of work processes, optimization of input utilization, and improvement of public administration. This means that projects with little social (in terms of employment) or economic content might have to be deferred or canceled in order to free resources needed for building communication and transport infrastructure. State enterprises with similar or complementary functions could be grouped together in order to utilize the productive capacity more efficiently. The restructuring of the Mexican economy should not be viewed (as has been the case with the de La Madrid administration) simply in terms of the sale, liquidation, and merger of Mexico's 1,100 state enterprises.[83] Privatization efforts may be neither necessary nor socially desirable for many state-owned enterprises if it is possible to improve their performance through programs of internal reform. In short, the restructuring of the Mexican economy should have less to do with ideology and more with the implementation of a set of economic and political reforms that lay the groundwork for a renewed collaborative relationship between the public and private sectors.

A prerequisite for realizing all of these programs is the institution of a fiscal system capable of mobilizing funds efficiently and equitably. Mexico's low utilization of its taxable capacity has been at the root of its many economic and financial problems. Relatively rich in resources, it registered a tax-to-GDP ratio of only 15.3 percent in 1981, below those of Chile (18.4 percent) and Brazil (18.1 percent).[84] The public sector could make the tax system responsive to growth of GDP by placing and/or raising taxes on those items for which the tax base grows at a faster rate than GDP—for instance, the income tax, sales taxes that exempt food but not services, and luxury consumption taxes. Such measures would not only improve the revenue-generating capacity of the tax system but would also contribute to redistribution of income. The Mexican government has already implemented some reforms designed to make direct taxation more equitable and to standardize indirect taxation. Among these were the addition of a 10 percent surtax, in 1983, on all taxpayers whose annual income is five times above the legal minimum wage (about 194,000 pesos in 1983); and a modification of the value-added tax (VAT) so that processed foods and patented medicines would be taxed at 6 percent and luxury goods at 20 percent, whereas food, house rents, and transportation, which are included in the basic wage basket, would be exempted. Other measures have been sought to eliminate anonymity in stock and security holdings, to triple the tax rate on domestic automobile tenancy, and to establish a single tax (of 110 percent) on a sale of gasoline and diesel fuel.[85] It remains to be seen whether these efforts prove to be the beginning of fundamental tax reform or merely stop-gap measures that will be removed once the immediate fiscal crisis abates.

Conclusion

This chapter has shown that the underlying roots of the economic and social crisis that has afflicted the Mexican people since 1982 can be traced to a growth strategy that has been characterized by the pursuit of highly restrictive import-substituting policies—even after the easy phase of import substitution was completed. The capital-intensive, protectionist nature of such policies led to an increase in both the concentration of income and the level of unemployment. Furthermore, as Mexico increased the attractiveness of producing for the home market, it failed to give similar encouragement to producing for export, thereby further reducing the foreign exchange earnings needed for the growth process. This failure to export, coupled with a reluctance on the part of policymakers to raise taxes in the face of growing public spending, drove the country to the printing press or to foreign capital as an adjustment mechanism. The recycling of petro-dollars to the country— though conducive to the investment process at the time—eventually paved the way for the crises of 1976 and 1982.

Meanwhile, the discovery of vast oil reserves in the late 1970s had the effect of deferring or canceling many pressing reforms in favor of free-spending policies aimed at rapid economic growth. The latter, by further exacerbating existing internal and external imbalances, contributed to accelerating inflation, large-scale capital flight, and the closing of foreign exchange markets in August 1982. To make matters worse, the IMF austerity program implemented during 1983–1986 has, at best, obtained cosmetic improvements at the cost of sharp reductions in real wages, soaring unemployment and underemployment, a lowering of nutritional and health standards, a collapse in investment, and a deterioration in the country's social and political climate. The social and economic costs of servicing the debt while allowing wealthy Mexicans to send vast amounts of capital across the border are politically unacceptable and economically unsustainable. Thus, unless Mexico obtains debt relief and restricts capital flight, long-term goals such as broad-based, self-sustaining growth along with an improvement in income distribution will remain elusive.

Notes

1. Banco Nacional de Mexico, S.A. (BANAMEX), *Review of the Economic Situation of Mexico,* Vol. 63, No. 734 (1987): 7–9.

2. A net transfer is defined as new money less debt service (interest and amortization payments). Net new borrowing is new money minus amortization payments (principal repayments on loans). In the case of Mexico, Professor William Cline of the Institute for International Economics projects that net transfers to creditors will be of the order of $9 billion in 1985 and $10.5 billion in 1987. William R. Cline, *International Debt: Systemic Risk and Policy Response* (Washington, D.C.: Institute for International Economics, 1984), p. 165.

3. Computed from Nacional Financiera, S.A. (NAFIN), *La Economia Mexicana en Cifras* (Mexico: NAFIN, 1978), pp. 19–45.

4. Ibid.

5. Computed from NAFIN, *op. cit.*, pp. 44–45; and the *World Development Report* (Washington, D.C.: World Bank, 1983).

6. Banco de Mexico, S.A., *Informe Anual* (Mexico, D.F.: Banco de Mexico, 1955–1976), various issues.

7. For further details, see René Villarreal, "The Policy of Import-Substituting Industrialization, 1929–1975," pp. 67–107, in Jose Reyna and Richard Weinert (eds.), *Authoritarianism in Mexico* (Philadelphia: Institute for the Study of Human Issues [ISHI], 1977).

8. Dwight S. Brothers and Leopoldo Solis M., *Mexican Financial Development* (Austin: University of Texas Press, 1966), p. 164.

9. Jorge E. Navarrete, "Las Dos Caras de la Moneda," in *Cuestiones Economicas Nacionales* (Mexico, D.F.: Banco Nacional de Comercio Exterior, 1971), p. 165; and Villarreal, *op. cit.*, Table 1.

10. For further details, see Miguel D. Ramirez, *Development Banking in Mexico: The Case of the Nacional Financiera, S.A.* (New York: Praeger Publishers, 1986).

11. Inter-American Development Bank (IDB), *Economic and Social Progress in Latin America, 1980–81 Report* (Washington, D.C.: IDB, 1982), p. 98.

12. Ibid., p. 102.

13. Another noteworthy development of the period was the decreasing importance of foreign direct investment (FDI) relative to foreign debt as a mechanism of adjustment. For example, in 1966 their cumulative values stood at about $1.9 billion each, and by 1975 total foreign debt registered a cumulative value of $10.6 billion—a figure that was two and a half times larger than that of foreign direct investment. In large measure this is explained by the Mexicanization process initiated during the administration of Adolfo Lopez Mateos (1958–1964). This strategy was implemented in order to regulate and control the activities of multinational corporations (especially U.S. ones) and to protect and promote the growth of Mexican industry. (For further details, see Weinert, *op. cit.*, Table 8.)

14. Rosario Green, *El Endeudamiento Publico Externo de Mexico, 1940–73* (Mexico, D.F.: El Colegio de Mexico, 1976), pp. 130–131; see also Green, "La Deuda Externa del Gobierno Mexicano," pp. 482–505, in Nora Lustig (ed.), *Panorama y Perspectivas de la Economia Mexicana* (Mexico, D.F.: El Colegio de Mexico, 1980), p. 187.

15. For further details, see Leopoldo M. Solis, *La Realidad Mexicana: Retrovision y Perpectivas*, 11th ed. (Mexico, D.F.: Siglo XXI Editores, 1981); see also Hollis B. Chenery, "Alternative Strategies for Development," *World Bank Staff Paper 165* (Washington, D.C.: World Bank, 1973); and Manuel Gollas, "Origenes de la Desigualdad en la Distribucion del Ingreso Familiar en Mexico," p. 141, in Nora Lustig (ed.), *Panorama y Perspectivas de la Economia Mexicana* (Mexico, D.F.: El Colegio de Mexico, 1980).

16. See Solis, *op. cit.*, pp. 244–280; Joel Bergman, "Income Distribution and Poverty in Mexico," *World Bank Staff Working Paper 234* (Washington, D.C.: World Bank, 1979); and Chenery, *op. cit.*, Appendix, Table 2.

17. Villarreal, *op. cit.*, p. 75.

18. Ann D. Witte, "Employment in the Manufacturing Sector of Developing Economies: A Study of Mexico, Peru and Venezuela" (Ph.D. dissertation, North Carolina State, 1971), Table 4.

19. The Congress of Labor is an umbrella organization composed of three major labor confederations: the Confederation of Mexican Workers (CTM), the Regional Confederation of Workers and Peasants (CROC), and the Regional Confederation of Mexican Workers (CROM). According to Barry Carr, "just over 5.3 million workers are members of labor unions, a figure that represented 26 percent of the economically active population (EAP) in 1982." Barry Carr, "The Mexican Economic Debacle and the Labor Movement: A New Era or More of the Same?" p. 91, in Donald L. Wyman (ed.), *Mexico's Economic Crisis: Challenges and Opportunities* (San Diego: Center for U.S.-Mexican Studies, 1983).

20. For futher details, see Michael C. Meyer and William L. Sherman, *The Course of Mexican History*, 3rd ed. (New York: Oxford University Press, 1987), p. 655.

21. Ibid.

22. For example, the Echeverría administration established the Workers Housing Fund (INFONAVIT), the National Fund for Workers Consumption (FONOCAT), and the National Rural Development Program (PIDE).

23. Leopoldo M. Solis, "Reflexiones sobre el Panorama General de la Economia Mexicana," in Hector Gonzales (ed.), *El Sistema Economico Mexicano* (Mexico, D.F.: La Real Jona Premia Editora, 1982), p. 340.

24. Computed from NAFIN, *op. cit.*, pp. 19, 353–354.

25. Ibid., pp. 225–226, 229–230.

26. For further details, see Leopoldo M. Solis and G. Ortiz, "Mexican Financial Structure and Exchange Rate Experience, Mexico 1954–77," *Journal of Development Economics*, Vol. 6, No. 4 (December 1979): 515–548.

27. Inter-American Development Bank (IDB), *External Debt and Economic Development in Latin America* (Washington, D.C.: IDB, 1984), pp. 176–181.

28. IDB, *Economic and Social Progress in Latin America, 1980–81 Report* (Washington, D.C.: IDB, 1982), p. 102.

29. See Solis, *op. cit.*, p. 344; see also Arturo Guillen, *Problemas de la Economia Mexicana* (Mexico, D.F.: Nuestro Tiempo, S.A., 1986).

30. Computed from NAFIN, *op. cit.*, pp. 380–387.

31. Comision Economica Para America Latina y El Caribe (CEPAL), *Notas Sobre La Economia y El Desarrollo*, No. 438/439 (December 1986), p. 15.

32. See PEMEX, *Memoria de labores 1970–81* (Mexico, D.F.: Subdireccion de Planeacion, 1984).

33. NAFINSA, *La Economia Mexicana en Cifras* (Mexico, D.F.: NAFINSA, 1984), p. 262.

34. IDB, *External Debt and Economic Development in Latin America* (Washington, D.C.: IDB, 1984), p. 176.

35. For further detail see Federal Reserve Bank of Chicago (FRB-Chicago), *International Letter 547* (Chicago: FRB-Chicago).

36. The emergency wage adjustment in March granted the following increases: 30 percent for wages under 20,000 pesos; 20 percent for wages between 20,000 and 30,000; and 10 percent for wages of more than 30,000 pesos. In January

of that year, an across-the-board increase of 34 percent in the minimum wage was granted (see Carr, *op. cit.,* p. 102). See also NAFIN, *La Economia Mexicana en Cifras* (Mexico, D.F.: NAFIN, 1986), p. 28.

37. The proportion of Mexico's debt financed at floating rates rose from 47 percent in 1975 to 77 percent in 1982. See *External Debt and Economic Development in Latin America* (Washington, D.C.: IDB, 1984), p. 93.

38. IDB, *Economic and Social Progress in Latin America, 1983 Report* (Washington, D.C.: IDB, 1984), p. 268.

39. FRB-Chicago, *op. cit.*

40. See *World Financial Markets* (New York: Morgan Guaranty Trust Company, May 1984).

41. See E. Chavez, "Exultacion en la Tribuna, Frente a la Indignacion Empresarial y Duda de Priistas," *Proceso,* No. 305 (September 1982): 6–8.

42. Nora Hamilton, "Mexico: The Limits of State Autonomy," p. 17, in Nora Hamilton and Timothy F. Harding (eds.), *Modern Mexico: State, Economy, and Social Conflict* (Beverly Hills: SAGE Publications, 1986).

43. See López Portillio's *State of the Union Message,* September 1, 1982, Mexico, D.F.

44. See *Wall Street Journal,* October 9, 1985, p. 26.

45. See Nora Hamilton, "State-Class Alliances and Conflicts," *Latin American Perspectives,* Vol. 11, No. 4 (Fall 1984): 6–32.

46. Sofia M. Mendez, "La Crisis Economica: Origenes y Consequencias," p. 138, in Guillermo Ramírez Hernández (ed.), *Mexico: Crisis Economica y Desarrollo* (Mexico, D.F.: Sociedad Cooperativa de Publicaciones Mexicanas, 1983).

47. Hamilton (1984), *op. cit.,* p. 25.

48. IDB, *Economic and Social Progress in Latin America, 1983 Report* (Washington, D.C.: IDB, 1984), p. 269.

49. See World Bank, *Poverty in Latin America: The Impact of Depression* (Washington, D.C.: World Bank, November 1986), p. 11.

50. Barry Carr, "The Mexican Economic Debacle and the Labor Movement: A New Era or More of the Same?" p. 106, in Donald L. Wyman (ed.), *Mexico's Economic Crisis: Challenges and Opportunities* (San Diego: Center for U.S.-Mexican Studies, 1983).

51. See Francisco J. Alejo, "Demographic Patterns, Labor Trends, and Market Trends in Mexico," pp. 86–89, in Donald L. Wyman, *op. cit.;* World Bank (1986), *op. cit.,* p. 11; and Daniel C. Levy and Gabriel Szekely, "Mexico: Challenges and Responses," *Current History,* Vol. 85, No. 507 (January 1986), pp. 16–20.

52. Ibid., p. 11. World Bank (1986), *op. cit.,* p. 11.

53. Carr, *op. cit.*

54. FRB-Chicago, *op. cit.*

55. For further details, see NAFIN, *La Economia Mexicana En Cifras* (Mexico, D.F.: NAFIN, 1986), p. 28; James D. Rudolph (ed.), *Mexico: A Country Study* (Washington, D.C.: American University, 1985), p. 184; and Alejo, *op. cit.,* pp. 79–89.

56. Computed from NAFIN (1986), *op. cit.,* Table 1.14, p. 28.

57. See *Wall Street Journal,* October 11, 1985, p. 1.

58. *Wall Street Journal,* September 26, 1985, p. 18.

59. *Wall Street Journal,* October 15, 1985, p. 10.

60. *World Financial Markets* (New York: Morgan Guaranty Trust Company, May 1984); and *Wall Street Journal,* October 3, 1986, p. 3.

61. Banco de Mexico, *Informe Anual* (December 1986), p. 93.

62. Arturo Fuente and Raimundo Arrolo, "El Poder Adquisitivo Del Salario, Productividad y Posicion Competitiva de Mexico." *Investigacion Economica*, vol. 45, no. 178 (October–December 1986), pp. 245–278.

63. Ibid.

64. Ibid., p. 259.

65. In 1981 Mexico's imports from the United States represented 67.6 percent of its total imports, whereas 55.2 percent of its exports were destined toward that country. See David R. Mares, "Prospects for Mexico-U.S. Trade Relations in an Era of Economic Restructuring," Table 2, in Donald L. Wyman, *op. cit.*

66. FRB-Chicago, *op. cit.*

67. Harold Lever and Christopher Huhne, *Debt and Danger: The World Financial Crisis* (New York: Atlantic Monthly Press, 1986), p. 132.

68. Other proposals include (a) a medium-term IMF facility providing emergency funds on concessional terms if Mexico suffers a sharp fall in oil prices; (b) a deferment of amortization payments along with a cap on interest payments at some percentage of Mexico's export earnings, with the unpaid interest converted into future debt (for further details, see David Felix, "How to Resolve Latin America's Debt Crisis," *Challenge*, Vol. 28, No. 5 [November–December 1985]: 50–51); (c) the limited (and gradual) implementation of a debt for equity swap program that gives preferential treatment to Mexican nationals; and (d) an increased allocation of Special Drawing Rights (SDRs) to Mexico.

69. David Felix, "How to Resolve Latin America's Debt Crisis," *Challenge*, Vol. 28, No. 5 (November–December 1985): 50–51.

70. For a radical perspective on the origins and consequences of the debt crisis, see Arthur MacEwan, "Latin America: Why Not Default?" *Monthly Review*, Vol. 38, No. 4 (September 1986), pp. 1–13.

71. For further details, see Hamilton (1986), *op. cit.*

72. Business Latin America, "Mexico's Rescue Plan Will Show Efforts to Keep Firms Afloat," *Weekly Reports to Managers of Latin American Operations*, February 16, 1983.

73. See *Financial Monthly Report*, No. 5 (September 1983), pp. 1–37.

74. Ibid., pp. 11–13.

75. Mexico has agreed to eliminate trade barriers over a period of eight years, with the possibility of being permitted an emergency assessment of 50 percent over and above previously negotiated tariff levels. After this period, the maximum tariff rate will be set at 50 percent. Mexico has also agreed to lift licensing requirements affecting 60 percent of its imports and to replace them with tariffs. Finally, three sectors will be subject to special attention in view of their strategic importance: agriculture, energy, and certain industrial subsectors, and some lines of capital goods. See BANAMEX, *Review of the Economic Situation of Mexico*, Vol. 62, No. 729 (1986):289.

76. *Maquiladoras* are foreign-owned factories that have their origin in the Border Industrialization Program, initiated by the López Mateos administration in 1961 to develop the northern region of the country—especially along the 2,000 mile border with the United States. Among other things, they are permitted to bring in raw materials and other inputs duty-free, to hire Mexican workers to assemble their products (e.g., filters for computers, machinery and electrical equipment, furniture, etc.), and to export the finished goods back to the United States for sale. Currently there are 700 *maquiladoras* operating in Mexico, and they provide jobs—both directly and indirectly— for more than 600,000 persons. See *New York Times*, January 19, 1986, p. 4F; and Sergio Rivas, "La Industria

Maquiladora en Mexico: Realidades y Falacias," *Comercio Exterior,* Vol. 35, No. 11 (1985), pp. 1071–1084.

77. BANAMEX, *Examen de la Situacion Economica de Mexico,* vol. 60, no. 709 (1984), pp. 720–721; and Sergio Rivas, "La Industria Maquiladora en Mexico: Realidades y Falacias," *Comercio Exterior,* Vol. 35, No. 11 (1985), pp. 1071–1084.

78. See Secretaria de Programacion y Presupuesto (SPP), *Estadistica Industrial Anual* (Mexico, D.F.: SPP, 1984).

79. This table compares the total value added (as a percentage of GDP) by the Maquiladora and Electricity industries during the 1975–1983 period (see Rivas, *op. cit.,* p. 1080).

Year	Maquiladoras	Electricity
1975	0.44	1.4
1977	0.38	1.5
1979	0.47	1.5
1981	0.41	1.5
1983	0.57	1.7

80. Rivas, *op. cit.,* p. 1080.

81. A step in this direction took place in early February 1987, when the New York–based Maidenform Inc. became the first U.S. company to open an assembly plant in the Yucatan region of southern Mexico. The plant is located outside the city of Merida and is expected to give employment to between 200 and 300 workers. For further details, see Michael J. Zamba, "In Bid to Diversify, México Seeks Plants Farther Inland," *The Christian Science Monitor,* February 24, 1987, p. 21.

82. For an informative discussion of the pros and cons associated with the pursuit of an export-substitution strategy, see Villarreal, *op. cit.*

83. As of September 1986, the Mexican state had sold over 200 "low-priority" state enterprises and had plans to dispose of an additional 180 unprofitable state agencies during the remainder of 1986 and 1987. Among the targeted enterprises are the country's oldest major steel mill in Monterrey (employing between 10,000 and 15,000 workers), Mexicana Airlines, and a large hotel chain. See IDB, *Economic and Social Progress in Latin America, 1983 Report* (Washington, D.C.: IDB, 1984), p. 317.

84. See IDB (1984), *op. cit.;* and A. Tait, W. Gratz, and B. Eichengreen, *International Monetary Fund Staff Papers,* Vol. 26, No. 1. (Washington, D.C.: International Monetary Fund, 1979).

85. See *Financial Monthly Report, op. cit.,* pp. 20–21.

7

Austerity Policies in Ecuador: Christian Democratic and Social Christian Versions of the Gospel

David W. Schodt

The austerity policies implemented during the 1980s in most of the Latin American countries are a direct response to the worst economic depression the region has faced since the 1930s.[1] The large external debt accumulated during the 1970s and early 1980s, rising interest rates, the sharp curtailment of access to world credit markets after 1982, and the sluggish performance of the industrialized economies since that date combined to precipitate a severe balance-of-payments crisis that required sharp contractions in the region's economies. The common nature of the economic crisis and the policies exacted by the IMF as prerequisites for its assistance imposed an element of consistency in the stabilization plans adopted by most of the Latin American countries. Nevertheless, in spite of a number of common characteristics, such as sharp contractions in import volumes, there are significant differences in the types of policies adopted by the region's governments, depending on the nature of the interest coalitions supporting those governments, the structure of the nations' domestic economies, and their linkages to the international economy.

This chapter explores the differences in austerity policies adopted by two successive democratic governments in Ecuador during the period 1981–1986: those implemented by President Osvaldo Hurtado in 1982 in response to the moratorium imposed on further private lending as a result of the threatened Mexican default; and those implemented by President León Febres Cordero beginning in 1984, when declines in the world prices of petroleum compounded Ecuador's existing problem of debt service. Hurtado, a Christian Democrat, was a former university professor whose perception of Ecuador's social and economic problems was decidedly structural.[2] Febres Cordero, nominally a Social Christian, was a former engineer and businessman elected on a platform promising to run Ecuador like a business, and surrounded by a team of advisers committed to a neoconservative approach to economic stabilization. An examination of the austerity policies pursued by these two governments is particularly revealing not only for the comparison it allows between the different economic measures adopted, but also for what the comparison demonstrates about the importance of political and economic factors to the efficacy of each.

The Petroleum Boom:
Prelude to the Crisis

Prior to the 1980s, Ecuador had had no experience with the radical stabilization experiments implemented elsewhere in the region. The debate between monetarist and structuralist approaches to stabilization that had so polarized economic policymaking elsewhere in Latin America during the preceding thirty years had not taken place in Ecuador.[3] Both the structure of the Ecuadorian economy and the highly restricted political system reduced the need for the types of policies adopted elsewhere. Price inflation had not been severe. Indeed, between 1950 and 1970, the average rate of inflation had been well under 5 percent; in only one year had it exceeded 6 percent.[4] Even during the petroleum boom years of the 1970s, the average rate of inflation did not exceed 12 percent. Balance-of-payments crises were frequent but typically occurred as a result of changes in external conditions, such as a drop in the world price for bananas, Ecuador's principal export. Domestic policy responses to deteriorating trade balances tended to be piecemeal, relying principally on import restrictions. But, given the small size of the industrial sector, such restrictions did not contract the economy as much as they would have in a country whose industrial sector depended more heavily on the import of raw materials and capital equipment. Exchange rates stayed remarkably constant until the 1970s.

The domestic political implications of Ecuador's recurrent balance-of-payments crises also differed from those in the more advanced countries in the region. Political participation was very limited. Prior to 1978, for example, no more than 18 percent of the population had ever voted in a presidential election. Sharp regional divisions and the small size of the industrial sector retarded the development of organized labor as a political force. Public expenditures, though historically large relative to GDP, were concentrated in traditional areas such as public works and education. Redistributive expenditures, for example, accounted for a relatively small share of total expenditures. Although Ecuador has very progressive labor legislation, only a very small portion of the population has benefited. Even though social security coverage expanded significantly during the petroleum period, as late as 1985 only 11 percent of the population and 23 percent of the labor force was covered by social security, making Ecuador sixteenth among Latin American countries in coverage.[5] Thus, even though balance-of-payments crises translated rapidly into public-sector deficits, contributing to an endemic political instability, Ecuadorian elites had little reason to fear that their control of the state would be seriously threatened by these changes of government.

The petroleum boom, which began in 1972, launched an unprecedented period of economic expansion and social change. By 1982 petroleum exports accounted for 65 percent of all export earnings; the petroleum sector generated nearly 10 percent of the country's gross domestic product.[6] Economic growth accelerated rapidly in the 1970s. During the last half of the preceding decade, real output had increased at an annual rate of just over 4 percent. Between 1970 and 1975, the growth of real output jumped sharply to an annual rate of 11.4 percent. Although this rapid rate of growth was not sustained during the latter half of the 1970s, the economy nevertheless grew at an average annual rate in excess of 6 percent throughout the remainder of the decade.[7] Formerly one of the poorest countries in South America, Ecuador by 1981 had attained a per capita income of $1,180, roughly equal to that of its neighbors Colombia and Peru.[8]

Industry, the most dynamic sector after services, also expanded rapidly during the 1970s, growing at an annual rate of 11.5 percent during the latter half of the decade. Between 1970 and 1980, the share of manufacturing in GDP rose from 16.8 percent to just under 18 percent.[9] The primary stimulus to industrial expansion was the broadening of the domestic market; a continuation of the government incentives for import-substitution industrialization begun in the mid-1960s, and an overvalued exchange rate that cheapened the price of imported raw materials and capital goods, also contributed to the growth of the sector. Thus, most of the expansion in Ecuadorian manufacturing was directed toward the expanding domestic market. Manufactured exports, though promoted by government policy, accounted for only 17 percent of the value of total manufacturing production in 1979. Moreover, semiprocessed cacao, which received heavy government subsidies, and petroleum derivatives contributed over three-quarters of the total value of Ecuador's manufactured exports.[10] If semiprocessed cacao and petroleum derivatives are excluded, manufactured exports (most destined for Andean Pact markets) never amounted to more than 9 percent of total exports (see Table 7.1).[11]

The public sector also expanded rapidly both in size and function during the 1970s. As public-sector expenditures were the primary conduit through which petroleum revenues flowed into the economy, growth of government spending closely paralleled the large increase in petroleum export earnings. Between 1970 and 1980, nominal public expenditures increased at an average annual rate of 27.5 percent, rising as a share of gross domestic product from 23 percent to a high of slightly less than 31 percent.[12] From 1974 through the end of the decade, two sectors—services (of which government services are the largest component) and manufacturing—accounted for more than three-quarters of

TABLE 7.1
Structure of the Ecuadorian Economy, 1950, 1980, and 1985
(Percentage Share of Gross Domestic Product)

Sector	Year		
	1950	1980	1985
Agriculture	38.8	12.1	13.6
Manufacturing	16.0	17.7	18.9
Services	15.2	23.2	17.5
Wholesale and Retail Trade	10.3	14.6	15.6
Transportation	4.8	7.9	8.6
Construction	2.7	7.4	5.4
Petroleum and Mining	2.3	12.2	17.0
Other	9.9	4.9	3.4

Sources: Figures for 1950 calculated from World Bank, The Current Economic
Position and Prospects for Ecuador (Washington, D.C., 1973), Statistical
Appendix, Table 2-3. Figures for 1980 and 1985 calculated from Banco Central
del Ecuador, Cuentas Nacionales No. 8 (Quito, 1986), pp. 55 - 56.

the growth of GDP. By the early 1980s, petroleum revenues financed approximately 40 percent of public-sector expenditures.[13]

Petroleum also provided an opportunity to expand the role of the public sector beyond its traditional functions. State-led development was the cornerstone of plans by the military government of General Rodríguez Lara (1972–1976) to transform Ecuadorian society. (He was replaced by a military triumvirate that held power from 1976 to 1979). The government's development plan for 1973–1977 stated that to achieve its objectives

> a more decisive intervention by the State in the economy [is necessary], as much to consolidate already initiated basic reforms . . . as to promote new reforms necessary to expand the potential for national development. The strategy implies transferring to the Public Sector those fundamental decisions that affect the economy and Ecuadorian society, those that today reside in foreign centers.

Most important, the military wanted the state to move beyond its traditional role as provider of services such as public works and education to direct involvement in production. As the plan noted, "the direct participation of the State in the productive process through the introduction of basic industries, which implies that the Public Sector should adopt a very active stance in the promotion of enterprises, is of fundamental importance."[14] State intervention in the financial sector was also advocated as a means of channeling petroleum revenues toward priority areas of the economy. Reflecting the government's priorities, value added by public enterprises rose from less than 2 percent of GDP in 1970 to 11.1 percent in 1980.[15] Similarly, in 1968 public financial institutions accounted for only 26 percent of total deposits and 36 percent of the total domestic credit supply; by 1981, however, these figures were 40 and 55 percent, respectively.[16]

Predictably, the large and rapid influx of petroleum revenues placed considerable stress on the Ecuadorian economy. Some of this stress was inevitable, some of it the consequence of policies pursued by the military governments in power during the 1970s. Price inflation began to accelerate, with the annual rate of increase rising from under 10 percent during the early 1970s to 22.7 percent by 1974.[17] The sources of this acceleration were various. Rising per capita incomes and stagnant agricultural production bid up food prices. Between 1970 and 1980, agricultural production for the domestic market declined an average of 2.4 percent annually.[18] Imports also rose both in volume and price, contributing to the increase in domestic prices. Large increases in the world price of petroleum in 1973 and 1974 led to a sharp rise in export earnings that became increasingly difficult to sterilize.

By 1975 a severe balance-of-payments crisis had developed, revealing an economy heavily addicted to petroleum income and highly sensitive to changes in the international economy. Ironically, the military had fallen into the very difficulty for which it had excoriated previous governments. As the 1973–1975 development plan had warned:

[Earlier] periods of boom which the country experienced were not sufficiently taken advantage of to develop and reform internal production, for different reasons which are ultimately explained by the country's social structure. The periods of relative bonanza were translated quickly into an economic instability manifested in balance of payments problems and a fiscal deficit greater in magnitude than those which characterized the period preceding the boom.[19]

Not only had the military failed to overcome structural weaknesses in the Ecuadorian economy but the changes that had occurred during the petroleum boom guaranteed that future stabilization policies would be more costly than they had been in the past, in terms of both reduced output and political opposition. Although the 1975 balance-of-payments crisis was temporarily resolved through increased foreign borrowing, the underlying conditions from which it had emerged were not addressed. Not surprisingly, as long as access to international credit markets was relatively unrestricted, governments chose to borrow rather than to pay the costs of economic adjustment. Particularly during the second half of the 1970s, public external debt rose rapidly from $461 million in 1975 to $3.3 billion by 1980.[20]

In 1979 the ruling military governments withdrew from power, succeeded by a democratically elected president, Jaime Roldós Aguilar, and his vice-president, Osvaldo Hurtado. By this time, however, the economic problems briefly exposed in 1975 had resurfaced. In 1981 the world price of petroleum began a sustained decline. Rapidly rising imports and sharply escalating interest payments also contributed to a dramatically worsening current-account balance, and inflation began to accelerate again. Public-sector deficits rose abruptly. In May of the same year President Roldós was killed in an airplane crash, leaving the presidency and the economy to his successor, Osvaldo Hurtado.

The Hurtado Administration and the Deteriorating Economy

Osvaldo Hurtado assumed the presidency under highly unpropitious circumstances. World petroleum prices had begun their downward slide, falling from a high of $32.20 in 1981 to $27.35 by the end of 1984. With export earnings unable to finance the country's import bill (between the end of 1980 and the end of 1982 the current-account deficit ballooned from $642 million to $1,195 million), the government turned to additional debt financing.[21] Ecuador's external public debt rose from $4.7 billion at the beginning of 1981 to $6.9 billion at the end of 1984.[22] The rate of growth of the economy in real terms declined from 3.9 percent in 1981 to a meager 1.2 percent in 1982.[23] Growth in the manufacturing sector slowed sharply, and the number of bankruptcies among firms in the private sector escalated. Unemployment, around 5 percent in the years immediately preceding the 1980s, rose to approximately 9 percent of the labor force by 1983. Underemployment increased from 24 percent in 1975 to between 40 and 60 percent by 1983.[24] Inflation began to accelerate, rising from 14.7 percent in 1981 to 48.1 percent by the end of 1983, and cutting into the purchasing power of lower income groups. Between 1980 and 1983, the purchasing power of a minimum-wage worker ultimately fell by 20 percent.[25]

Keenly aware of his own precarious position, the new president's inaugural address was simultaneously a call for austerity by both public and private sectors, and a plea for support from all sectors of the population. The balancing act he was called upon to perform between competing economic and political demands was a particularly difficult one, since the austerity policies required to address economic problems such as the large public-sector deficit and the deteriorating current-account balance would be certain to cost him scarce political resources. Not only was Osvaldo Hurtado an unelected president but the party he headed, the Christian Democrats, had a small base that was largely confined to the sierra provinces. Committed to democratic reform, he struggled to build an enduring constituency for his policies. His inability to do so left him politically isolated as opposition mounted from business elites and organized labor, clearly revealing the way in which the dramatic economic change occurring during the petroleum boom had not been accompanied by concomitant political change.

Private-sector opposition to President Hurtado was immediate and vehement. Even during Roldós' 1979 presidential campaign it was his running mate, Hurtado, who had evoked the greatest cries of alarm from the business community. His Christian Democratic background had evoked charges denouncing his "foreign ideology." Rightist critics, citing his concern, widely known from his writings, for redressing some of the glaring inequities in Ecuadorian society, and his desire to greatly expand political and economic participation, portrayed him as a socialist or "quasi-Marxist." To be sure, some injudicious comments Hurtado had made after his and Roldós' first-round victory provided fuel for his critics' remarks, but even then the moderate reformist character of his proposals was apparent to most careful observers. As vice-president, Hurtado had emerged as a leading spokesman for fiscal restraint. His proposals on assuming the presidency in 1981 offered little explanation for the eruption of criticism from business leaders, orchestrated primarily through the chambers of production, which were the regional associations of business elites. (There are chambers of agriculture, industry, and commerce.)

In considerable measure, the hostility expressed by the private sector was prompted by a combination of the sharp reduction in its access to policy formulation experienced since 1972, and the deterioration in economic conditions that was particularly evident after 1981. As Hurtado emphasized in a television address to the nation in December 1981, "large economic interests [that] perhaps for the first time in history encounter a government to which they cannot give orders, in which they do not have employees to represent their interests, combat it solely for this reason."[26] But the lack of access was nothing new; it had been an issue of private-sector resentment of varying degrees since the Rodríguez Lara government (1972–1976). In general, the petroleum-induced socioeconomic changes were contributing to the development of a less elitist, more inclusionary political system, as evidenced by the growing strength of center-left parties. In addition, the elimination of functional representation in the legislature with the adoption of the 1978 constitution had further narrowed traditional channels of elite influence. Most important, however, the exhaustion of the petroleum boom and the diminishing recourse to international sources of credit meant that, in contrast to periods of rapid economic expansion, few decisions could be undertaken without imposing significant costs on a number of groups in society. In this context, private business elites were all the more anxious to regain their traditional privileged access to public policy formation.

During the petroleum boom, the state had also acquired a degree of autonomy relative to the private sector unprecedented in Ecuadorian experience. The shift in revenue dependence from taxation of the private sector, primarily foreign trade, to the direct receipt of petroleum revenues greatly reduced the ability of Ecuador's economic elites to veto policies that they opposed through their manipulation of public revenues. In 1965, for example, a shutdown of commercial activity organized by the

Quito and Guayaquil chamber of commerce contributed to the overthrow of the ruling military Junta; in March 1983 a similar shutdown of commercial activity had little effect on the government. As one of the leaders of the 1965 commercial strike lamented, "we were able to bring down the government then. . . . Today when we organize such a stoppage, the government can laugh at us."[27] With traditional avenues of influence weakened, regaining direct control of the state became an issue of increasing concern to the economic elites—a concern undoubtedly reinforced by Hurtado's sincere commitment to significantly expanding the political participation of formerly excluded groups in Ecuadorian society.

The growth of the public sector also contributed to private-sector antagonism. Business elites excoriated the growing "statism" of the Hurtado administration, citing the public sector's expansion as evidence in support of what they perceived to be growing attacks on the private sector. Certainly by virtue of the state's much greater involvement in the economy, most of which had taken place during the immediately preceding military governments, public-sector decisions had assumed far greater importance for the public sector than they had held before 1972. Public-sector expenditures as a share of gross domestic product, which had peaked in 1980, remained relatively constant from 1981 to 1984. Undoubtedly, the concomitant expansion of public enterprises and financial institutions during the 1970s contributed to charges that the state was usurping private property rights. In considerable part, however, the private sector's criticism of the Hurtado government reflected its continuing frustration over the petroleum-induced shift in the locus of economic power from private elites to the public sector—a shift particularly galling to Guayaquil's coastal economic elites, who also saw the regional balance of power tilt from the coast toward Quito in the highlands.

Certainly there were grounds for some private-sector complaints over the size of the public sector. The expanding bureaucracy placed a growing burden on private economic transactions. Guayaquil businesses, in particular, were irritated by what they perceived as increasingly obstructionist policies emanating from the Quito government. In February 1973, the Rodríguez Lara government had established the Superintendencia de Precios to regulate prices on a broader scale than had been undertaken previously. The following year a new public enterprise, the Empresa Nacional de Almacenamiento y Comercialización de Productos Agropecuarios (ENAC), whose function was to store and distribute basic foods, was added to a system of public food stores, the Empresa Nacional de Productos Vitales (ENPROVIT), established in 1971 by President José María Velasco Ibarra. The rationale for both price regulation and the two public enterprises was to control the prices of basic commodities produced or distributed by a highly concentrated and protected Ecuadorian industry. Price regulation attacked the problem directly; the public enterprises introduced an element of competition into what was otherwise perceived as a highly monopolistic sector. Direct price regulation certainly did become increasingly cumbersome, contributing to shortages of some products such as wheat. Both ENAC and ENPROVIT competed with private business, providing fuel for charges of statism. Although in this case there was a fairly compelling argument for their creation on grounds of social efficiency, there were other public enterprises whose creation was less easily defended.

Organized labor, in spite of initial support for the new democratic administration, had already begun to oppose the government before Roldós' death. After the hard line taken toward labor by the military triumvirate after 1976, the return to democracy in 1979 and the election of a government pledging social and economic reforms was openly welcomed by most labor groups. During the early months of the Roldós administration, minimum wages were increased, antilabor laws issued by the triumvirate were rescinded, and new legislation was introduced facilitating labor organizing. By the end of 1980, the new administration had been responsible for the approval of 22 percent of all active labor organizations established since 1966.[28] Despite these actions, the government's lack of progress in implementing its reform program disillusioned its labor supporters, bringing charges that the Roldós administration had betrayed its popular base of support.

Part of organized labor's frustration was undoubtedly a consequence of its high expectations for rapid change; and part was due to its limited participation in formal politics. Of the political parties, only the mainstream communist Broad Leftist Front (FADI) and the Maoist Popular Democratic Movement (MPD) had well-developed linkages to labor, and these parties had won only two seats between them in the 1979 congressional elections. Thus, with the abolition of functional representatives, organized labor had virtually no representation in the legislature. In addition, no labor leaders held important administrative posts. But, in contrast to the breakdown of communication between the government and the economic elites, the striking characteristic of the period after 1979 was an almost constant dialogue between the minister of labor and the national labor federation, the Unitary Workers' Front (FUT). It was when this dialogue failed that labor took to the streets with mass demonstrations. At the same time, admittedly, FUT leaders had some interest in a certain number of mass demonstrations as a means of strengthening their control over the country's fragmented labor organizations, and over their rank-and-file members, who had demonstrated a tendency to vote for nonleftist candidates in national elections.

Austerity Policies

By mid-1982, the economy had deteriorated to the point where Hurtado had little choice other than to adopt potentially painful austerity measures, despite the virtual certainty that, at least in the short run, these policies would exacerbate the economic decline and further erode his already tenuous political base. In May, Hurtado announed a 32 percent devaluation of the sucre. In October, this was followed by a package of policies that (1) raised taxes on beer, cigarettes, and luxury vehicles; (2) doubled the domestic price of gasoline; and (3) eliminated the subsidy for wheat. In November, in an effort to reduce the burden on lower-class groups and to forestall increased opposition from organized labor, the minimum wage was increased by 15 percent and an additional payment was mandated to compensate for the increased cost of transportation following the gasoline price increase. But these measures were insufficient to check mounting opposition from labor, which angrily denounced the government as "antipopular" and "pro-oligarchic." The Unitary Workers' Front charged that the policies "sharpened the general and fiscal crisis, accelerated inflation—[already] aggravated by the last monetary devaluation—all this to the benefit of the country's oligarchy."[29] Large national strikes were held in September 1982 and barely a month later in October to protest the government's policies. The government found itself under attack from business as well as from labor. The chambers of commerce and industry condemned the devaluation, which pushed up costs for importers and import-dependent industries. Large private-sector borrowing from international banks in dollars during the late 1970s and early 1980s exacerbated the negative effects of a devaluation on Ecuadorian business. From the end of 1975 to the beginning of 1980, privately held external debt grew twelve-fold; from 1980 to the end of 1982, it rose an additional 130 percent to a high of $1.6 billion.[30] Already weakened by the economic crisis, the private sector panicked as the devaluation not only increased the costs of imported inputs but also drove up the burden in sucres of their external dollar debt. After the May 1982 devaluation, 32 percent more sucres had to be earned in order to repay the same dollar amount of debt.

The economic crisis deepened in 1983. Burdened by natural disasters, falling petroleum prices, and the government's austerity program, Ecuador's gross domestic product declined by 2.8 percent. Severe flooding caused by a shift in ocean currents along the coast (the "El Niño") devastated the economically critical coastal agriculture. Both export crops and food for domestic consumption were destroyed. A potato blight in the highlands cut sharply into harvests of that staple food. Inflation, already accelerating from the effects of import restrictions and currency devaluation, exploded as food prices jumped 80 percent.[31] By mid-1982, alarmed by Mexico's threatened default, international banks had virtually closed off credit to Latin America, forcing Ecuador to begin talks with the International Monetary Fund (IMF) for assistance in renegotiating its external debt. In 1983, bolstered by IMF insistence on a reduction in public-sector expenditures, Hurtado finally managed to implement his own previously expressed concerns over the need for austerity in the government sector.[32] Facing vehement opposition from public-sector employees over proposed cuts in current expenditures, Hurtado chose to make his largest cuts in public investments. As a result, government spending as a share of GDP fell by 20 percent.[33] A second devaluation in March 1983 decreased the value of the sucre relative to the dollar by a further 21 percent, and a program of automatic "mini-devaluations" was set in place, triggering yet another round of protest from both organized labor and business elites. Even exporters, the primary beneficiaries of a devaluation, were disgruntled by the simultaneous abolition of export subsidies. On March 23, 1983, the democratic government confronted its fourth national strike. At the same time, the Quito and Guayaquil chambers of commerce, composed largely of importers, organized simultaneous commercial shutdowns in the two cities. Rumors of a military coup began to circulate openly, as some of the more conservative business leaders openly called for removal of the president.

Ironically, by the middle of 1983, as economic conditions grew progressively worse, political opposition to the government moderated. Organized labor, although it opposed many of the government's policies, had never sought its overthrow and began to realize that continued opposition would likely provoke a military coup. Recognizing that any military government would likely take a much harder line against labor, moderate leaders of the FUT "allegedly reached a private agreement with the government to restrain labor unrest."[34] Organized labor protest diminished after the March 1983 national strike, the last called against the Hurtado government.

Opposition from the chambers of production also abated, though for quite different reasons. First, during the early part of 1983, the government began discussions with the private sector over its external dollar debt. The devaluations had progressively increased the debt burden on the private sector, whose representatives charged that they had been "forced" to borrow dollars by the government's tight money policy, which had dried up domestic sources of funds. The government, for its part, initially maintained that the private-sector enterprises knew the risks of borrowing in dollars and that at least part of the liquidity problem was due to the movement of capital out of the country and into investments such as Miami real estate. But antagonism between government and business over this issue moderated as it became clear that failure to act would result in increasing the rate of bankruptcy, worsening unemployment, and a growing probability of failure of some of the country's largest banks. By the second half of 1983, the government had agreed to a program of *sucretización*, under which the government absorbed some of the private debt, stretched out payment periods, and essentially assumed the risk of further exchange-rate fluctuations. Criticized by organized labor and leftist groups as a sell-out to the country's economic elites, the program did serve to help restore private-sector confidence and to moderate attacks from the business chambers.

Second, as the scheduled 1984 presidential elections approached, the private sector's attention turned increasingly toward launching the candidacy of its long-time spokesman, León Febres Cordero. Considered a leading candidate, his election would give the political right direct control of the presidency for the first time in many years. Given the weakness of the traditional rightist parties, business elites began to convert the chambers of production into the primary vehicles for organizing Febres Cordero's campaign. Elected at the head of a coalition of rightist parties, the National Reconstruction Front (FRN), Febres Cordero assumed office on August 10, 1984.

Leon Febres Cordero and Policies of Economic Liberalization

Economic conditions facing León Febres Cordero at the time of his inauguration, although they continued to be serious, were nevertheless significantly improved relative to the situation that had confronted his predecessor, Osvaldo Hurtado. As shown in Table 7.2, the rate of growth of real output had turned around from a dismal negative 2.8 percent in 1983 to a relatively robust 4.0 percent in 1984. Inflation had moderated from 48.1 percent in 1983, the highest level recorded in more than 20 years, to 30.4 percent by 1984. Over the same period, investment as a share of gross domestic product had fallen slightly, from 16.6 to 15.4 percent—far less than the precipitous drop recorded during the previous year.

Yet despite this improvement, the Ecuadorian economy remained delicately balanced on the performance of its external sector. Although the country's external debt had risen only marginally since 1981, Ecuador still owed $6.85 billion to its foreign creditors. And whereas debt service as a percent of export earnings had fallen sharply from the high levels recorded prior to 1983, interest payments alone consumed just slightly more than one-third of all export earnings. Petroleum revenues, which accounted for more than 70 percent of the value of all exports, remained relatively constant only because production increases had managed to offset a steady deterioration in world prices.

Nor was an uncertain economy the only obstacle Febres Cordero faced. Elected without a strong popular mandate for his economic policies, he faced an opposition congress in which he was able to count on only 16 of the 71 delegates for unquestioned support. His victory in the run-off election was scarcely overwhelming, with a significant proportion of his support based not on his economic proposals but on regionalism or protest against the conditions of economic austerity experienced during the Hurtado administration. Febres Cordero's cabinet appointments, drawn almost entirely from the business community (especially from Guayaquil), did nothing to strengthen his support from the parties constituting the National Reconstruction Front (FRN), which had anticipated considerable patronage opportunities in the new administration. With Febres Cordero's strongest base of political support narrowly confined to the business community, the legitimacy of his administration rested primarily on his ability to generate broad-based economic growth that would expand employment opportunities and raise standards of living.

TABLE 7.2
Economic Indicators: 1979-1986

Indicator	Year							
	1979	1980	1981	1982	1983	1984	1985	1986
GDP (1975 U.S. dollars) (Percent change)	5.3	4.9	3.9	1.2	-2.8	4.0	3.8	1.7
CPI (Annual percent change)	10.1	12.8	14.7	16.4	48.1	30.4	28.0	23.0
Exchange Rate (free market)	27.8	28.0	31.3	51.3	84.8	98.7	117.2	151.9
Exchange Rate (nominal rate for exports)	24.8	24.8	24.8	30.2	45.4	67.0	84.6	121.9
External Debt (billions, U.S. dollars)	3.6	4.7	5.9	6.2	6.7	6.9	7.4	8.2
Debt Service/Exports (Percent)	64.5	47.4	71.3	72.6	33.7	34.6	29.9	38.1
Current - Account Balance (billions)	-0.63	-0.64	-1.0	-1.2	-0.14	-0.25	-0.12	-0.64
Minimum Wage[a] (Percent Change)	32.0	91.0	0.0	25.7	17.3	24.4	31.4	34.1
Wage Share[b] (Percent)	30.3	34.8	33.3	31.6	26.4	24.1	23.9	23.9
Gross Fixed Investment/GDP (Percent)	23.7	23.6	22.3	22.7	16.6	15.4	16.1	18.7
Money Supply[c] (Percent Change)	17.1	28.0	11.7	20.2	30.4	42.4	23.8	20.1

[a]Includes complementary remunerations and other benefits. (See Memoria 1985, pp. 202-203.)
[b]The wage share is calculated from the Ecuadorian national accounts as wages ("remuneracion de empleados") divided by profits ("excedente bruto d explotacion") plus wages.
[c]Currency plus demand deposits.

Source: Banco Central del Ecuador, Memoria 1985 and Memoria 1986, (Quito); World Bank, An Agenda for Recovery and Sustained Economic Growth, (Washington, D.C.); Banco Central del Ecuador, Cuentas Nacionales del Ecuador, Nos. 7 (1985), 8 (1986), and 9 (1987), (Quito).

Thus, where economic circumstances had forced Hurtado to begin his presidency with a plea for support for policies of austerity, Febres Cordero began his with promises of prosperity. Once installed in office, Febres Cordero lost no time implementing the policies that would not only restructure the Ecuadorian economy along free-market lines but also, he believed, produce the economic growth he had promised. Condemning the Hurtado administration for economic policies they claimed had left the nation's economy in a state of near ruin, Febres Cordero and his advisers proposed unshackling the economy from what they saw as the burden of excessive government regulation. They also favored reorienting industrialization policy from its emphasis on import substitution toward one promoting exports, particularly those of man-ufactured goods. These objectives were to be accomplished by the removal of government controls over prices and exchange rates, the elimination of import tariffs, and the active solicitation of the participation of foreign capital. In a significant deviation from his neoliberal ideology, Febres Cordero had committed himself during the campaign to a major program of public housing construction. Aside from this program, he stressed economic growth and the anticipated accompanying expansion of em-ployment opportunities as the means by which the benefits of economic liberalization were expected to reach lower income groups. No public-sector redistributive policies, such as land reform, were part of these proposals.

The new administration argued that the basic problem with the Ecuadorian economy was that producers were subjected to government policies that not only distorted market prices but, because of the erratic application of these policies, also increased the degree of uncertainty for businesses. Thus, in simple terms the administration's strategy was to eliminate government controls—to "get prices right"—and, once this was accomplished, to avoid future policy shifts. Currency devaluation occupied a prominent position in these arguments. The exchange rate was believed to be the most important price to get right in an economy like that in Ecuador, where foreign trade plays such a major role. As Alberto Dahik, president of the Monetary Board, emphasized, the ex-change rate is "a fundamental variable which must never give the wrong signals to the economy."[35] Ecuador's historical tendency toward over-valued exchange rates, it was believed, had discouraged exports while stimulating imports, thus contributing to the country's chronic balance-of-trade deficits.

In addition to price reforms, a second component of the argument for economic liberalization involved opening the country to foreign capital. Consistent with the general ideological commitment to eliminating government regulation over all aspects of economic activity, the anticipated inflow of foreign capital was also seen as a means of solving the problem of low domestic investment and of alleviating the current-account deficit. In the short run, foreign capital was necessary to increase petroleum exports through its financing of new exploration and development. In the long run, given Ecuador's large external debt and the heavy outflows of capital this entailed, it was only with inflows of foreign capital that economic growth could be rekindled and the economy reoriented from its current emphasis on import-substitution industries to those producing manufactured goods for export.

Febres Cordero's proposals for economic liberalization were not new; similar policies had been tried before in other Latin American countries during the 1960s and 1970s. What distinguished the proposals made by the Ecuadorian administration was that government's determination to implement within a democratic political system the kinds of policies that previously had been attempted primarily by highly authoritarian governments. Without question there was a need for some of the policies of economic liberalization proposed by the Febres Cordero government. The heavy debt burden and the falling price of petroleum mandated some immediate change. Ecuador's history of boom-and-bust export cycles suggested that a diversification of exports was certainly desirable. But, at least in the short run, the major reorientation of the Ecuadorian economy proposed by Febres Cordero and his advisers would almost certainly depress the economy. Devaluations could be expected to raise domestic costs of production as the price of imported inputs rose, to accelerate the pace of inflation, and to increase the burden of private-sector debt. Bankruptcies would be likely to become more frequent, and, along with them, unemployment would be expected to rise. As for the employed, stagnant production and rising prices would be likely to lead to falling real wages. To be sure, in the long run, the expected expansion of export industries may provide a new source of economic growth. But the benefits from export expansion are likely to be weakly linked to the rest of the economy unless the new export industries are highly labor intensive.

Such changes necessarily imply a realignment of costs and benefits across social groups relative to the previous development model of import-substituting industrialization. Traditional exporters are the clearest and most immediate winners from a policy of economic liberalization; losers include industrialists producing for the domestic market, importers, organized labor, and civil servants. Particularly in a time of economic austerity, this realignment of economic costs and benefits carries with it the potential for heavy political costs. It is by no means coincidental that most previous Latin American experiments with economic liberalization have been associated with authoritarian political regimes.

Well aware of the negative results of similar policies adopted some years earlier by military governments in Chile, Argentina, and Uruguay, the Febres Cordero administration argued that it would not repeat the mistakes of these prior experiments in economic liberalization.[36] Yet its view of these mistakes was a largely technocratic one. A belief firmly held by Febres Cordero and the business elites who supported him was

that what Ecuador needed along with "getting prices right" was a dose
of sound management practices. Febres Cordero campaigned on this
assertion, appealing to businessmen like the Quito industrialist who is
reported to have commented that "a country is not too different from
a company. . . . If you run a company inefficiently it goes bust; otherwise
it makes profits."[37]

Less than a month after his inauguration, Febres Cordero announced
the details of his policies for economic liberalization. Central among
these was a decree shifting most of the country's exports and imports
from a fixed to a theoretically floating rate of exchange (an intervention
market was established in the Central Bank with an exchange rate that
paralleled the free market but never actually floated). Simultaneously,
all import quotas except for those on automobiles were lifted, and import
tariffs on industrial raw materials were reduced by one-half. Some tariffs
on a limited number of consumer goods imports were also reduced to
retard the growing contraband trade. Given Febres Cordero's vitriolic
attacks on the Hurtado administration's economic policies and his pro-
fessed commitment to economic liberalization, these measures were
surprising. Febres Cordero's policies did not appear to represent a
significant departure from those begun under Hurtado, and, as a news-
paper generally critical of the government noted, "the measures are
moderate with respect to the economic policies that were being attributed
to the government."[38] However, the exchange rate and tariff changes
were only the first part of Febres Cordero's program for economic
liberalization. In early September 1984, the government announced the
elimination of price controls on most domestically produced goods.
Interest-rate ceilings were raised and floating rates established for some
types of deposits. In late December, gasoline prices were raised by 70
percent.

Policies to open the country to foreign investment and to attract new
sources of foreign capital also proceeded apace. Petroleum companies
had expressed renewed interest in Ecuador following the Hurtado administration's adoption of new risk-contract legislation. Agreements with
Occidental and Exxon/Hispaniol petroleum companies, initiated by the
Hurtado government but suspended just prior to the elections, were
signed by Febres Cordero during the early months of 1985 with the
hope that known reserves could be doubled by 1987.[39] During the next
year, five additional petroleum companies signed risk contracts. Seeking
to encourage foreign investment in other areas of the economy as well,
the administration announced its intention not to be bound by Decision
24 of the Andean Pact agreement, which established common restrictive
standards for the treatment of foreign investment by signatory nations.[40]
In November 1984, Febres Cordero had signed legislation resurrecting
for the first time since 1971 Ecuador's agreement with the Overseas
Private Investment Corporation) (OPIC), a body that provided insurance
to U.S. corporations against the event of expropriation. With the exception

of the petroleum sector, however, direct foreign investment did not show the kinds of gains hoped for by the administration. Undoubtedly, the lukewarm response from foreign investors to these initiatives was attributable in part to a general reluctance to invest anywhere in the debt-ridden Latin American region. In addition, falling petroleum prices and the escalating political conflict between Febres Cordero and the opposition-dominated legislature did little to inspire investor confidence in Ecuador.

Increased foreign borrowing formed a key component of Febres Cordero's economic plan. In early 1985 Ecuador concluded an agreement for refinancing its foreign debt that stretched out the repayment period to twelve years, and allowed an initial three-year grace period during which the country would not have to make payments on principal.[41] In January of the following year, Febres Cordero capitalized on his close ties to the United States and his commitment to free-market principles by securing $319 million in new public loans. Proclaiming the Ecuadorian government "the best in Latin America," the U.S. administration appeared ready to make Ecuador a test case under Treasury Secretary James A. Baker's plan for assistance to the indebted developing countries.[42]

The economic consequences of these policies at the end of 1985 were mixed, and difficult to disentangle from other changes in the domestic and international economies. Real gross domestic product increased by 3.8 percent, down slightly from the 4.0 percent growth registered in 1984. The rate of inflation declined somewhat, from an annual rate of 30.4 percent in 1984 to 28.0 percent in 1985. These price figures, however, mask a deceleration in the rate of inflation through October 1984 and a renewed acceleration after this date as the new government's price decontrols and exchange-rate policies took their toll on price stability.[43] Wage increases do not appear to have been a source of inflationary pressure, as the minimum wage in real terms increased only 6.4 percent between December 1983 and December 1985.[44]

The external sector performed well, with the current-account deficit falling from $248 million to $120 million. Petroleum exports made a significant contribution to this performance, as increases in volume were able to offset a continued softening of world petroleum prices. The traditional exports—bananas, coffee, and cacao—all showed gains in 1985, with both price and volume increases contributing to their showing. Some part of the gains in traditional exports, however, are attributable to the recovery of production following the flooding in 1983. The increase in the value of banana exports from 1984 to 1985, for example, was due almost entirely to the recovery of domestic production.

Public expenditures constituted a key component of Febres Cordero's political strategy. Elected with a narrow political base and committed to policies that, at least in the short run, would be likely to impose heavy costs on lower income groups, the president sought to broaden his appeal to voters through a vigorous program of public works expenditures. The pattern of spending during the first year and a half of his administration, for example, shows a marked shift from expenditures for economic and social development to those for general services and public works.[45] Publicly funded construction projects in Guayaquil, the principal locus of Febres Cordero's popular support, grew at a much faster rate than projects in Quito.[46]

Through 1985 petroleum revenues were sufficient to accommodate the public spending requirements of the president's strategy. The public-sector accounts had shown a surplus since 1983. In 1985 the surplus rose from the 0.4 percent of GDP registered the preceding year to 1.5 percent, the largest surplus since 1970. Yet this improvement was not attributable to decreases in expenditures, which increased markedly over the period; rather, it was the result of revenue increases, notably those from petroleum. The state budget, about 46 percent of total public-sector expenditures, registered a surplus for the first time since 1973, as increased petroleum revenues were also diverted to this account.[47] But the dependence of the public sector on petroleum revenues increased from 47.6 percent in 1983 to 51.7 percent in 1985, warning of the sensitivity of this strategy to the stability of world petroleum prices.

In early 1986 world petroleum prices again began to fall, dropping from their 1985 average of $26 per barrel to an average of slightly less than $13 over the course of the next year. In the absence of significant new discoveries of petroleum, volume increases could not be expected to offset the decline in price. As petroleum revenues fell, the administration was forced to make even greater efforts to increase the inflow of foreign capital. Traditional, nonpetroleum exports did show encouraging gains during 1986: They increased by 16 percent and thus lent some credence to the administration's pro-export policies.[48] Coffee, shrimp, and bananas, which collectively accounted for 70 percent of nonpetroleum exports, performed well. Nontraditional exports, such as gold and the newly developed cut-flower industry, also showed impressive gains, even though their contribution to total export earnings remained relatively insignificant. Nevertheless, the gains in nonpetroleum exports failed to offset the drop in petroleum earnings. The current-account deficit, which had narrowed in 1985, again began to widen, reaching $700 million by the end of 1986.

Although its earlier overtures to foreign investors had met with only limited success, the Febres Cordero government continued its efforts to attract new investment. On December 5, 1986, the Monetary Board approved guidelines for debt-equity swaps that would allow investors to acquire discounted public debt under the condition that they agree to purchase local equity worth the sucre equivalent of that debt.[49] Yet, despite the administration's earnest courtship of foreign investors, new investment outside the petroleum sector failed to increase significantly.[50]

With the current-account deficit widening and direct foreign investment showing little increase, the administration aggressively sought new loans.

In 1986 alone, Ecuador's external debt rose by 10 percent, from \$7.4 billion to approximately \$8.2 billion. But this new borrowing, rather than financing economic growth as the government had planned, went largely to offsetting the decline in petroleum earnings and, thus, to temporarily delaying the costs of economic adjustment to lower export prices.

The performance of the Ecuadorian economy in 1986 deteriorated along with the fall in petroleum prices. Economic growth slowed to a discouraging annual rate of 1.7 percent. Restrictive monetary policy helped to hold down the rate of inflation, which averaged 23 percent for the year, but it contributed to the slow rate of economic growth. Per capita incomes fell to their lowest levels since 1978. Open unemployment reached the historically high level of 12 percent, up from 10.4 percent in 1985, and underemployment touched levels near 40 percent. Debt service obligations rose from 29.9 percent of exports in 1985 to 38.1 percent in 1986.

Political support for the president also weakened. Opposition from the national labor organization, the Unitary Workers' Front (FUT), which had been relatively ineffective up to this point, intensified. Whether primarily because of worsening economic conditions, reduced fears of repression, or the organizing efforts of its leadership, an important development during 1986 was the FUT's increased ability to draw support from outside its immediate membership. Even among the country's economic elites, Febres Cordero's strongest supporters, there were some signs of discontent as it became clear that not all business groups would benefit from the administration's liberalization policies. The Quito chamber of commerce, whose members are principally importers, criticized the government's policies, calling for a "revision of 'multiple aspects' of the measures adopted to offset the falling price of oil."[51] Military support remained a question mark. A revolt in March 1986, led by Air Force commander, General Frank Vargas, was successfully defused by the administration. Apparently inspired by internal military disputes, the revolt nevertheless reflected a growing re-politicization of the armed forces, thus increasing uncertainty about the military's intentions and contributing to the general erosion of support for Febres Cordero.[52] A plebiscite held in June, intended to increase the government's support among independent voters, was turned into a referendum on the president's policies by the opposition. An overwhelming defeat for Febres Cordero (the plebiscite lost in every single province) was widely interpreted as signaling a new willingness by the administration to compromise. By mid-June, the secretary of public information, Marco Lara, was announcing the administration's willingness to correct its errors, and Febres Cordero was issuing a personal call for dialogue with the opposition.

On August 11, 1986, despite his conciliatory assertions two months earlier that the Ecuadorian economy could not tolerate further adjustment policies, the president responded by unilaterally adopting new economic measures to meet the immediate crisis and, in a bold move, put the finishing touches on his program of economic liberalization. Most import and export transactions were moved to the free market, effectively devaluing the sucre by 35 percent. Export subsidies were removed and import tariffs reduced. Most interest-rate ceilings were removed and bank reserve requirements reduced. Nine days later, public-sector foreign exchange transactions, including petroleum, were devalued by 50 percent. In an effort to prevent these moves from triggering a new round of inflation, the rate of growth of the money supply was reduced, adding to the recessionary tendency of the economy.[53] Despite these measures, however, by the beginning of 1987 it had become clear to the Febres Cordero administration that its debt servicing obligations could not be met. In mid-February, in a surprising shift of course for a government that had prided itself on its reputation as a model debtor, debt service payments were suspended and negotiations to secure more favorable terms for payment of Ecuador's external debt were reinitiated.

On March 5, 1987, a major earthquake shook the country, rupturing the trans-Andean pipeline and dashing any hopes for economic recovery. Facing a predicted loss of petroleum revenues of nearly $400 million and reconstruction costs estimated to be at least $600 million, Febres Cordero was obliged to adopt emergency economic measures. The prices of fuel and public transport were raised by 80 percent and 25 percent, respectively. Basic food commodity prices were frozen, and the president called for across-the-board cuts in government expenditures.

A natural disaster of this magnitude might have been expected to at least temporarily moderate opposition to the president. Yet Febres Cordero's emergency economic measures ignited a new round of broad-based opposition, pointing to a deep erosion of legitimacy for his government and to his failure to firmly consolidate a base of political support.

Conclusions

Osvaldo Hurtado and Febres Cordero assumed the presidency with decidedly different perceptions both of Ecuador's problems and of the policies most appropriate to their solution. Hurtado's understanding of Ecuadorian reality was particularly influenced by structuralist perspectives. Sincerely committed to reducing social and economic inequality, he saw the expansion of political participation and the strengthening of democratic institutions, along with government reformist policies, as keys to their reduction. Febres Cordero, in contrast, saw Ecuador's problems in largely neoconservative terms. For him, government policies were a large part of the problem; only by reducing the role of government in the economy and by "getting prices right" could these problems be redressed. His attitude toward democracy was equivocal. Certainly his conduct in office, characterized by one Ecuadorian analyst as that of a "muscular presidency," suggested a willingness to break with democratic procedure in pursuit of his ends.

Yet, despite the marked ideological differences between these two presidents, their economic policies in the short-run were notably similar, shaped by the nature of the continuing economic crisis and by the requisites for IMF assistance. However, there were differences in implementation. Although both administrations devalued the sucre, Hurtado chose to implement a system of regularly scheduled "minidevaluations"; Febres Cordero initially opted for relatively large unannounced devaluations and, finally, for floating rates. The point in each president's term at which austerity policies had to be imposed also differed. Economic conditions were deteriorating as Hurtado assumed office. Access to international credit markets was abruptly curtailed, the rate of growth of inflation-adjusted GDP fell from 3.9 in 1981 to −2.8 in 1983, and Hurtado was obliged to immediately implement policies of economic austerity. Febres Cordero, in contrast, took office just as the economy was beginning to recover. Although his policies of economic restructuring would begin to redistribute income among social groups, these initial changes were moderate and somewhat masked by relatively robust rates of economic growth in 1984 and 1985 of 4.0 and 3.8 percent, respectively. In addition, Febres Cordero was able to continue borrowing. It was not until 1986, when the price of petroleum began to fall precipitously, access to foreign capital was sharply restricted, and the rate of economic growth slowed to 1.7 percent, that he was forced to adopt severe austerity policies.

Although both Hurtado and Febres Cordero were obliged to oversee policies of economic adjustment that depressed incomes, the political implications of these policies differed. Both men had assumed the presidency with narrow political bases. Hurtado was an unelected president heading a minor party. Under severe attack from business elites, he sought to reconstruct the traditional structuralist alliance of industrialists producing for the domestic market and urban lower-class groups, while simultaneously seeking to incorporate new groups such as rural workers. Yet, despite his efforts, he found himself under attack from broad sectors of society. Industrialists producing for the domestic market were a small fraction of Ecuador's business elites, and many were distrustful of Hurtado's reformist objectives. Members of organized labor saw their real incomes fall 15 percent between 1981 and 1983 as the economic crisis deepened.[54] Policies intended to benefit rural groups, such as literacy programs and community development projects, were severely constrained by the deteriorating economic conditions. Regionalism also played a role in Hurtado's inability to garner support. His political base was largely confined to the sierra. In the short-run, the lack of revenue and his personal distaste for the populist tactics of public works spending limited his ability to recruit support from the coast, particularly from the electorally pivotal Guayaquil voters. Ironically, it would seem that Hurtado's efforts to spread the costs of his austerity policies across social groups resulted in a situation where no group could easily identify itself as a beneficiary of the government's actions.

Febres Cordero's political base was also very narrow; indeed, it was principally confined to the country's business elites. His policies, although they promised to favor lower income groups through economic growth, guaranteed immediate benefits only to agricultural exporters and the financial sector. Other business groups, such as importers and industrialists, who began to realize that their interests might not be served in the short run, were nevertheless initially restrained in their criticism of the president out of a sense that Febres Cordero was one of their own. Organized labor, although it actively opposed the president's policies, was not able to do so effectively until the end of 1986. The inflation-adjusted minimum wage had risen by 6.4 percent from 1984 to 1985 but then fell by 9.8 percent in 1986.[55] As living standards eroded, Febres Cordero's principal claim to legitimacy—namely, his ability to deliver economic growth—was increasingly questioned. Yet as opposition to Febres Cordero began to mount, the president continued to eschew efforts to build consensus, relying instead on increasingly authoritarian tactics for implementing his economic proposals.

Thus, although both Osvaldo Hurtado and Febres Cordero responded to the economic crisis with similar economic policies of austerity, both the means by which these policies were implemented and the long-run objectives of the two administrations differed markedly. Whereas Hurtado sought to build political support for his reformist policies by expanding political participation and strengthening democratic institutions, Febres Cordero has imposed policies of economic restructuring that he expected to build consensus through their rekindling of economic growth. The latter's relative success is a reflection not only of the different economic constraints imposed on the two administrations by external events but also of the relative weakness of organized opposition groups in Ecuadorian society.

Notes

1. Portions of this chapter are revised versions of material drawn from *Ecuador: An Andean Enigma* (Boulder, Colo.: Westview Press, 1987).

2. See, for example, Osvaldo Hurtado, *Political Power in Ecuador* (Boulder, Colo.: Westview Press, 1985).

3. See, for example, Rosemary Thorp and Laurance Whitehead (eds.), *Inflation and Stabilisation in Latin America* (New York: Holmes and Meier, 1979); and Alejandro Foxley, *Latin American Experiments in Neo-conservative Economics* (Berkeley: University of California Press, 1983), for good discussions of this debate.

4. Banco Central del Ecuador, *Series de Estadísticas Básicas* (Quito, 1977), Table 4.1, p. 28.

5. *Cifra*, No. 9, Quito (December 12, 1985), p. 7.

6. Banco Central del Ecuador, *Memoria 1985* (Quito), p. 264.

7. Banco Central del Ecuador, *Cuentas Nacionales No. 5* (Quito, 1983), Cuadro 3, pp. 15–16.

8. World Bank, *World Development Report 1983* (New York: Oxford University Press, 1983), Table 1, p. 148.

9. These calculations are based on Ecuadorian national accounts data.

10. Calculated from World Bank, *Ecuador: An Agenda for Recovery and Sustained Growth* (Washington, D.C.: World Bank, 1984), Table 2.2, p. 120.

11. Cristián Sepúlveda, *El Proceso de Industrialización Ecuatoriano* (Quito: Instituto de Investigaciones Económicas [Universidad Católica], 1983), p. 48.

12. David W. Schodt, "The Ecuadorian Public Sector During the Petroleum Period: 1972–1983," Technical Paper Series No. 52 (Austin: Office of Public Sector Studies, Institute of Latin American Studies, University of Texas, 1986), Table 4, p. 19.

13. World Bank, *An Agenda*, p. 38.

14. *Plan Integral de Transformación y Desarrollo 1973–1977* Resumen General (Quito: Editorial "Santo Domingo," 1973), pp. 4, 5.

15. Banco Central del Ecuador, *Cuentas Nacionales*, Nos. 2 and 7 (Quito: Cuadro Económico de Conjunto, 1982 and 1985). These figures almost certainly understate the degree of state involvement in production, given that only those enterprises with 50 percent or greater state ownership are defined as public enterprises.

16. Rob Vos, "Financial Development: Problems of Capital Accumulation and Adjustment Policies in Ecuador, 1965–1982," Working Paper (Subseries on Money, Finance and Development) No. 9 (The Hague: Institute of Social Studies, November 1983), p. 13.

17. Banco Central del Ecuador, *Memoria 1985*, p. 199.

18. Rob Vos, "El modelo de desarrollo y el sector agrícola en Ecuador, 1965–1982," *El Trimestre Económico*, Vol. 52(4), No. 208 (Mexico, October–December 1985), Cuadro 3, p. 1110. Both the volume and value of agricultural production declined.

19. *Plan Integral*, p. 3.

20. World Bank, *An Agenda*, p. 22.

21. Banco Central del Ecuador, *Boletín Anuario*, No. 7 (Quito, 1984), p. 120.

22. *Memoria 1985*, p. 276.

23. Banco Central del Ecuador, *Cuentas Nacionales No. 6* (1984), Cuadro no. 8, p. 32.

24. Banco Central del Ecuador, *Memoria 1983*, p. 71; and *Boletín Anuario*, No. 7 (1984), p. 198.

25. *Boletín Anuario*, No. 7 (1984), pp. 101, 202.

26. Osvaldo Hurtado, address given to the nation on network television (December 7, 1981), in *Democracia y Crisis*, Vol. 2 (Quito: SENDIP, 1984), p. 111.

27. Quoted in Howard Handelman, "Elite Interest Groups Under Military and Democratic Regimes: Ecuador, 1972–1984," paper presented at the annual meeting of the Latin American Studies Association, Albuquerque, New Mexico (April 17–20, 1985), p. 9.

28. Gilda Farrell, *Mercado de trabajo urbano y movimiento sindical* (Quito: IIE-PUCE/ILDIS, 1982), pp. 38, 39, in Nick D. Mills, *Crisis, Conflicto y Consenso* (Quito: Corporación Editora Nacional, 1984), p. 186.

29. *El Comercio* (September 18, 1982), in Nick D. Mills, *Crisis, Conflicto y Consenso: Ecuador 1979–1984* (Quito: Corporation Editora Nacional, 1984), p. 165.

30. Banco Central del Ecuador, *Memoria 1983*, p. 123.

31. Banco Central del Ecuador, *Boletín Anuario*, No. 7, p. 103. Inflation averaged about 14.6 percent from 1980 to 1982, but it had risen to 48 percent by 1983. Although even 48 percent is low by the standards of many Latin American countries, it was more than double the highest rate recorded in Ecuador during the preceding twenty years.

32. *Análisis Semanal*, Año XII, No. 40 (October 11, 1982).

33. Schodt, "The Ecuadorian Public Sector During the Petroleum Period: 1972–1983," pp. 19–20.

34. Howard Handelman, "The Dilemma of Ecuadorian Democracy, Part II: Hurtado and the Debt Trap" (Hanover, NH.: University Field Staff International, No. 34, 1984), p. 6.

35. *Latin American Weekly Report*, WR-86-09 (February 28, 1986), p. 7.

36. See, for example, *Latin America Weekly Report*, WR-86-09 (February 28, 1986), pp. 6–7.

37. *Latin America Regional Reports Andean*, RA-84-07 (August 31, 1984), p. 7.

38. *Hoy* (September 7, 1984), quoted in *Análisis Semanal*, No. 36 (September 10, 1984), p. 440.

39. Michael Crabbe, "Foreign Oil Investment Encouraged," *Petroleum Economist* (July 1985), p. 246.

40. Ecuador signed an agreement to this effect with the United States in November 1984. Other member nations, also eager to attract additional foreign investment, were expected to follow. See *Latin American Regional Reports Andean*, RA-84-10 (December 14, 1984).

41. *Análisis Semanal*, No. 50 (December 26, 1985), pp. 615–616.

42. *Latinamerica Press*, Vol. 18, No. 6 (February 20, 1986), pp. 1–2.

43. CORDES, "Coyuntura Económica Ecuatoriana, 1985–1986," Apunte Tecnico No. 5 (Quito, May 1986), pp. 28–29.

44. Calculated from Banco Central del Ecuador, *Memoria 1985*, p. 54.

45. CORDES, "Coyuntura," p. 21.

46. *Latin American Weekly Report*, WR-86-14 (April 11, 1986), p. 5.

47. Banco Central del Ecuador, *Memoria 1985*, pp. 205–206.

48. *El Bimestre*, Año 4, No. 1 (January-February 1987), p. 51.

49. *El Expreso* (December 5, 1986), in *El Bimestre*, Año 3, No. 6 (November-December 1986), p. 26.

50. *Análisis Semanal*, No. 18 (May 12, 1986), pp. 222–226; Ibid., No. 51 (December 29, 1986), pp. 629–630.

51. *Latin America Weekly Report*, WR-86-14 (April 11, 1986), p. 5.

52. *Latin America Weekly Report*, WR-86-11 (March 14, 1986), p. 1.

53. *Latin America Weekly Report*, WR-86-33 (August 28, 1986), pp. 2–3.

54. Calculated from Banco Central del Ecuador, *Memoria 1985*, p. 54. Labor had received a large increase of 57 percent in 1979, which both Roldós and Hurtado had opposed.

55. Ibid., pp. 198, 202.

8

Venezuela: Austerity and the Working Class in a Democratic Regime

Jennifer L. McCoy

Conventional wisdom indicates that pluralist democracies are more likely to favor popular sectors in formulating economic policies than are authoritarian regimes.[1] Likewise, democracies are allegedly less amenable to the successful imposition of economic stabilization or adjustment programs that require sacrifices on the part of any large group of the electorate. This chapter examines the Venezuelan democratic regime from 1979 to 1986 in order to determine the extent to which regime type makes a difference regarding the consequences of economic austerity. Are the poor and the working class more likely to be favored under democratic austerity than under authoritarian austerity; or do they tend to bear similar burdens under different regime types? What other variables may explain differential sacrifices of social groups under similar conditions of austerity? This analysis does not attempt to evaluate the success of democratic regimes in implementing stabilization programs; rather, it examines the consequences of those efforts (to the extent they are imposed) for the working class and the poor in Venezuela.

Following an overview of the recent political and economic crises and the austerity measures in Venezuela since 1979, this chapter assesses the relative burden born by different social classes and groups. Where comparable data are available, comparisons are made with other Latin American cases so that we can put in perspective the Venezuelan case and draw initial and limited conclusions regarding the costs of austerity and regime type. Concluding remarks offer an explanation for the Venezuelan experience.

Recession and Austerity in Venezuela

As the fourth largest debtor in Latin America and with an economy in recession, Venezuela has faced a dilemma common to other Latin

TABLE 8.1
External Debt of the Six Largest Latin American Debtors: 1985

Country	Total External Debt[a]			Long-term Debt[b] as % of GNP
	Millions of dollars	% short-term	Per capita (dollars)[c]	
Argentina	48,444	12.3	1588	43.8
Brazil	106,730	10.3	787	56.4
Chile	20,221	8.2	1671	123.9
Mexico	97,429	5.6	1236	52.8
Peru	13,688	8.2	736	74.9
Venezuela	32,079	32.0	1854	46.1

[a] Includes private and public short- and long-term debt.
[b] Refers to medium- and long-term debt with maturity of more than one year.
[c] My calculations.

Source: World Bank, World Development Report 1987 (Oxford: Oxford University Press, 1987), Tables 1, 16, 18.

American debtors—how to meet its external financial obligations, reactivate the domestic economy, and simultaneously sustain the well-being of its citizens. As Table 8.1 indicates, Venezuela's total external debt (public and private) in 1985 was $32 billion, almost all of which was owed to private creditors.[2] In comparison with the experiences of other large debtors in the region, the Venezuelan situation varies depending on the indicator used. Table 8.1 shows that Venezuela's per capita debt is the highest among the six largest Latin American debtors. It also has the highest proportion of short-term debt among the top six Latin American debtors.

On the other hand, Venezuela is in a relatively good position regarding debt ratios, as indicated in Table 8.2. As a percentage of exports, both its total debt service and its service on the public debt was lowest among the top five Latin American debtors in 1985. This position did not change in 1986.[3] In terms of GNP ratios, Venezuela does not fare quite as well. Tables 8.1 and 8.2 show that data for both debt service and total external debt as a proportion of GNP put Venezuela in the middle of the pack.

After twenty years of positive growth,[4] the Venezuelan economy began to stagnate in 1979 and went into recession in 1980. To speak of GDP can be misleading in the Venezuelan case, however. Because of accounting procedures using volume rather than value of petroleum exports, real GDP measured in constant 1968 dollars (the base year used by the Venezuelan Central Bank until 1987) understates the tremendous growth in oil revenues experienced in 1973–1974 and 1979–1980. Table 8.3 shows both the 1968 base figures and adjusted figures so as to take into account the rise in oil prices in the 1970s. The alternative methodology,

TABLE 8.2
Debt Service Ratios[a] for Selected Latin American Countries, 1985

Country	Total Long-term Debt Service as percentage of:		Long-term Public Debt Service[b] as percentage of:	
	GNP	Exports	GNP	Exports
Argentina	n.a.	n.a.	6.1	41.8
Brazil	4.9	34.8	3.7	26.5
Chile	14.7	44.1	8.7	26.2
Mexico	8.5	48.2	6.5	37.0
Peru	3.8	16.0	1.9	7.9
Venezuela	8.7[c]	30.0[c]	4.6	12.8

[a]Refers to interest and principal payments on long-term external debt.
[b]Refers to interest and principal payments actually made.
[c]Refers to interest and principal on long-term debt, plus interest on short-term debt.

Sources: World Bank, World Development Report 1987, Tables 17 and 18; for Venezuelan total long-term debt service, The Economist Intelligence Unit, World Outlook 1987 (London: The Economist Publications, 1987), p. 170, and my calculations.

as developed by VenEconomy, divides oil GDP in current bolívares (including crude petroleum, natural gas, and refining) by the nonoil economy's implicit deflator for each year.[5] This method provides a more realistic estimate of oil's role in the economy by taking into account the dramatic changes in the price of oil since 1973. The result produces markedly different estimates not only of GDP growth but also of the importance of the oil sector to the Venezuelan economy.[6]

Volatile changes in the petroleum sector can also mask important trends in the rest of the economy. After extremely high growth in the mid-1970s, the nonoil economy stagnated and then declined after 1978, despite the spectacular rise in oil revenues. This was due in large part to the contractionary economic policies followed by both a Christian democratic (COPEI) administration and a social democratic, Acción Democrática (AD) administration since 1979.

Upon his inauguration in March 1979, *copeyano* President Luis Herrera Campins continued a contractionary economic policy begun during the last year of the previous administration in response to the overheated economy and the financial and economic disequilibria produced by the tremendous rise in oil revenues in the mid-1970s. Trade deficits, government budget deficits, and foreign debt emerged and grew in 1977 and 1978, while inflation continued unabated. The Sixth Plan of the Nation (1981–1985) emphasized the goals of growth with redistribution and growth with stability. The latter goal soon overshadowed the former, however.

The stabilization policies followed by the Herrera Campins administration included cutbacks in government expenditures, slower growth

TABLE 8.3
Venezuela: Annual Real Growth Rates in GDP, 1969-1986

Year	GDP	Non-oil Economy	Petroleum Sector[a]	GDP	Petroleum Sector
	(% change with 1968 base)			(adjusted % change)[b]	
1969	4.1	5.8	-0.9		
1970	7.6	8.4	5.1		
1971	3.0	5.3	-4.8		
1972	3.2	6.4	-9.0		
1973	6.3	6.3	6.2		
1974	6.1	9.8	-11.1		
1975	6.1	11.1	-22.1		
1976	8.8	9.8	0.8		
1977	6.7	7.8	-2.5	4.6	-3.6
1978	2.1	2.5	-1.7	-1.8	-18.0
1979	1.3	0.8	6.9	8.6	41.3
1980	-2.0	-1.5	-6.9	1.4	7.7
1981	-0.3	0.0	-3.4	-0.6	-5.8
1982	0.6	1.4	-7.2	-8.0	-26.6
1983	-5.6	-5.7	-4.7	-8.5	-17.4
1984	-1.5	-2.2	0.3	4.9	33.1
1985	-0.4	0.6	-3.2	-3.4	-15.1
1986	2.5	3.3	0.1	-5.7	-37.2

[a]Includes crude petroleum and natural gas production, and refining.
[b]Adjusted to reflect the growth in purchasing power of petroleum.   See text
for explanation.

Sources: For base 1968 data (1969-1983), Banco Central de Venezuela, Anuario
de Series Estadísticas, various issues.   For adjusted figures (1977-1982),
American Embassy Caracas, "Venezuelan National Income and Product Account,"
December 20, 1982.   For all data (1983-1986), Veneconomy, The Economic Outlook
for Venezuela, 1987-1992 (Caracas, June 1987).

rates of credit and monetary liquidity to curb inflation, lowering of
certain import tariffs to encourage domestic competitiveness and efficiency, and a gradual freeing of previously controlled prices. Concerning
the first two stabilization measures, the Herrera Campins administration
effectively slowed the growth in money supply to 9 percent in the first
year (compared with 16 percent in 1978 and a high of 50 percent in
1975) and continued to restrict it until late 1981, when it was allowed
to expand once again to stimulate the economy. Central government
expenditures were also effectively cut, declining half a percent in 1979.
The 55 percent increase in oil revenues after the second spectacular rise
in oil prices in 1979–1980, however, temporarily eliminated current-
account and fiscal deficits, and government expenditures once again shot
up over the next two years. Thus, despite its intended fiscal restraint,
the Herrera administration spent in its first three years nearly the same
amount that the Pérez administration spent in all of its five years in
office (1974–1978).[7]

Table 8.3 shows that, in response to relative scarcity of credit, higher interest rates, falling domestic demand, and rising costs of inputs, the nonoil economy began to stagnate in 1979, with particular losses in textiles, transport equipment, electrical machinery, and construction. Both supply and demand growth rates dropped sharply as public and private investment slowed (falling 20 percent in 1979), and consumption declined in response to a sharp rise in inflation and to the declining purchasing power of wages in 1979. Thus, even while the oil economy boomed in 1979–1980, the nonoil economy grew only 0.8 percent in 1979 and continued to stagnate throughout the Herrera Campins administration. By the end of Herrera's term, the nonoil economy was in recession with a real growth rate of −5.7 percent in 1983. It would not recover until 1986.

Whereas Mexico alerted the world to its pending external debt crisis in August 1982, the extent of the Venezuelan crisis became known as late as February 1983, when the government suspended convertibility of the bolívar. The government's action was taken in response to several factors that were precipitating the financial crisis. First, capital flight surged in the early 1980s. Between 1980 and 1982, net private short-term capital outflows quadrupled, from US$1.3 billion in 1980 to US$5.3 billion in 1982.[8] Although this flow was primarily attributable to the attraction of higher interest rates abroad, Venezuelan interest rates were freed in August 1981. Nevertheless, capital flight continued to increase sharply in response to speculation as the economy deteriorated. By early 1983 rumors of an impending devaluation or exchange control measures, coupled with eroding confidence in government management of the economy, caused an even larger surge in capital flight. In January and February of 1983 alone, US$2 billion left the country, as compared to US$1.3 billion for all of 1978.[9]

Second, the combination of a current-account deficit and capital flight caused a precipitous decline of international reserve assets beginning in 1982. The central bank began the year with US$8.6 billion in official international reserves, with the state oil company, Petroleos de Venezuela, S.A. (PDVSA), holding an additional US$8.5 billion and the state investment authority, Venezuelan Investment Fund (FIV), holding another US$2.5 billion. By late September 1982, foreign exchange outflows had cut the central bank reserves in half, and the administration was forced to revalue gold and take control of the foreign exchange holdings of PDVSA. Although these measures boosted the Central Bank reserves, by November 1 the country had experienced a net reduction of at least US$6 billion in total foreign reserves.[10]

Third, the need to refinance the external public debt was increasingly urgent, whereas the willingness of foreign lenders to refinance was rapidly evaporating in the wake of the Mexican debt crisis. More than the absolute size, it was the structure of the Venezuelan debt that had become particularly troublesome. A large part of the debt was short

TABLE 8.4
Venezuela: Total Outstanding Public External Debt (in Millions of U.S.
Dollars)

Outstanding (as of December 31, 1982)	6,610
Due in:	
1983	13,090
1984	2,556
1985	2,403
1986	1,865
1987 and beyond	5,137

Source: Ministry of Finance and BCV, "Venezuela: Recent Developments and
Prospects" (Caracas, February, 1983).

term, maturing in 1983–1984.[11] The Public Credit Law passed in August
1981 authorized the refinancing of $13 billion of short-term debt contracts
by the decentralized state nonfinancial agencies. But with half of that
debt still to be refinanced in December 1982, and with additional
outstanding external debt, more than half of the total US$25 billion was
to come due in 1983 (see Table 8.4). The inability to refinance all of
the debt due further weakened Venezuela's international reserve position
in 1983.

Finally, oil revenues started their decline, with a 20 percent drop in
1982.[12] The resulting current-account deficit, combined with the rapid
depletion of reserve assets and the huge amount of debt due, finally
forced the administration to take drastic measures. For political reasons
it had tried to delay any such measures until after the December 1983
presidential elections; but on February 13, 1983, the president imposed
strict exchange controls, declaring a freeze on foreign exchange transactions and establishing a complicated three-tiered exchange rate. Under
this system, the state would retain a preferential rate of 4.3 bolívars
(Bs) to the dollar (the old fixed rate) for repayment of public debt and
imports of essential goods. A rate of Bs6 per dollar was set for other
trade transactions, subject to exchange control. Finally, a free-floating
rate was established for travel, financial transactions, and other international transactions. Private-sector access to dollars for debt servicing
was disputed for several months, until eventually it, too, was granted
the preferential rate. Within a month, the free-floating bolívar had declined
to only one-third of its original value. To control inflation, the administration also enacted price controls that lasted almost six months.

While the administration was in disarray following the exchange
controls, negotiations to restructure the debt stagnated. The commercial

banks wanted an IMF-approved program even though Venezuela did not have any IMF loans. Election year campaigning, however, caused the Herrera Campins administration to delay negotiations with the IMF until after the election. In addition, paralysis in the administration following the exchange controls and a public dispute between the head of the Central Bank and the finance minister over the private-sector debt reflected the tension and lack of unity within the administration and caused delays in negotiating the public debt with the banks.

During the next three years, a series of new austerity packages were announced. Upon its inauguration in February 1984, the new AD administration of Jaime Lusinchi (1984–1988) was forced to propose new austerity measures immediately in order to facilitate debt negotiations with the IMF and commercial banks, although it was unclear if the administration would actually negotiate with the IMF. The first package was announced in March 1984, with the following major points. First, the three-tiered exchange-rate system was replaced with a more complicated four-tiered system under which the preferential rate of Bs4.3 to the dollar was reserved for food and medical imports, and public and private debt principal payments; the Bs6 rate was retained for imports and exports of the state oil and iron industries; a new rate of Bs7.5 was applied to most other authorized imports, public and private debt interest payments, and student study abroad grants; and a free-floating rate was established for travel, most exports, personal financial transfers, and luxury imports.[13] Note that the new main official rate of Bs7.5 per dollar constituted a 74 percent devaluation for interest payments and most imports. Second, wages were frozen. Third, interest rates were again to be fixed by the Central Bank, and they were expected to fall from about 16 percent to 12 percent.[14]

The idea behind the new package was to avoid formal IMF negotiations while following an IMF-like program to obtain informal IMF approval and to facilitate negotiations with the commercial banks. To enhance business support of the program, the government also decided to delay the legislation of new tax laws that were expected to bring business opposition. Thus, business reaction was generally favorable except with regard to the higher exchange rate for interest payments on foreign debt. In contrast, organized labor was unhappy with the economic package despite a series of measures by presidential decree to make the package more palatable to workers. These included a requirement that private employers increase employment by 10 percent, an emergency public job-creation program, a transport pass for workers earning less than Bs2,000 per month, and a rise in the minimum wage from Bs900 to Bs1,500 per month.[15]

As in the case of the early stabilization plan of the Herrera Campins administration, the results of this one were mixed. On the positive side, the decline in the growth rate was slowed to −1.5 percent in 1984 (with adjusted GDP showing a nearly 5 percent growth rate), and consumption of imported goods, historically extremely high in Venezuela, was cut in half between 1982 and 1984. The effectiveness of import restrictions, exchange controls, and devaluation was also reflected in the rebuilding of the Central Bank international reserve position from US$11 billion at the end of 1983 to US$13.7 billion by the end of 1985. On the negative side, inflation rose to 18 percent, and the poor and the working class seemed particularly hard hit (as will shortly be discussed).

The effect on the debt negotiations appeared to be positive. Although Venezuela had actually been criticized in the Cartagena group summit during the summer of 1984 for its low profile and conciliatory attitude toward its creditors, by September that attitude and its economic policies had apparently paid off. The government and the bank advisory committee signed an agreement in principle to restructure US$21.2 billion of the US$26.4 billion public external debt. The terms included an interest rate of 1.125 percent over the London Inter-Bank Offer Rate (LIBOR),[16] with the maturity to be stretched out over a 12.5-year period and no grace period. In addition, Venezuela would make a down payment of US$750 million in principal payments upon signature. Venezuela thus became the first major debtor to renegotiate its debt without prior IMF approval, although it would take two more years for the agreement to finally go into effect, for the reasons discussed below.

Another series of stabilization packages in 1986 affected the entire Venezuelan society. First, in the context of renewed debt renegotiations with the commercial banks in January–February 1986, the government devalued the currency again by unifying the exchange rate (a move long recommended by the IMF) at Bs7.5 to the dollar; the exception was public and private debt amortization, which would continue at the preferential rate of Bs4.3 to the dollar. The devaluation meant a large increase in the cost of imported food (upon which Venezuela depended for one-third of its food consumption and half of its agricultural commodities in 1984).[17] The parallel floating rate would continue for non-essential imports and travel. The banks for their part accepted a Venezuelan demand for a two-year moratorium on the repayment of US$923 million in principal due between July 1985 and December 1986. Faced with the possibility of a hardened Latin American debt position at the upcoming Cartagena summit in February 1986, the banks signed the rescheduling agreement two days before the summit (the agreement had initially been signed in principle by the advisory committee in September 1984), with a new contingency clause providing for renegotiations if Venezuela's economic position deteriorated.[18]

Dramatically falling oil prices in early 1986 forced the government to take additional measures.[19] Venezuela signed its first loan in a decade with the Inter-American Development Bank to help finance an industrial credit plan for the private sector, and the government announced new import restrictions on automobiles, metal-working products, and pharmaceutical and wheat purchases.[20] Then in mid-1986, as oil prices hit rock bottom, President Jaime Lusinchi announced a new 21-point economic program that included the following points: (1) a partial devaluation of the bolívar, with all debt now to be repaid at Bs7.5 (in contrast to principal payments previously at Bs4.3); (2) liberalization of the foreign investment code; (3) new restrictions on agricultural imports and finished manufactured products; (4) "modernization" of the tax system; and (5) promotion of nontraditional products.[21] Both the banks and the private sector reacted angrily to the devaluation—the banks because they feared default on the private sector debt, and the private sector because of the cost. But this latest devaluation helped the government finance its budget through foreign exchange sales. Nearly 10 percent of the 1987 budget was to be financed through the sale of foreign exchange to the private sector for debt payments.[22]

The program also included some measures for the poor. It called for US$666 million to be spent on low-cost housing; an apprentice job program for 50,000 youth; a program to retrain government employees for the private sector; the maintenance of price controls on thirty basic food items; and free milk for school children and pregnant women.

Finally, a third package of economic measures was announced on December 6, 1986, including the following: (1) a devaluation of the official exchange rate to Bs14.5 to the dollar for essential imports (with the exception of basic food and medicine, retained at Bs7.5); (2) an increase in the minimum urban wage from Bs1,500 to Bs2,000 per month and the agricultural minimum wage from Bs1,200 to Bs1,500 per month; (3) continued price controls on essential goods and services, with additional subsidies for domestic fertilizer and other agricultural items; and (4) a plan to provide the private sector with a stable exchange rate for servicing of its foreign debt.

This third plan paved the way for a new restructuring agreement for external public debt in February 1987. In light of the Mexican accord signed in the fall of 1986, and in response to falling oil revenues, Venezuela demanded easier terms in its debt accord, invoking a contingency clause from the February 1986 accord to that effect. The new accord granted Venezuela a lower interest margin (reduced from 1 and ⅛ to ⅞ of 1 percent over LIBOR) over fourteen years, effectively lowering interest payments from US$3.82 billion to US$1.35 billion between 1987 and 1989.[23]

In short, the core of the government's response to the economic and debt crises has been devaluation of the currency to protect the trade balance and continued timely payments on its foreign debt. The bolívar was devalued 237 percent between 1983 and 1986 at the official rate, and nearly 500 percent at the free-floating rate. With regard to its foreign debt, Venezuela maintained an exceptionally good record in interest payments, although a partial moratorium on principal payments was regularly extended with creditor approval from 1983 until the 1986 agreement finally went into effect. Consequently, Venezuela has also been successful at restructuring its debt on relatively good terms. The consequences of this approach to the crisis for Venezuelans, and for the working class in particular, are discussed below.

Consequences of Austerity

The global recession, foreign debt crisis, and collapse of the oil market hit Venezuela hard in the 1980s. Although the country continued to have the highest per capita income in the continent,[24] it experienced the second largest percentage drop in per capita consumption in constant dollars in the region, falling nearly 20 percent between 1980 and 1985.[25] The effect on a nation accustomed to consumerism and foreign travel for the middle and upper classes was profound. After the devaluation, imports were cut in half and the cost of foreign travel immediately rose to three—and eventually six—times what it had been before devaluation, as the bolívar declined from Bs4.3 to the dollar to Bs12 in 1983 and to as low as Bs25 in 1986.

The impact of the recession and devaluation on different segments of Venezuelan society is analyzed in this section. Several indicators, including wages, unemployment, and prices and subsidies, are examined to determine the consequences of austerity for the working class. In addition, the impact of devaluation and tax reform on the private sector is discussed. The data for some of the measures are reliable; the data for others vary considerably across sources. In most cases where the sources disagree, I have used only those data that are corroborated by at least one other source. Exceptions are noted in the discussion.

The role of the national labor confederation (the Confederation of Venezuelan Workers, or CTV) and that of the national business peak association (the Federation of Chambers and Associations of Commerce and Production, or Fedecámaras) in shaping government policy is also discussed. The CTV, by far the largest labor confederation in the country, represents 25–30 percent of the work force. Dominated by Acción Democrática, it is a pluralist organization that also has factions representing COPEI and the smaller leftist parties. Not tied to any political party, Fedecamaras is a national organization that represents major councils for the commercial, industrial, and financial sectors.

Austerity and the Working Class

Wages. Although wage statistics for Venezuela vary according to source, all sources indicate a sustained fall in real wages after 1979.[26] After growing sharply in 1977–1978, real wages declined precipitously in 1979 as inflation shot up and collective bargaining failed to compensate. In response, organized labor pressed for compensatory action, demanding a presidentially decreed wage increase. National labor leaders, including the president of the dominant CTV, threatened to call a national strike if the government did not respond to labor's demands. President Herrera's continued refusal to mandate a general wage increase finally led labor leaders to seek an alternative way to reach their goals—by introducing legislation in the national Congress through the major opposition party, AD, and smaller leftist parties with ties to labor. The legislation that was passed in November 1979, despite the opposition of the administration, granted a sliding scale of wage and salary increases from 30 percent for low wage earners to 5 percent for higher wage earners, with a cap of Bs6,000 (US$1,395) per month.[27] Although the wage increase did slow the decline in purchasing power in 1980, the year of its implementation,[28] Table 8.5 shows that real wages continued to fall until 1985 as labor failed to achieve another legislated wage increase and collective bargaining failed to sustain the pre-austerity purchasing power of workers.

How do Venezuelan workers fare compared with the rest of the continent? Table 8.5 shows the change in real wages for selected Latin American countries, using data from the Inter-American Development Bank. Looking at the accumulated change in real wages between 1981 and 1984, we find that Venezuela shows a decline of nearly 18 percent compared to a regional average of −12.8 percent. It falls exactly in the middle of the pack in rank order of accumulated change.

On the basis of this limited data, we can conclude that regime type does not appear to have a direct effect on the ability of workers to achieve salary gains. There is no apparent correlation between regime type and direction of accumulated change. Two intriguing results do emerge from this comparison, however. First, note that strikingly positive gains or turnarounds in wages have been achieved during the first year of a new democratic regime in several cases: Argentina (1983–1984), Bolivia (the year following its return to democracy in 1982), Brazil (1985), and Uruguay (1985). These cases indicate that it may be a context of regime *change* (and in these cases a change to democracy), rather than the existence of democratic politics per se, that explains the ability of governments and social groups to press for policy change and income gains. The political space created by abrupt regime change may allow for the implementation of any new policy or strategy, whether it is austerity or expansion.[29] As I have discussed elsewhere, change in administration under the democratic regime may have a similar effect in the Venezuelan case.[30]

A second striking aspect of the data in Table 8.5 is the relationship between positive wage gains and economic growth. Virtually all of the cases of real wage increases coincided with positive growth in GDP (23 out of 24 cases). On the other hand, loss of purchasing power does not necessarily occur only in recessionary times. Only 25 of 40 cases (or 62 percent) of negative wage change coincided with negative GDP growth. The implication is that while a growing economy may be a necessary condition to achieve positive wage gains, it is not a sufficient condition, and other factors must be taken into account. Obviously, these

TABLE 8.5
Change in Real Wages and Real GDP for Selected Countries: 1980-1985 (in Percentages)

Country	1981 Wage	1981 GDP	1982 Wage	1982 GDP	1983 Wage	1983 GDP	1984 Wage	1984 GDP	1985[a] Wage	1985[a] GDP	Wage Change: 1981-1984
Argentina[a]	-10.7	-6.5	-10.5	-5.2	29.3	3.4	16.0	2.4	-14.5	-4.4	24.1
Bolivia	-6.4	-0.3	-1.5	6.6	16.6	-7.3	-43.6	-3.1	-28.7	-2.1	-34.9
Brazil	-1.3	-1.6	0.5	0.9	-11.4	-3.2	-7.5	4.5	3.0	8.3	-19.7
Chile	8.9	5.5	-0.2	-14.1	-10.7	-0.7	0.1	6.3	-4.2	2.0	-1.9
Colombia	2.0	2.3	5.0	0.9	6.1	1.0	6.0	3.2	-3.0	2.8	19.1
Costa Rica	-9.1	-2.3	-19.9	-7.3	11.4	2.9	7.8	7.5	4.5	1.6	-9.8
Ecuador	-12.8	3.9	-2.7	1.2	-12.6	-3.1	-7.0	4.1	5.7	3.2	-35.1
Mexico	1.6	7.9	-9.6	-0.5	-18.2	-5.3	-7.4	3.7	-1.3	2.7	-33.4
Panama	-2.3	4.2	0.3	5.5	7.2	0.4	n.a.	-0.4	n.a.	3.3	5.2[b]
Paraguay	5.3	8.7	-2.8	-0.1	-7.1	-3.0	-3.5	3.1	-2.2	4.0	-8.1
Peru	-1.7	3.1	2.2	0.9	-16.7	-12.0	-15.3	4.7	-15.7	1.5	-31.5
Uruguay	7.5	1.9	-0.3	-9.4	-20.7	-5.0	-9.2	-3.3	16.0	0.7	-22.7
Venezuela	-5.4	-0.3	-0.1	0.7	-7.2	-5.6	-7.2	-1.4	0.3	-0.4	-17.9
Regional Average											-12.8

[a] Estimated
[b] 1981-1983

Source: Inter-American Development Bank, Economic and Social Progress in Latin America: 1986 Report and 1987 Report.

TABLE 8.6
Real Average Minimum Wages[a] in Selected Latin American Countries, 1979-1982
(Percent Change)

Country	1979	1980	1981	1982
Argentina	-7.3	17.5	-2.5	-8.4
Brazil	0.0	2.3	-1.1	-0.5
Colombia	11.0	32.6	-2.2	n.a.
Costa Rica	2.3	-0.4	-9.9	-8.7
Chile	-0.9	0.2	-0.9	-0.3
Mexico	-2.6	-6.5	0.6	-1.0
Peru	1.8	23.8	-15.6	n.a.
Venezuela	-10.9	62.7	-12.9	-6.6
Regional Average	-2.2	4.1	-1.6	-2.0

[a]Calculated from an index of 1970 = 100.

Source: James Wilkie, Statistical Abstract of Latin America, Vol. 24 (1985), Table 1406.

relationships must be subjected to much more systematic analysis before we can draw any firm conclusions; they are presented here primarily for illustrative purposes.

Minimum-wage data are incomplete for Venezuela and somewhat problematic for analysis. Although the Venezuelan Constitution of 1961 guarantees a minimum wage, it was not enforced until 1974 when a nationwide minimum wage (excluding agricultural and domestic workers) of Bs15 per day (US$3.50) was decreed by President Carlos Andrés Pérez. The Law of General Salary and Wage Increases passed by Congress in 1979 included a provision for minimum wages, doubling the 1974 figure to Bs30 (US$7.00) per day.

The impact of this act is evident in Table 8.6, which shows a large increase in the real minimum wage for Venezuela in 1980. According to one study, the legislation helped to reduce urban poverty in that the proportion of urban wage earners who earned less than the subsistence-level income fell from 32 percent in 1979 to 13 percent in 1980.[31] In subsequent years, however, real minimum wages fell even faster than the regional average, again indicating that a relatively long-lived and stable democratic regime does not guarantee any better distribution of the costs of austerity than do other regime types. In 1984 the minimum wage was raised again from Bs900 to Bs1,500 per month—a two-thirds increase.

Meanwhile, accumulated inflation reached 71 percent between 1980 and 1984, indicating a loss in purchasing power in real terms of 6 percent, despite the decree of 1984. Workers in small enterprises were especially hard hit. A 1985 survey indicated that, although only 15 percent of workers in large companies earned the minimum wage or less, 24 percent of those in medium-sized companies and 44 percent of

TABLE 8.7
Urban Unemployment in Venezuela (in percentages), 1975-1986

Year	Rate
1975	7.2
1976	6.0
1977	5.5
1978	5.1
1979	5.8
1980	6.6
1981	6.8
1982	7.8
1983	10.5
1984	14.3
1985	13.3
1986	11.8

Sources: UN-ECLA, Economic Survey of Latin America (1979, 1983); Interamerican Development Bank, Economic and Social Progress in Latin America: 1986 Report and 1987 Report.

workers in small companies earned the minimum wage or less.[32] In December 1986 another increase was granted, raising the urban minimum wage by one-third and rural minimum wage by one-quarter. As discussed below, however, projected inflation in 1987 will most likely negate most of those gains.

Unemployment. Table 8.7 shows that unemployment in Venezuela increased every year from 1978 to 1984, with a slight tapering off in 1985 and 1986. Official rates peaked in 1984 at 15 percent, rising to as much as 30–35 percent in the depressed construction industry, but unofficial estimates go much higher. The CTV estimated 18–20 percent overall unemployment, and an independent estimate went as high as 23 percent for 1985.[33] Official unemployment data have always been controversial, with the CTV claiming that official data underestimates real unemployment. The problem of accurate measurement is compounded by the problems of underemployment and employment in the informal sector in Venezuela. For example, the Inter-American Development Bank estimates that the informal sector constituted 40 percent of total employment in Caracas in 1981, whereas in nine major countries of the region the average share of the informal sector in urban employment was only 25 percent for the same year.[34]

During the oil boom, unemployment was quite low, averaging 5.95 percent between 1975 and 1978 (although underemployment remained a problem). However, as the internal (nonoil) economy stagnated after 1978, particularly the construction and service sectors, Venezuela's unemployment problem worsened relative to the rest of the region. According to one source, Venezuela fell from the third lowest urban unemployment in 1978, to seventh out of thirteen countries surveyed in the region in 1983.[35] A second source reports that Venezuela fell from fifth lowest in open unemployment (1978–1980 average) to the fifth highest out of fifteen countries surveyed in the region in 1984.[36] Thus, although the entire region suffered growing unemployment, Venezuelan workers became relatively worse off.

Although Venezuela has one of the highest rates of unionization in Latin America (25–30 percent of the labor force), more than two-thirds of workers are not covered by collective contract. Furthermore, the size of the enterprise determines to a great extent the coverage by collective contract. Nearly all workers in large enterprises (employing more than 100 workers) are helped by collective contracts, whereas only about 20 percent in small enterprises, and practically none in micro-enterprises (1–5 workers), are helped.[37]

For all of these reasons, the CTV was more concerned about employment than about wages during the height of the economic crisis in 1983–1985. This concern explains the political position taken by the CTV during the same period, in support of measures that would promote private-sector investment and productivity, and thus prevent bankruptcies and further loss of jobs. For example, the CTV supported the private sector's demands for access to dollars at the preferential exchange rate for debt servicing, as discussed below. In addition, it refrained from calling for a new general wage and salary increase until the end of 1985, preferring instead to rely on the collective bargaining method to promote wage increases in only those sectors that showed recovery.

Prices and Subsidies. The final indicator to be considered regarding the costs of austerity for the working class is the change in the subsidy and pricing policies of the government, and the resulting inflation. Venezuelan governments since 1958 have traditionally relied on price controls and state-subsidized goods to maintain a minimum standard of living for the electorate. Although direct government subsidies to basic food producers had for a long time been a standard mechanism to combat rising food prices, especially benefiting the poor, it was not until 1974 and the doubling of the inflation rate that subsidies began *en masse.* In that year, the central government spent Bs249 million (US$57 million) in food subsidies; and during the remainder of the Pérez administration, that figure grew to an average of Bs1 billion per year. As of 1981 the government was spending Bs4.8 billion (US$1.11 billion) annually.[38]

As part of its efforts to combat the fiscal deficit and improve productivity, the Herrera administration sought to significantly reduce subsidies and price controls. Theoretically, inflation would also be kept under control because international competition would force greater efficiency of domestically produced goods. Thus, in August 1979 the administration announced a policy of *liberación de precios* and listed 150 items to be decontrolled. The one significant exception to the policy were the goods of greatest importance to the popular diet, which would continue to be controlled.

TABLE 8.8
Caracas Metropolitan Area Consumer Price Index: Annual Variation, 1970 - 1986

Year	General Prices (in percentages)	Food, Drink, and Tobacco (in percentages)
1970	1.0	1.4
1971	3.2	3.5
1972	2.9	4.9
1973	4.1	7.6
1974	8.3	12.7
1975	10.2	14.7
1976	7.7	8.8
1977	7.8	12.4
1978	7.2	9.3
1979	12.3	16.6
1980	21.6	33.1
1981	16.2	18.5
1982	9.6	9.7
1983	6.3	7.8
1984	18.0	33.0
1985	12.6	N.A.
1986	11.5	N.A.

Sources: Banco Central de Venezuela, Informe Económico. (1970-1983). For 1984 data, the source was U.S. Department of Commerce, Foreign Economic Trend Report: Venezuela (Washington, D.C.: June 1985). For 1985-1986 data the source was Revista SIC (Caracas, January 1987), p. 41.

Former president Luis Herrera Campins explained his policy this way: The former government had produced an

artificial acceleration of the economy that began to show signs of disequilibria in the last years, and that provoked a great indebtedness in the country. . . . When I came into office, we tried to free prices in the belief that reducing state price controls to a minimum would enter private enterprises into a healthy competition in the areas of prices and quality. It was a belief of good faith that turned out to be wrong.

What happened instead? Instead of that competition, perhaps because of the oligopolistic nature of the Venezuelan economy, the private sector, in agreement, raised prices of all products. In response, AD approved the Law of General Increase in Wages and Salaries at the end of 1979, and this was the principal impulse of inflation. We then had to reimpose controls.[39]

The result of the pricing policy was indeed refueled inflation, with the consumer price index rising 12.3 percent in 1979 and 21.6 percent in 1980 (see Table 8.8). Food and beverage prices rose even faster, to 33 percent in 1980. Furthermore, since exchange and interest rates continued to be set by government policy, producing an overvalued bolívar and interest rates lower than international rates, private investment began a sustained fall, declining 20 percent in 1979 and producing negative growth in the internal (nonoil) economy in 1980.

Though low compared to much of the rest of the continent, these inflation rates were extremely high by Venezuelan standards. Historically, a strong currency and cheap imports helped to restrain inflationary pressures in that they provided an escape valve through which the government could meet rising domestic demand by relaxing import controls. As long as imported products were cheaper than domestic products, price stability could be maintained. In the early 1970s, however, the wholesale price index for imported products rose higher than that for domestic goods, and world inflation was reflected in the Venezuelan economy as well. The inflationary impact was greatly exacerbated by the expansion of the economy after the rise in oil revenues in 1974. Thus, whereas the CPI rose on average of only 2.3 percent annually from 1970 to 1972, it tripled to 7.5 percent per year between 1973 and 1978, as shown in Table 8.8. The pricing policies of the Herrera Campins administration contributed to new heights of inflation in 1979–1980.

In addition to the freeing of prices, a partial elimination of subsidies was begun in 1979 and continued through 1982. Although the administration had promised to control the prices of goods important to the popular diet, it eliminated subsidies on four basic food items in January 1982: white corn flour, rice, sugar, and coffee. The elimination of fertilizer subsidies in March 1981 had already caused those prices to jump 400 percent. By 1983 only milk and concentrated animal feed subsidies remained, and the latter were removed later that year.

The Lusinchi administration continued the policy of eliminating subsidies. During its first month in office it announced the removal of a US$850 million per year subsidy of domestic gasoline. Prices for low-octane fuel immediately rose 166 percent.[40] Later in the same year, the government reduced a major food subsidy—dairy products—causing the prices of pasteurized milk to rise 120 percent and powdered milk 85 percent.[41] Prices were determined according to three classes of goods: (1) The 1984 Law of Costs, Prices, and Salaries returned 150 products of basic necessity to price controls; (2) price increases for another group of noncontrolled goods and services were made subject to a 60-day notice; and (3) prices for a third class of goods could rise without government permission.[42]

Lusinchi administration policies caused inflation to soar to 18 percent in 1984, with a rate of 33 percent for food and beverages (see Table 8.8). The poor and working class seemed particularly hard hit. One source estimated that, in 1985, the average food costs for a family of five would be Bs1,700, which exceeded the new monthly minimum wage of Bs1,500.[43] Inflation was slowed in 1985–1986; but with a new devaluation in December 1986 and strict curbs on imports, combined with increased public-sector spending and a compensatory wage bonus in mid-1987, the annual rate of inflation for the second quarter of 1987 reached 55 percent. As of August, analysts expected 1987 inflation to total 35–40 percent or higher.[44]

During the first two and a half years of the economic crisis, from February 1983 to September 1985, organized labor took a cooperative stance regarding wages and salaries and refrained from demanding a general salary increase to compensate for the resurging inflation of 1984–1985. Instead, the CTV focused on protecting salaries through the collective bargaining process, pressing for "salary adjustments" only in those sectors showing a recovery. With this kind of restraint, the CTV indicated its cooperation with the government program to stabilize the economy first, and then to revive it.

One element in the debate about how to achieve economic recovery centered on the so-called "reactivation project," which was introduced in the Seventh Five-Year Plan presented in November 1984. Initial plans called for an unbudgeted Bs18 billion to be spent on reactivation projects; however, this was cut to Bs6.5 billion in 1985, and its implementation was largely delayed until 1986. The government had sought to constrain current spending in order to prevent a fiscal deficit, while spurring reactivation of the economy through extrabudgetary public investment. Instead, delays in implementation resulted in very little spending for "reactivation" and actually produced a fiscal surplus in 1985.

As the economy failed to "recover" and talks among government, business, and labor faltered, the CTV changed its stance from patient cooperation to challenging demands. In the fall of 1985, the CTV renewed its calls for implementation of the reactivation project and shifted its wage policy from a demand for "salary adjustment" through collective bargaining to a demand for an across-the-board salary increase of 30–35 percent over a three-year period. Advancing the thesis that the country should spend its way out of the recession, the CTV ran into opposition from both the government and the private sector—an opposition arising from their fears of renewed inflation.

Although the government effectively ignored the demands for across-the-board salary increases, a change in policy in 1986 produced sharply higher public spending through the Triennial Investment Plan (which had replaced the Seventh Five-Year Plan for 1986–1988) and resulted in an expansionary economy for the first time since 1978. The apparently successful "reactivation," however, was stimulated primarily by government spending, as indicated by the fiscal deficit (for the consolidated public sector) of 4.6 percent of GDP in 1986, rather than by any sustained improvement in the economy. Indeed, the government chose to follow its plan of economic recovery through public spending, after two years of economic stabilization, despite the sharp fall in oil revenues in 1986. Although the 1986 deficit was financed chiefly by a drawing down of international reserves, this mechanism would no longer be feasible in 1987, when consolidated public-sector deficits were estimated to reach 8–10 percent of GDP.[45]

Finally, on April 29, 1987, the government decreed a "compensatory bonus" of 20–30 percent to all employees earning less than Bs20,000 per month, along with a 120-day price freeze and a freeze on employee dismissals. The compensatory bonus was apparently intended to be a "one-shot" bonus rather than a salary increase. Nevertheless, the Lusinchi administration had finally responded to the political pressures of labor's demands. The combination of a demand-stimulus public policy (greater public spending and mandatory wage increases) with import controls and devaluation in 1986 and 1987 produced strong inflationary pressures reaching 40 percent in 1987 that wiped out the wage gains from the April bonus.

Austerity and the Private Sector

Workers have not borne all of the costs of austerity, however. The private sector has faced the burdens of a tax reform resulting in higher taxes for business, as well as higher costs of imports and debt servicing resulting from the successive currency devaluations. When the Lusinchi administration first came into office in 1984, the issue of tax reform was put on the back burner in order to avoid alienating the private sector. However, in mid-1986, the government revived the issue and began to "modernize" the taxation system, in effect raising taxes on corporations and taxing profits earned abroad.[46]

One of the most controversial issues in government-business relations since the exchange crisis of 1983 has been the rate of exchange for private-sector servicing of its external debt. Along with the exchange controls and initial devaluation of February 1983, the Herrera Campins administration announced a three-tiered exchange rate that provided dollars at the preferential rate of Bs4.3 (the old rate) only for public-sector debt servicing. Private-sector access to dollars was not resolved until several months later, when the preferential rate was finally granted for private-sector debt servicing as well. The debate, involving a public dispute between the finance minister and the head of the Central Bank, revolved around several issues.

The private sector argued that it should not be discriminated against in the issue of debt repayment, and that a devaluation would further hurt growth. Organized labor, concerned about a loss of jobs, supported private-sector demands for cheap dollars because it feared that labor-intensive small businesses would fail if forced to make debt service payments at the higher rate. Critics, however, argued that insufficient record keeping would allow the private sector access to cheap dollars in excess of the amounts needed to meet debt payments. In addition, some argued that the huge amount of capital flight, which peaked in early 1983, directly contributed to the debt crisis by draining international reserves.[47] Not only was the capital not being repatriated but owners stood to make a windfall profit with successive devaluations.

The private sector was finally granted the preferential rate in late 1983, but on the condition that its debt be rescheduled with a three-year maturity period—not an easy task. In a series of devaluations in 1984–1986, the private sector was granted the same rate as the public sector for debt servicing. Then in December 1986, a third devaluation forced a revision in private-sector access to preferential dollars. Whereas the bolívar was devalued to Bs14.5 to the dollar for most transactions, private-sector debt servicing was to retain the Bs7.5 rate. However, a new premium of Bs4.5 for the purchase of dollars made the effective rate for the private sector Bs12 to the dollar.[48]

The devaluations had various effects on the private sector. In general, devaluation benefits export sectors by bringing in more revenues, and it hurts import sectors by raising the price of imported goods. It thus has the effect of transferring income to exporting sectors and industries with import-substitution capacities. In the case of Venezuela, the public sector is the primary exporter, controlling more than 90 percent of export revenues, whereas the private sector is a net importer.

Nevertheless, helped by higher costs of competing foreign goods, import restrictions, and state subsidies, some private-sector industries showed impressive growth in 1986. Import restrictions on automobiles, metal-working products, and pharmaceutical products helped those domestic industries in particular. In addition, spectacular growth rates in agriculture (6.8 percent in 1986), after nearly two decades of slow growth and periods of stagnation, were stimulated by government support including a renewed fertilizer subsidy and improved provision of farm credit,[49] and by protection measures producing domestic prices that at times were higher than international prices, even at the free-floating exchange rate.[50]

Private investors with funds outside of Venezuela, many of whom had speculated before the exchange crisis of February 1983, emerged in an especially strong position with the successive currency devaluations. Finally, although the private sector did face much more costly debt payments with the devaluations, continued access to preferential dollars shielded business from the much higher free-floating rate (which reached Bs25 in the fall of 1986 and Bs35 in the fall of 1987).

On the other hand, the devaluation and import restrictions hurt those sectors depending on imports. Stringent import restrictions and foreign exchange controls produced a cut in imports from US$13 billion in 1981 to US$7.6 billion in 1985 and US$6 billion in 1986.[51] Only goods essential to the state-owned petroleum and iron ore industries, and basic food and medical imports, were granted preferential rates of exchange. Higher import prices and restrictions on imports produced shortages in some sectors and contributed to rising inflation.

Many in the private sector were critical of government policy, citing the failure to provide a coherent export-promotion policy that would benefit the private sector. Two factors in particular received criticism in

1987: the lack of sufficient trade credits to promote private-sector exports, and the government decision in December 1986 to change the exchange rate for exports from the free-market rate (at that time Bs25 per dollar) to a rate of Bs14.5 per dollar. As a result of the latter policy, exporters were required to exchange their dollar receipts at the Central Bank for a rate of only Bs14.5 to the dollar, rather than the higher free-market rate. The effect of this policy was to increase public-sector revenues, since the government could then sell those dollars at the much higher free-market rate, at the expense of private-sector exporters.

Explaining the Costs of Austerity
in Venezuela

As this analysis has indicated, both workers and private capital have shared in the burdens of austerity and debt servicing in Venezuela. Workers have faced deteriorating purchasing power in the past seven years as a result of falling real wages (tied to the rising cost of living and to the reduction of subsidies) and rising unemployment. The private sector has faced an increasingly burdensome debt service and rising costs of imports due to successive devaluations of the bolívar.

Although the indicators in this analysis do not allow for a direct assessment of the relative burdens borne, it is clear that both classes have perceived sacrifice on their part. As one economic adviser to Consecomercio (the Council of Commerce) noted, "One cannot say the [Lusinchi] government favored the popular or the private sector more. It's more ambiguous. In the beginning, the policy granting preferential dollars [for private-sector debt servicing] favored the private sector; later, subsidized prices favored the popular sectors. It's a trade-off."[52]

A former president of Conindustria (the Council of Industry), Gerardo Lucas, commented on the social pact and the economic policy of the Lusinchi government: "Because the CTV has gained a great amount of power in AD, . . . Lusinchi's economic program has been the program of the CTV. Especially in the first two to two and a half years, the measures were for the CTV." Another critical issue for the former president was the expansion of the public sector at the expense of the private sector: Public investment was funding projects low in productivity at the expense of private-sector investment that would generate employment and nontraditional exports. As Lucas put it, "We are falling into a pattern of statism at any cost."[53]

In explaining the hardening of the CTV position in late 1985 and 1986, CTV President Juan José Delpino said:

> During economic crises in free market economies in general, the greatest responsibility always falls on the shoulders of the workers because they are the wage-earners . . . and the cost of living is reflected immediately in the purchasing power of that wage. For this reason we sought economic measures to benefit workers and improve purchasing power. There was

TABLE 8.9
Venezuelan Debt Service on Internal and External Public Debt as a Percentage of
Consolidated Central Government Expenditures, 1979 - 1984

1979	1980	1981	1982	1983	1984
17.2	16.8	11.9	15.2	21.0	25.0

Source: Calculated from IMF, Government Finance Yearbook (1986), pp. 945, 947.

not a positive response [from the government] to our requests; on the
contrary, they let it pass, and unemployment grew and salaries deteriorated
more.[54]

As Table 8.9 indicates, the government has responded to the debt
crisis by devoting an increasingly large portion of expenditures to debt
servicing (though not necessarily any greater percentage than the other
large Latin American debtors).[55] As a result, Venezuela has maintained
a good record in servicing its debt. The priority given to debt servicing
has several implications for Venezuelan society. Not only did the government spend a growing portion of funds on debt servicing, but it also
maintained a budgetary surplus in 1984 and 1985, thus inhibiting the
reactivation of the economy through increased public expenditures.

The initial strategy of the Lusinchi administration was to stabilize
the economy in the first two years, and then to reactivate the economy
through public spending and investment in the third year. Despite the
collapse of the oil market in 1986, the government carried out the plan
to reactivate the economy that year and the next. The decision to shift
to an expansionary policy in 1986 was most likely motivated by several
factors, including the growing pressure from labor (traditionally a strong
faction within AD), the successful renegotiation of the foreign debt, and
the relatively strong international reserve position at the beginning of
1986. Thus, the fiscal surplus of 1984–1985 became a deficit in 1986,
financed by internal borrowing, by the drawing down of reserves, and
by the sale of currency for profit. The plan did succeed in spurring
economic growth at a real rate of 3 percent in 1986. As noted earlier,
however, this model of growth, driven by deficit spending, contains real
limits that were already becoming apparent in 1987 as international
reserves fell 29 percent between January 1986 and January 1987 (from
US$13.8 billion to US$9.8 billion).

An even larger 1987 government budget projected a 38 percent increase
in fiscal revenues, nearly 70 percent of which resulted from the 1986
devaluations.[56] The state's ability to sell to the private sector and
consumers currency earned at Bs7.5 per dollar for Bs14.5 or the even
higher floating exchange rate thus apparently financed much of the 1987
budget increase. Yet the increased fiscal income was, for the most part,
neither being reinvested in the domestic economy nor being spent on

demand creation. Instead, more than half of the increase was to go to service the public debt, whereas only 21 percent was to be spent on wage increases and renewed subsidies.[57] Income was thus being transferred from the private sector and consumers to external creditors for the public debt.

Venezuela's ability to achieve this transfer of income was facilitated by the nature of state-society relations there. Historically, organized labor has been closely tied to political parties, and the national labor confederation, CTV, has been dominated by leaders affiliated with Acción Democrática for most of its existence. Party-union ties largely explain the role of the CTV under alternating political parties in power. The CTV has traditionally supported the economic programs of AD governments (as evidenced by restrained strike activity, acceptance of wage restraints, and assured labor peace) while at the same time acting as a "loyal opposition" under COPEI governments to protest economic programs through such actions as renewed strike activity and wage demands. Under no circumstances, however, has the CTV posed a systemic threat to the democratic regime. Instead, the orientation of the dominant national labor confederation since 1959 has been predicated on a doctrine of class compromise and conciliation with active support of the democratic regime. Even though some evidence indicates a growing autonomy on the part of the labor movement, ironically due largely to early state support of the CTV, challenges to government programs and the established system of industrial relations remain within strict and explicit bounds.[58]

Acción Democrática has historically been the party of the masses, with early strength among peasants and rural and urban workers, whereas COPEI, a Christian Democratic party, garnered support from the middle sectors and business. Nevertheless, the evolution of Venezuelan politics into a two-party dominant system, with AD and COPEI alternating control of the government since 1963, reflects the increasing centricity of both parties. This centricity is particularly evidenced by COPEI's multiclass vote since the 1960s and by AD's successful wooing of the private sector in the past decade and a half.

Furthermore, the rhetoric of a "social pact" among organized labor, private capital, and the state has embodied AD's attempts to address economic crises. After the paralysis and incoherence of the *copeyano* Herrera Campins administration (1979–1983) in addressing the exchange crisis of 1983, the *adeco* Lusinchi administration (1984–1988) imposed a series of economic stabilization measures centering on devaluation of the currency, despite AD's image as the party of the masses.

Building on a tradition of *concertación* and class compromise, Lusinchi in particular has used the notion of the social pact to deal with economic austerity and debt. The re-creation of tripartite commissions, composed of labor representatives from the CTV, business representatives from Fedecamaras, and state representatives, theoretically provides a structured forum for discussion and negotiation of accords to address national economic and industrial relations issues, as well as for the articulation of demands and responses from the respective participants. In actuality, the tripartite commissions, at the national level at least, have not produced significant substantive agreements and may play a more important symbolic than substantive role. For example, the National Commission of Costs, Prices, and Salaries (Conacopresa), proposed by labor and established by law in 1984 to study requests for price increases and salary adjustments, was dominated by the state and lasted less than a year before the private sector walked out.[59] A new presidential-level tripartite commission to analyze national economic policy was created in 1985 and replaced the Conacopresa (which was to continue to function as an advisory body to the new commission). In its first year, however, the national commission failed to resolve the fundamental issues of wage adjustment and reactivation of the economy.

Throughout 1986 the government had successfully implemented its stabilization policies while preventing severe social disruption. The long-term success of the "social pact" model in legitimating austerity in Venezuela is by no means guaranteed, however. In 1987, after eight years of austerity, social tensions erupted into demonstrations and protests, organized labor split with the governing faction of AD over the 1988 presidential nomination, and business continued to express its dissatisfaction and lack of trust through capital flight and falling investment. Nationwide student protests and a university faculty strike in March and April 1987 reflected the strains produced by the prolonged recession and austerity, in addition to specific university grievances. Within the governing party, AD labor leaders split with the Lusinchi faction to support former President Carlos Andrés Pérez over Lusinchi's candidate Octavio Lepage for the 1988 nomination. Finally, after three years of labor peace and low strike activity, three major strikes disrupted the economy in the spring of 1987: the port workers' strike, which closed La Guaira for three weeks in April; the teachers' strike in February; and the university professors' ten-day strike in April.

The Venezuelan case cannot be explained in terms of state-society relations and the role of the government exclusively, however. The nature of the Venezuelan debt and the structure of its economy not only set it apart from other Latin American countries but also help to explain the successful renegotiation of its external debt (as of 1987) in particular.

Between 1978 and 1985, Venezuela maintained a current-account and general balance-of-payments surplus every year except for 1978 and 1982, the years immediately before and after the world oil price boom produced by the Iran-Iraq War in 1979. Despite declining oil revenues in 1985, Venezuela posted the largest current-account surplus in the region, for the most part due to successful import restrictions.[60] In addition, Central Bank international reserves were built back up from US$10 billion at the end of 1982 to nearly US$14 billion at the end of

1985.[61] Falling oil prices in 1986, however, caused a deterioration in both of these areas.

The nature of the debt itself is problematic in that an unusually large portion of it is short term. In 1983 nearly half of the external public debt was due in less than one year, thus compelling the government to seek a rescheduling agreement to stretch out its payments. The new accords negotiated in 1986 and 1987 successfully stretched to twelve years the payments of the external public debt maturing between 1983 and 1988. Owing to its favorable reserve position, Venezuela sought a rescheduling of its debt rather than new money. Only in 1987, when reserves dipped below US$10 billion, did serious political controversy arise over the wisdom of restructuring the debt without guarantees of new money. Moreover, Venezuela retained good standing in terms of its interest payments due to government priorities given to debt servicing. The combination of these factors facilitated Venezuela's ability to negotiate some of the most favorable terms in the continent.

Conclusions

Does regime type make a difference in determining who pays the costs of austerity? The Venezuelan case between 1979 and 1986 indicates that regime type alone does not determine who pays the costs, at least in terms of workers. The drop in consumption and the fall in real wages in democratic Venezuela are comparable to those in other Latin American countries under both military and civilian regimes. Furthermore, the Venezuelan state has been both willing and able to impose an austerity program requiring sacrifices from both workers and the private sector.

At least three other intervening factors are indicated by the Venezuelan case. First, the nature of state-society relations is obviously crucial. In this case, a party-dominated labor movement facilitates the capacity of the state to impose austerity without risking severe social disruption, at least when that party is in control of the government. But even when the opposition party has been in control, the basic class compromise and system of concertation has ensured the survival of the democratic regime as both labor and capital have refrained from making any serious threats to it. The recent "social pact" in Venezuela reflects the mechanisms and institutions created in the early consolidation of the democratic regime nearly thirty years ago. But while such pacts provided legitimacy to government austerity programs by enabling important interest groups to participate in the decisionmaking process (at least symbolically), they have not guaranteed that the working class in Venezuela is any better off under austerity than the working class in countries without such mechanisms. Furthermore, the growing strains of the model in 1986–1987 indicate that it may not be viable in the long term.

Second, the structure of Venezuelan exports is such that the state controls virtually all export revenue, due to the state-owned oil, iron ore, steel, and aluminum industries. This factor creates a situation in which the private sector is dependent on state-determined exchange rates and access to dollars for imports and debt service; at the same time, the state is provided with an important revenue-generating mechanism as it buys dollars at one rate (the official rate for public-sector imports and exports) and sells them at a much higher rate to the private sector and consumers.

Finally, given Venezuela's initial credit-worthiness as an oil economy and its excellent international reserve position, the country's foreign debt has been owed to private creditors rather than public institutions. The adoption of a series of stabilization packages, including measures recommended by the IMF, was designed in part to obtain informal IMF approval while avoiding the political liability of formal negotiations with the IMF. These factors, along with Venezuela's relatively good debt service performance, facilitated the government's ability through 1987 to renegotiate its debt without formal prior approval from the IMF. As a result, the legitimacy of government policy was enhanced, even though that policy required sacrifices from various sectors of the society in carrying out the austerity program.

Notes

1. Portions of this chapter previously appeared in "The Politics of Adjustment: Labor and the Venezuelan Debt Crisis," *Journal of Interamerican Studies and World Affairs*, Vol. 28, No. 4 (Winter 1986–1987), pp. 103–138.

2. Venezuela was the only country in the region to actually reduce its external debt in 1985 (from US$34.2 billion in 1984), primarily due to payments made on the public-sector debt.

3. The Economist Intelligence Unit, *World Outlook 1987* (London: The Economist Publications, 1987).

4. Annual real growth in GDP averaged 5.61 percent in the years 1959–1978. During the oil boom years of 1974–1978, average annual real growth of GDP was 6.42 percent, and the nonpetroleum economy grew at an average annual rate of 8.64 percent. See Banco Central de Venezuela, *Anuario de Series Estadísticas* (various years).

5. Robert Bottome and John Sweeney, *The Economic Outlook for Venezuela, 1987–1992*, VenEconomy report (Caracas: VenEconomia, June 1987).

6. As time passes after the base year of 1968, the data calculated from constant figures become more and more distorted. This is the case because constant data are calculated by multiplying the volume of production in each year by the prices of the base year. Particularly with the dramatic changes in oil prices in 1973–1974, 1979–1980, and 1986, the relative importance of the oil sector (crude petroleum and natural gas, and refining) in the Venezuelan economy as measured in 1968 prices thus becomes very under- or overstated. For example, in 1974 current prices, oil jumped to account for 40 percent of total GDP, whereas in constant 1968 prices, oil appeared to account for only 15 percent of GDP. Similarly, in 1980 current prices, the oil sector accounted for 29 percent of GDP, compared to only 9 percent if measured in 1968 prices. Thus, between 1973 and 1985, data using the base year of 1968 consistently understate the

importance of the oil sector for the economy. On the other hand, the rapid decline of oil prices in 1986 produced a distortion in the opposite direction: In current prices, oil accounted for only 15 percent of total GDP, whereas in constant 1968 prices, it accounted for 24 percent, thus overstating the importance of oil in the economy. (These figures were calculated from Central Bank data.)

7. These data were derived from Banco Central de Venezuela, *Anuario de Series Estadísticas* (various years).

8. Ministry of Finance and Banco Central de Venezuela, "Venezuela: Recent Developments and Prospects" (Caracas, unpublished report, February 1983), Table 11, p. 19.

9. Eduardo Mayobre, "The Renegotiation of Venezuela's Foreign Debt During 1982 and 1983," in *Politics and Economics of External Debt Crisis: The Latin American Experience*, edited by Miguel S. Wionczek (Boulder, Colo.: Westview Press, 1985), pp. 325–347.

10. U.S. Department of Commerce, *Foreign Economic Trends Report: Venezuela* (Washington, D.C.: GPO, January 1983).

11. Mayobre, in "The Renegotiation of Venezuela's Foreign Debt," estimated in 1982 that 45 percent of the Venezuelan debt was due in 1983–1984, compared to only 19 percent for Brazil and Argentina, and 30 percent for Mexico.

12. Mayobre, "The Renegotiation of Venezuela's Foreign Debt," p. 326.

13. U.S. Department of Commerce, *Foreign Economic Trends Report: Venezuela* (Washington, D.C.: GPO, June 1985).

14. *Latin American Weekly Report*, March 2, 1984.

15. Judith Ewell, "Venezuela: Interim Report on a Social Pact," *Current History* (January 1986), p. 27.

16. The interbank lending rate in the Eurodollar market was used as a reference point for floating-rate loans.

17. U.S. Department of Commerce, *Foreign Economic Trends Report: Venezuela* (Washington, D.C.: GPO, June 1985).

18. *Latin American Weekly Report*, February 26, 1986.

19. Although the 1986 budget was based on a projected price of $24 per barrel (see Ewell, "Venezuela: Interim Report"), during the course of the year prices dropped as low as $8 per barrel. The average price per barrel for 1986 was $13.50, a little more than half the projected price in the budget. See *Latin American Monitor* (London), Vol. 4, No. 3 (April 1987), p. 408.

20. *Latin American Weekly Report* (London), January 6, 1986.

21. *New York Times*, July 22, 1986.

22. *Latin American Weekly Report* (London), October 23, 1986.

23. *New York Times*, March 19, 1987.

24. The islands are excluded from this generalization. In 1984 current dollars, Venezuela's per capita income was US$3,410, whereas the next highest, that in Argentina, was US$2,230. See *World Development Report 1986* (Oxford: Oxford University Press, 1986), Table 1.

25. Bolivia had the largest drop in per capita consumption of 28.7 percent between 1980 and 1985. See Inter-American Development Bank, *Economic and Social Progress in Latin America: 1986 Report* (Washington, D.C.: IDB, 1986), Table 3.

26. In addition to the IDB data presented here, the Venezuelan Central Bank and two Venezuelan scholars report a sustained decline in real wages between 1979 and 1984, following a period of positive growth in the 1970s. See Asdrubal Baptista Troconis, "El Salario Real en Venezuela," *Revista SIC* (April 1985), p.

148; Miguel A. Rodríguez, "Aumento Salarial y Recuperación Económica," *Revista SIC* (June 1986), p. 18.

27. Hernández and Lucena estimated that in 1980, the year the legislation was implemented, the general salary and wage increase produced an average monthly increase of US$102. In contrast, increases obtained through collective bargaining averaged only US$66 for salaried employees and US$59 for wage earners. See Oscar Alvarez Hernández and Hector Lucena, "Political and Economic Determinants of Collective Bargaining in Venezuela," *International Labour Review*, Vol. 124, No. 3 (May–June 1985), p. 373.

28. Banco Central de Venezuela reports that real wages for nonagricultural workers fell only 1 percent in 1980, compared to a decline of 23 percent in 1979. See *Anuario de Series Estadísticas* (1980).

29. For a discussion of the effect of regime type on the implementation of austerity policies, see Karen Remmer, "The Politics of Economic Stabilization: IMF Standby Programs in Latin America, 1954–1984," *Comparative Politics*, Vol. 19, No. 1 (October 1986), pp. 1–22.

30. J. McCoy, "The Politics of Adjustment: Labor and the Venezuelan Debt Crisis," *Journal of Interamerican Studies and World Affairs*, Vol. 28, No. 4 (Winter 1986–1987), pp. 103–138.

31. Vanessa Cartaya, "Empleo e Ingresos en Venezuela," manuscript, Instituto Latinoamericano de Investigaciones Sociales (ILDIS), Caracas (September 1986), p. 187.

32. Ibid., p. 188.

33. See Ewell, "Venezuela: An Interim Pact"; and *Latin American Weekly Report*, December 20, 1985.

34. Definitions of the informal sector vary, but the IDB defines it, in practice, as all self-employed workers (excluding professionals), nonremunerated household workers and domestic workers, and nonhousehold workers who work in microenterprises and whose compensation takes the form of wages or payment by work done. See *Economic and Social Progress in Latin America: 1987 Report*, pp. 124–126. Another source reports that 20 percent of the nation's total work force was employed in the informal sector in 1986. See *VenStrategy: A Quarterly Economic and Political Report*, Vol. 1 (September 1987), p. 35.

35. UN-ECLA, *Economic Survey of Latin America and the Caribbean: 1983*, Vol. 1 (Santiago, Chile, 1985), p. 18.

36. Inter-American Development Bank, *Economic and Social Progress in Latin America: 1986 Report*.

37. Cartaya, "Empleo e Ingresos en Venezuela," p. 182.

38. Ignacio Purroy, "Cambio en la politica de subsidios," *Revista SIC*, No. 442 (February 1982), pp. 68–71.

39. Interview with author, August 1987, Caracas.

40. *Latin American Weekly Report* (London), March 2, 1984.

41. *Latin American Weekly Report* (London), January 18, 1985.

42. U.S. Department of Commerce, *Foreign Economic Trends Report: Venezuela* (Washington, D.C.: GPO, June 1985); *Latin American Weekly Report* (London), February 5, 1978, p. 2; and interview with Dr. Emetério Gómez, economic professor and adviser to Consecomercio, Caracas, August 10, 1987.

43. Ewell, "Venezuela: An Interim Pact."

44. *VenStrategy: A Quarterly Economic and Political Report*, Vol. 1 (September 1987), p. 9.

45. Ibid., p. 38.

46. *Latin American Weekly Report*, September 11, 1986.

47. Miguel Rodríguez argues that it was the massive export of capital between 1973 and 1983 that caused the Venezuelan debt crisis, rather than an excess of public spending and investment. He estimates that the value of external investment and earnings on that investment is now equivalent to the total external public and private debt. See "Los Mitos y Realidades del Endeudamiento Externo Venezolano," Instituto de Estudios Superiores de Administración, manuscript (Caracas, 1984).

48. *Latin American Index* (London), December 15, 1986; and *Revista SIC* (January 1987), pp. 19, 41.

49. For details, see *Latin American Weekly Report*, September 13, 1985.

50. Purroy, "Médidas para Crecer más Pobres," *Revista SIC* (January 1987), p. 17.

51. The Economist Intelligence Unit, *World Outlook 1987*, p. 170.

52. Author's interview with Emetério Gómez, professor of economics, Caracas, August 10, 1987.

53. Author's interview with Gerardo Lucas, former president of Conindustria (1986–1987), Caracas, August 18, 1987.

54. Interview with author, Caracas, August 18, 1987.

55. The *Latin American Weekly Report* estimated that 30 percent of government expenditures would be spent on servicing the public debt in 1986 and 1987 (January 6, 1987, and July 24, 1987).

56. Purroy, "Médidas para Crecer más Pobres," *Revista SIC* (Enero 1987), pp. 19–20.

57. Ibid.

58. For a discussion of party-union ties in the creation and consolidation of the organized labor movement in Venezuela, see Stuart Fagan, "Unionism and Democracy in Venezuela," in *Venezuela: The Democratic Experience*, edited by John Martz and David Myers (New York: Praeger Publishers, 1977). For a discussion of the growing autonomy of the CTV and its implications, see J. McCoy, "Labor and the State in a Party-Mediated Democracy: Institutional Change in Venezuela," *Latin America Research Review* (forthcoming). For a discussion of recent challenges from independent unions and dissident unions within the CTV, see Daniel Hellinger, "Venezuelan Democracy and the Challenge of 'Nuevo Sindicalismo,'" paper presented at the 1986 meeting of the Latin American Studies Association, Boston, October 23–25, 1986.

59. Accounts of the dispute vary, but apparently the CTV was angered because the commission focused initially on price increases, including the approval of a 120 percent increase in milk prices, rather than salary adjustments; the private sector was dissatisfied with new pricing restrictions. A CTV representative denied reports that the CTV was planning to leave the commission in protest, and claimed that Fedecamaras left because all of its demands were not met, even though business had benefited disproportionately during the first year of the commission (confidential author's interview with CTV Executive Committee member, Caracas, August 1985). See also *Latin American Weekly Report*, July 19, 1985, p. 5.

60. Inter-American Development Bank, *Economic and Social Progress in Latin America: 1986 Report*.

61. See *Barclay's Economic Report: Venezuela* (June 1986).

9

The Costs of Austerity in Nicaragua: The Worker-Peasant Alliance (1979–1987)

David F. Ruccio

Adjustment programmes carry costs, which raises the question of who bears the burden of adjustment. It is a sad comment on the state of economics that the statistics necessary to give a definitive answer to this question are usually unavailable; nonetheless, with the use of some imagination, one can hazard a guess as to the answers.

—Victor Bulmer-Thomas[1]

We have sacrificed the working class in favor of the economy as part of the strategic plan.

—Tomás Borge[2]

Austerity and Revolution

The ongoing economic crisis in Nicaragua has been comparable in severity and duration to the desperate situation in the remainder of Central America.[3] Since at least 1980, all five countries have experienced deteriorating external accounts and domestic stagflation. Although the immediate economic problems faced by these countries have been similar, their causes have been different. Some factors of external origin (increased real international interest rates, declining external terms of trade, etc.) have negatively affected all of these countries; at the same time, United States foreign policy, war, and domestic political upheaval have had less uniform consequences in the region. Naturally, then, all countries in the region have been forced to adopt programs of economic stabilization and adjustment; however, because these programs have been forged under radically different economic and political conditions, they have had contrasting effects on domestic social sectors and classes.[4]

One of the distinguishing characteristics of the Nicaraguan case is that an economic austerity program has been carried out without the backing of the International Monetary Fund (IMF). This sets it apart from much of the rest of Central—and South—America.[5] The Nicaraguan government has apparently not needed IMF support to enforce its particular austerity program. In addition, the weight of the United States in the IMF and Nicaraguan attempts to redefine national sovereignty would have made any official IMF program doubtful. Still, the similarities between the Nicaraguan program of stabilization and adjustment and traditional IMF conditions has been the focus of attention since the February 1985 announcement of the Nicaraguan policy package.[6]

The general issue of the relationship between traditional austerity programs and the nature of austerity in a revolutionary situation clearly needs to be addressed. We might expect, on the one hand, that a revolutionary government would carry out a macroeconomic program quite different from those of right-wing military dictatorships or clearly pro-capitalist civilian regimes. On the other hand, we would probably expect a relatively small peripheral country to share with other foreign exchange–constrained economies the limitations imposed by the short-term inflexibility of restructuring either demand or supply.[7] What are the differences between austerity under different regimes, and how can these differences be explained? How much room for maneuver is there—especially in the context of a crisis-ridden world economy, not to mention a continuing external aggression? Can the revolutionary project stay alive under such conditions? Unfortunately, these questions have tended to be neglected.

This relative lack of attention is explained, at least in part, by the presumption that austerity is a singular phenomenon in all economies, generally associated with traditional IMF-style programs. Orthodox austerity policies are often aimed at restoring the conditions of profitability in the domestic economy by changing the balance of power between classes. The differential consequences of these programs for different social sectors and classes have long been suspected; they are now being explored in some detail.[8]

Still, the general problem of stabilization and adjustment, and the costs of austerity, cannot be dismissed in the Nicaraguan revolutionary context by assuming that the government in power represents the popular sectors, or that the economy is centrally planned, or finally that the economic problems are all externally generated. First, notwithstanding appeals to the "logic of the majority" (whereby economic policy is designed to satisfy the basic needs of the majority of the population instead of the interests of the ruling minority, as under the previous regime),[9] the early revolutionary economy is still characterized by a complex combination of capitalist and other forms of production and distribution; the pre-revolutionary class structure has been transformed, not abolished. Second, there is generally much less central economic control than is presumed by the Ministry of Planning, economic advisers, or outside observers.[10] Finally, even if the causes of the economic crisis can be attributed to the pre-revolutionary economic legacy and external "shocks" (whether international economic conditions or the war, or both), the revolutionary program itself can be expected to create its own share of economic imbalances. Moreover, these internal and external disequilibria, regardless of origin, have effects that need to be addressed. Thus, the revolution forgets about the problem of stabilization and adjustment at its own peril. This is certainly one of the lessons of Chile under the Popular Unity government; it is also an issue that goes back at least as far as Lenin's New Economic Policy.[11]

In the case of revolutionary regimes in the Third World, it is important to assess the costs of austerity through the lens of the "worker-peasant alliance." The worker-peasant alliance has a twofold meaning in this context. On the one hand, workers and peasants are key participants in the tensions and conflicts that provoke a revolutionary crisis in society; they are also the projected beneficiaries of the policies and programs of the revolutionary government. On the other hand, the worker-peasant alliance refers to the project, supported by an even wider constellation of social forces, of transforming social relations—especially the class aspects of those relations—in both urban and rural areas of the country.

The use of the worker-peasant alliance as an "entry point" into the problem of austerity in a revolutionary context has the advantage of focusing on just those class dimensions of austerity that are usually left out of typical economic and political analyses. Attempts to understand austerity in terms of simple private-sector/public-sector or party/non-party dichotomies view the problem in terms of competing claims on resources based on property ownership or the ability to wield political power. Property and power are placed at the center of the analysis; they are substituted for class. The result is that many of the issues that arise in the course of building, maintaining, and redefining the worker-peasant alliance—the complex class dynamic of a society undergoing revolutionary change that, in turn, affects and is affected by changes in property ownership and the ruling political party—tends to fade into the background, or disappear completely.

At the same time, maintaining the revolution's bases of peasant and worker support and its goal of class transformation cannot just be assumed, especially within the context of economic crisis and the government austerity measures. Does austerity call into question short-term support for the revolution by popular classes in urban and rural areas? Are there conflicts between workers and peasants that emerge in the course of responding to difficult economic and political conditions? What about the long-term goals of the alliance: How are they affected by the costs of austerity? The present chapter begins to answer these questions for the Sandinista Revolution in Nicaragua.

The nature, scope, and consequences of austerity for the Nicaraguan Revolution cannot be understood without an analysis of the main features of the Nicaraguan economy and economic policy since the overthrow of the Somoza regime; such an analysis appears in the first section. The second section involves a relatively brief discussion of the costs of the insurrection and the economic situation within the revolution through 1984. The third section presents a critical assessment of the austerity program that was adopted in early 1985. The fourth part of the analysis focuses attention on the costs of austerity in the cities and in the countryside. Finally, the immediate and long-term consequences of these costs are addressed in the last section.

Adjustment and Stabilization (1979–1984)

The worker-peasant alliance attempts to transform the key features of the inherited model of development. The initial measures taken by the government, together with the gains made by social movements outside the state, tend to alter the macroeconomic balances of the pre-revolutionary economy. In addition, the insurrection against the old regime disrupts "normal" economic life. This chapter's first general thesis, therefore, is that a revolution is forced to confront the twin problems of revolutionary transformation and macroeconomic balance from the moment it is ushered into power.

In the case of Nicaragua, the knife-edge of transformation and balance has been further sharpened by the inherited economic situation, a general deterioration of world economic conditions, and the military and economic aggression sponsored by the U.S. government. From the beginning, then, the Nicaraguan Revolution has been forced to devise an appropriate program of stabilization and adjustment. The changing response to the economic crisis during the last eight years may conveniently be divided into three phases. The first phase, covering the 1979–1981 period, involved a recovery from the pre-1979 depression. Starting in 1982 and lasting until the elections in 1984, the second phase was characterized by central economic controls and state-led growth—the Nicaraguan attempt at "stabilization with equity." The subsequent austerity phase was provoked by the accumulated imbalances and the escalation of the war; it was officially announced in 1985 and continues to the present.

Phase 1 (1979–1981)

Many of the early measures of the Government of National Reconstruction were aimed at reviving the "stagnationist" Nicaraguan economy.[12] The last years of the Somoza regime witnessed a balance-of-payments crisis caused in large part by capital flight. Beginning in 1977 and continuing through the first year of the new government, the "flight to safety" for wealthy Nicaraguans totaled $685 million.[13] These capital exports, officially classified as short term for balance-of-payments accounting purposes, were presumably converted into a unilateral, long-term movement once the Somoza regime was deposed. Therefore, although long-term capital inflows totaled $811 million during the same period and the accumulated external debt reached $1.6 billion by the time

Somoza left the country, only $3 million remained in the official reserves of the Central Bank when the new government assumed power.

Strict capital controls are arguably the most effective mechanism for stemming capital flight. One of the first acts of the new government was, in fact, nationalization of the banking and foreign trading systems. However, by that time, the bulk of the capital flight had already taken place. This is certainly one of the macro policy dilemmas of revolutionary governments: It is possible to close the floodgates, but only after government institutions have been seized from the old regime—and by then the level of capital outflows has already crested.

In the end, the Nicaraguan economy had already "adjusted" to this pre-revolutionary balance-of-payments crisis: Although total exports exceeded pre-insurrectional levels, imports fell by approximately 22 percent in both 1978 and 1979. The immediate cause was the depression generated by the destruction and general disruption of the insurrection itself. Real gross domestic product (GDP) dropped by 7.1 percent and 25.5 percent in 1978 and 1979, respectively.[14]

Against the backdrop of intense political struggle for control of the revolution, Nicaragua was able to begin the process of recovering from the damages and disruption caused by the insurrection. The economic slide was reversed, and, although GDP growth rates were below the overly optimistic expectations of the first two economic plans, national product grew at an annual average rate of 5 percent during 1980–1981.[15]

The three key features of the stabilization during this period were an inflow of external resources, an expansionary fiscal policy, and liberal credit distribution. Net long-term capital inflows rose from $120 million (in 1979) to $343 million (1980) and $596 million (1981), the product of widespread support from official donors and creditors around the world.[16] The importance of fiscal expenditures more than doubled during this period, rising from an average of 8.7 percent of GDP during 1970–1978 to 15 percent in 1979, 19.6 percent in 1980, and 22.3 percent in 1981.[17] However, the growth of tax revenues fell behind that of expenditures; therefore, the fiscal deficit increased steadily during the same period (6.8, 9, and 10.4 percent of GDP for the same years, respectively).[18] The third leg of the recovery passed through the nationalized banking system: Total credit grew by 46.7 percent from 1979 to 1980 (and again by 26.8 percent in 1981), with the largest part aimed at rural producers.[19] In addition, the combination of negative real interest rates and the low rate of loan repayment magnified the expansionary impact of the credit bonanza.

The general increase in national output was accompanied by an increase in basic consumption, as employment and real standards of living of peasants and workers increased. Unemployment, which had risen to 22.9 percent in 1979 (from a 1978 level of 14.5), fell to 17.8 percent in 1980.[20] In addition, workers experienced increases in wages. These increases were mostly the result of raising, enforcing, and narrowing the differential between rural and urban minimum wages. Even in this first phase, however, no attempt was made to allow the total real monetary wage bill to rise significantly. Rather, the emphasis was on expanding social services (the "social wage") through state-sponsored programs in health and education, and on the buying power of individual incomes, in the form of government subsidies to basic consumer goods and services and decreased housing and land-rental rates.

The success of these measures in raising national output and basic consumption expenditures, together with the 1980 renegotiation of the inherited external debt, won plaudits from foreign and domestic observers alike. However, the growth-oriented stabilization of the Nicaraguan economy was not a uniform success. Already, at this early stage, cracks were beginning to appear in the armor of economic recovery. The availability of foreign finance to cover the fiscal deficit (47.9 percent of the deficit in 1980) was beginning to fall off;[21] continued expansion in government programs would require increasing use of domestic borrowing, especially new Central Bank funds. Still, the domestic inflation rate fell by 50 percent between 1979 and 1981.[22] The effects of the expansion were felt, instead, on the external account: Whereas exports fell by 26 percent from 1979 to 1980 (and continued to oscillate around levels far below the pre-revolutionary peak), imports jumped 78 percent in 1980 and slackened only slightly in 1981. The result was a deficit on current account of $491 million in 1980 and $563 million in 1981. New adjustment measures were therefore necessary.

Phase 2 (1982–1984)

The first flush of success in consolidating a worker-peasant alliance and in growing out of the pre-revolutionary recession was followed by a series of attempts to control the growing imbalances in the domestic economy and the external sector.

Import controls and export incentives were introduced with the aim of closing, and reducing the need to finance, the persistent current-account deficit. Measures such as multiple exchange rates, import surcharges, and foreign exchange rationing succeeded in lowering total imports by 20 percent in 1982.[23] Exports, however, continued to decline, even in the face of increases in guaranteed export prices. Part of the problem was the slowdown in nontraditional (mostly manufactured) exports to the Central American Common Market, caused in turn by the economic crisis in the remainder of the isthmus. At the same time, Nicaraguan agro-exporting capitalists responded less enthusiastically than expected to the class compromise offered by the revolutionary government. Traditional super-profits in agro-export production had probably declined as a result of the combined effect of the fall in labor productivity (as agricultural laborers shortened their workday) and the appreciation of the real exchange rate; presumably, exporters were also reacting to their now limited access to foreign exchange, the 1981 agrarian reform law, and political changes in the country as a whole.[24] The export-import imbalance did, however, fall by 20 percent during 1982.[25] This decrease, in turn, slowed the rate of growth of external debt.

On the domestic side, the government attempted to prevent inflation by continuing to limit increases in nominal wages and salaries. Any increase in standards of living would come from government social welfare programs and access to consumer goods at official prices. The aim was to increase the percentage of domestically produced goods provided by the state itself through the intermediary of institutions such as the Nicaraguan Enterprise for Basic Foods (ENABAS) at official (and therefore subsidized) prices. The rate of increase in food prices was slowed to 23.9 percent (from 25.9 percent in 1981), whereas the overall inflation rate remained at less than 25 percent.

One of the immediate effects of this second phase of adjustment was a decline in GDP of 0.8 percent in 1982. Total consumption fell by a comparable amount, although the consumption "mix" continued to change: "Social consumption" (basic plus public consumption) barely decreased, whereas nonbasic consumption fell by almost 30 percent.[26] Instead of traditional retrenchment, the government was attempting to carry out a program of "stabilization with equity."[27]

The second nontraditional element was the boom in state spending during this period. The government was not going to let economic activity slow to a standstill in order to solve the accumulating disequilibria. Rather, decisions were taken across the various government ministries to expand public-sector spending not only on defense but also on new investment projects.

The emphasis on state investment was inaugurated with the initial flood of foreign funds during 1980 and 1981; it continued to be justified both by the near disappearance of private capitalist investment and by the objective of transforming the existing productive structure of the country. The strategy from the beginning was for the state to serve as the "center of accumulation."[28] The majority of new investment projects was centered in the agro-industrial sector.[29] The result was that investment as a percentage of GDP rose from negative 9.3 percent in 1979 to 19.5 percent in 1980, falling back to the more reasonable 15.9 percent in 1983.[30]

Although investment ratios reached levels unmatched in the rest of Central America, the remainder of the economy was subject to more typical policies designed to curb inflation and close the current-account deficit. Wages and salaries were kept constant in nominal terms; with an inflation rate slowly climbing to above 30 percent, real remuneration continued to decline. The responsibility of maintaining standards of living fell on government programs, both health and education expenditures, and subsidies for basic consumption goods. As a result, transfer payments for such welfare programs reached 7 percent of GDP in 1984.

Government attempts to balance the external account also contributed to the fiscal deficit. The official exchange rate was kept pegged at 10 córdobas to the dollar (the level established in an IMF agreement just before Somoza was deposed): High-priority inputs and basic consumption goods were offered at the official rate, while export proceeds were surrendered at rates somewhat higher (each product had a different rate)—implying a de facto devaluation for exporters while the external terms of trade continued to decline. Again, the effect was to add an additional component to the fiscal deficit. Although government revenues increased every year, the rate of increase did not match that of expenditures; the resulting public-sector borrowing requirement peaked at 30 percent of GDP in 1983, falling back to 24.8 percent in 1984.[31]

Notwithstanding the price incentives, exports continued at levels far below both the pre-revolutionary period and the current level of imports. Nonbasic consumption items (including nonbasic food) had been squeezed out of the import bill, but the attempt to maintain domestic industrial production, the state investment program, and import-intensive exports (especially cotton) meant an increasing deficit on current account.[32] The accumulated result was a growth in external debt from $2.6 billion in 1981 to $4.4 billion by the end of 1984.[33] The scarcity of foreign exchange and the "overheating" of the domestic economy were finally exhibited in the widening gap between the official and black-market exchange rates: Whereas the official rate remained pegged at 10 córdobas to the dollar throughout this phase, the number of córdobas for each dollar on the black market soared from 29 in 1981 to 276 during 1984.

The final destabilizing tendency throughout this period was the external aggression. The war with the "contras" represented both a direct shock to the fiscal deficit and a direct and indirect factor that disrupted production throughout the country. The most recent data, through the middle of 1987, are presented in Table 9.1.[34]

The "exhilarationist" tendencies of the Nicaraguan economy were increasingly visible in 1984. In macroeconomic terms, these tendencies meant that capacity and foreign-exchange limits were such that continued economic expansion resulted in growing internal and external disequilibria, especially inflation and a current-account deficit. In fact, the 1984 economic plan (drawn up at the end of 1983) called for a series of macroeconomic adjustments. However, the necessity of calling for national elections in November 1984 put off any change in economic policy until 1985. On February 8, newly elected President Daniel Ortega announced the initial measures of an economic austerity package.

The Austerity Program (1985–1987)

The aim of the new economic policy was obvious: A general policy of "belt-tightening" was called for, and special attention would be given to so-called strategic sectors. Thus, the government assigned the highest priority to the war effort—in particular, to the state's defense budget and, in matters of distribution, to the combatants and residents of the

TABLE 9.1
The Costs of War in Nicaragua (1980–1987): Direct Material and Financial
Losses, and Effects on GDP (in millions of dollars)

Years	Material			Financial			Total of Direct Losses	Effects on GDP
	Destruction of Wealth[a]	Production Losses	Sub-Total	Blocked Loans	Commercial Blockade	Sub-Total		
1980	0.5	1.0	1.5	—	—	—	1.5	—
1981	4.0	3.4	7.4	8.2	—	8.2	15.6	241.0
1982	11.0	21.2	32.2	38.3	—	38.3	70.5	326.0
1983	58.6	106.6	165.2	61.3	14.0	75.3	240.5	331.0
1984	27.7	170.2	197.9	92.1	15.0	107.1	305.0	458.0
1985	18.4	97.8	116.2	73.0	79.4	152.4	268.6	682.0
1986[b]	14.2	89.8	104.0	92.0	79.4	171.4	275.4	783.0
1987	10.1	41.5	51.6	—	—	—	51.6	779.0
Total	144.5	531.5	676.0	364.9	187.8	552.7	1228.7	3600.0[c]

[a]Capital stocks and inventories
[b]To April 30, 1987
[c]Estimated, to end of 1987

Source: Unpublished data from the Nicaraguan Institute of Statistics and Censuses.

war zones. The "formal sector" of the economy oriented toward the production of goods and services, both rural and urban, received the next highest priority; finally, government policy would attempt to squeeze the urban "informal sector."

The policy that drew the most attention was the change in the foreign exchange rate: For the first time since 1979, the córdoba was officially devalued, declining from 10 to 28 (with multiple rates rising to 50 córdobas) to the dollar. The devaluation was aimed, in part, at reducing the foreign exchange losses of the Central Bank: By 1984, total losses from purchasing dollars (from exporters) at a price greater than they were sold (for imports) reached 5.5 percent of GDP; these losses were reduced to 2.8 percent of GDP in 1985.[35] It was also aimed at closing the current-account deficit by changing the relative prices of imports and exports. Additional incentives to exporters included an increase in guaranteed prices for cotton and coffee, and the first step of a complicated policy of surrendering a portion of export earnings in dollars to cattle-ranchers.

The fiscal deficit was attacked from both sides of the ledger. New taxes were imposed on capital gains and the incomes of independent professionals; however, the revenue generated by these direct tax increases tended to be offset by the decline in enterprise profits and the growth of the nontaxed "informal" economy. The main source of new revenues were indirect (consumption and excise) taxes. On the expenditure side, the government instituted a hiring freeze, a cutback in the state investment program, and the elimination of consumer subsidies. This last measure contributed to a rise of 376 percent in the 1985 price index for food—compared to 220 percent for the overall consumer price index.[36]

There was a simultaneous attempt to tighten monetary policy. For example, interest rates, which ranged from 5 (for loans to rural cooperatives) to 19 percent (for 5-year deposits) in 1984, were raised to 6 and 27 percent, respectively, in 1985. The percentage of production costs covered by state credit was also lowered from 100 to 80 percent.

These traditional (in terms of typical IMF programs) austerity measures were accompanied by less traditional moves to stem the fall in real wages and salaries. The official wage and salary scale was adjusted upward in February, and then again in both March and May. This attempt to index wages and salaries was designed both to protect deteriorating standards of living and to attract workers back into formal-sector employment. As we shall see, however, wages and salaries did not keep pace with accelerating inflation.

The results of the new policy package were mixed: The fiscal deficit continued to fall from the 1983 high of 30 percent of GDP to 23.3 percent in 1985, even as defense expenditures soared to 35.6 percent of total government expenditures.[37] Imports grew at a slower pace than in 1984, but total exports continued to fall, leaving a current-account deficit of $627 million. Finally, the recession induced by the new measures meant that 1985 GDP fell by 4.1 percent.

The overall decline in economic activity was the expected result of the war-economy package. The other effect of the 1985 "shock" was a spiraling inflation rate: The general price level, which had been increasing at an average annual rate of 50 percent through mid-1985, was growing by 334 percent by year's end. Typical explanations of inflation, based on fiscal deficit financing and escalating wage costs, are clearly not applicable: The government deficit, as noted above, had declined during both 1984 and 1985; real wages, not withstanding the nominal adjustments, also fell (as discussed in detail below). The immediate causes must be sought elsewhere—in the elimination of consumer subsidies and the freeing of the prices of consumer goods, in the redirection of consumer goods away from civilians and toward combatants, and in the increased prices of imported goods.

This heterodox austerity program continued to be applied in the subsequent two years. In 1986 the official exchange rate was devalued once again, to 70 córdobas per dollar. Dollar incentives were extended to cotton and coffee exporters. Interest rates on loans and deposits were again raised; in addition, payments by check were required for large transactions. The official wage and salary scale was increased in both January and March. Finally, the government responded to the shortage of consumer goods by raising producer prices on basic grains and other domestic foodstuffs.

According to the available preliminary data, the fall in real GDP actually slowed in 1986, to −0.4 percent.[38] Similarly, the fiscal deficit fell to 17 percent of GDP, with the largest part continuing to be financed by credit from the Central Bank. The external sector gap, however, widened even further: Exports fell to $274.5 million whereas imports rose to $1.1 billion. Thus, the accumulated external debt, as expected, reached $7.2 billion by year's end.[39] The unemployment rate continued to hover at 22.5 percent while inflation skyrocketed to 681.6 percent. Nicaragua's successes in the *contra* war were clearly taking their toll on the domestic economy.

The economic plan for 1987 called for a continuation of the austerity program. All sectoral programs were based on the continuing difficulties caused by the foreign exchange bottleneck. Production targets were set by calculating the guaranteed availability of foreign exchange and the need to negotiate additional foreign loans and donations. The economic plan also demonstrated the difficulty of planning in a situation in which economic survival and military defense mean making unforeseen decisions in an ever-changing context. For example, the drafting of the 1987 plan was based on three key presumptions: (1) There would be an increase in wages and salaries; (2) coffee prices would rise (by 13.5 percent); and (3) the córdoba would not be officially devalued.

The situation during 1987 evolved in a dramatically different way. International coffee prices remained constant. Nominal wages and salaries, on the other hand, were allowed to rise. On March 1, the official scale was increased by 56 percent (on average) and the scale itself was expanded from 28 to 39 categories. Additional increases were granted in June, July, and August. It was finally announced that wage and salary increases would be granted on a monthly basis according to the percentage increase in the official prices of a basket of 54 products. Additional measures to make the official scale more flexible included the payment of bonuses based on length of service, technical qualifications, and productivity increases that, according to recent estimates, trebled the actual salary base.

Finally, the córdoba continued (and continues) to face downward pressure in the desperate attempt being made to close the current-account deficit. Surcharges have been applied that raise the import exchange rate from 70 to 170 for essential imports (such as fertilizers and medicines) and to 370 for goods classified as nonessential imports. Export prices were also raised to the extent that the average implicit exchange rate fell to 560 córdobas to the dollar. The growing scarcity of foreign exchange, by mid-year, had driven the parallel exchange rate to 6,000 and the black-market rate to 9,500.

The Costs of Austerity

The Nicaraguan economic crisis and the macroeconomic policies that have been followed in the last eight years have had predictably severe costs. For example, GDP per capita, after rising slightly between 1979 and 1983, fell by more than 15 percent during the 1984–1986 period. That tendency should continue for 1987. However, in the context of the Nicaraguan Revolution, the decline in the average availability of goods and services for the population as a whole tells us little about the effects of austerity on the class composition of the country and, therefore, about the class dynamics of the revolution itself. An analysis of the consequences of austerity in the cities and the countryside focuses attention on the current status of the worker-peasant alliance. It is also a key ingredient in assessing the tensions that the revolution will have to confront in the postwar period.

Austerity in the City

Important crosscurrents have affected the urban class structure in Nicaragua during the 1979–1987 period. The fact that the struggle to overthrow the Somoza regime had been based in large part on urban social groups meant that the workers' struggles earned them a share of benefits from government policy that, at least in the early years of the revolutionary process, probably surpassed the workers' percentage (or numerical weight) in the population as a whole. It also meant that the cities, especially Managua, have swelled considerably during that last eight years, on the basis of rural to urban migration.[40] However, the period of austerity proper (1985 to the present) has witnessed a shift in priority away from the cities to the countryside, as the program of adjustment and stabilization has responded to the exigencies of the war.

The early measures of the revolutionary government, together with the postinsurrection economic recovery, led to an improvement in conditions in the urban centers. The combined effect of the nationalization of Somoza's enterprises, the creation and expansion of government-sponsored social services, and the general resurgence in economic activity was an increase in jobs for the urban unemployed. Although increases in nominal wages were kept low, urban workers benefited from new health and education programs and the organization of new trade unions, as well as from the availability of domestic and imported consumer goods distributed through the state marketing system at officially controlled prices. It may also be inferred that, except for the few domestic capitalists whose enterprises were nationalized along with those owned by the Somoza family, other urban social groups (shopkeepers, owners of small industry, state employees, and urban professionals) benefited as well from the program of economic recovery during the early years of the revolution.

Beginning with the first phase of adjustment and stabilization in 1982, the relative benefits began to shift. Import controls, the scarcity of foreign exchange, and the first assault on nonbasic consumption negatively affected the traditional living standards of such urban groups as managers and professionals. At the same time, the state responded to their threat of emigration by offering them incentives in the form of housing, vehicles, and other goods. Although inflation remained at manageable levels, the slower increases in nominal wages and salaries meant that by the end of 1982 their purchasing power had declined by 19 percent with respect to 1980 (see Table 9.2).

The economic situation of the urban working class has provoked numerous tensions within the revolutionary process. For example, the purchasing power of individual wages and salaries could be allowed to decline as long as the state was able to distribute basic consumption goods and maintain the social wage in the form of health and education services to the majority of the population. However, the increased scarcity of goods available at official prices through the state distribution system, as well as eventual cutbacks in state welfare expenditures, reduced the ability of workers to achieve their customary standard of living by purchasing goods in nonstate markets at prices many times higher than the official ones. The decline in purchasing power and the instability of industrial employment (as production declined due, among other factors, to the shortage of imported inputs) led to a fall in productivity, higher levels of absenteeism, and eventually to increased participation in so-called informal-sector activities.

The organization of an official wage and salary scale (SNOTS) in February 1984 was aimed not at stemming the decline in purchasing power but, rather, at equalizing the level of remuneration for similar

TABLE 9.2
Nicaragua: Real Wages and Salaries, 1980-1986

	1980	1981	1982	1983	1984	1985	1986
Nominal wages and salaries	100.0	113.0	125.2	141.3	182.8	460.6	1223.6
Consumer price index	100.0	123.9	154.6	202.6	274.4	876.7	6852.5
Real wages and salaries	100.0	91.2	81.0	69.7	66.6	52.5	18.0

Notes: 1980 = 100 for all indices.   Data on nominal wages and salaries are based on monthly averages for workers registered with the Nicaraguan Social Security Institute.   The consumer price index covers Managua; it represents the average for each year.   Real wages and salaries were calculated by the author as the ratio of nominal wages and salaries to the consumer price index.

Sources: United Nations Economic Commission for Latin America and the Caribbean, Estudio económico de América Latina y el Caribe, 1986: Nicaragua (LC/L. 425/Add. 11, November 1987) for nominal wages and salaries; and unpublished data from the Nicaraguan Institute of Statistics and Censuses for the consumer price index.

types of work. Employers responded to the movement of workers from formal- to informal-sector activities by offering payment in kind and other incentives.[41] In the state, the movement of employees between different government agencies soared as administrators competed for skilled workers by offering positions that were in a higher SNOTS category and other "perks." Industrial capitalists, in both state-owned and private enterprises, reacted by supplying a portion of output (shoes, textiles, etc.) to compensate for the decline in the purchasing power of wages in order to keep workers from shifting to informal-sector activities.[42]

The urban sector that has suffered the greatest increase throughout this period had been the so-called informal activities sector. Both the movement of urban workers pushed out of formal-sector employment because of the decrease in real wages *and* rural-to-urban migrants have swelled Managua's informal sector. The estimates of the Secretariat of Planning and Budget of the relative size of nonagricultural informal-sector employment are presented in Table 9.3.

Though significant in terms of its role in urban economic life, the informal sector is also the subject of numerous myths. For example, it is common in Nicaragua to observe that all participants in the informal sector have acquired great wealth in comparison to the rest of the population. In fact, the rate of depreciation of the córdoba is evidence that large incomes can be earned through speculative activities—not only on imported goods but also on domestic foodstuffs. An internal study by the Ministry of Foreign Trade concluded that the activities of

TABLE 9.3
Nicaragua: Formal and Informal Sector Employment (Percentage of Total
Employment in Each Category)

	Formal Sector	Informal Sector
Manufacturing	53.2	46.8
Energy and Water	98.8	1.2
Construction	70.2	29.8
Commerce	19.5	80.5
Transport & Communication	62.3	37.7
Finance	97.9	2.1
Services	63.0	37.0

Source: Secretariat of Planning and Budget, "Nicaragua: Plan económico
nacional, 1987" (December 1986), mimeo, p. 145.

a typical *buhonero* (a government-licensed private importer) would earn
a 32 percent rate of return on a single transaction. However, the number
of private importers has been drastically reduced, and, although no
reliable data have been produced, low-income "proletarian" informal-
sector workers probably far outnumber those whose activities are the
source of elevated incomes.

The other powerful myth concerning the informal sector is that all
activities are speculative, commercial ones. Again, exact data are not
available. However, the merchants of Managua's Eastern Market co-exist,
there and elsewhere in the city, with a large number of producers of
goods and services (furniture, shoes, car repair, etc.). Government attempts
to "squeeze" the informal sector have been hampered by the role of
both informal-sector incomes and goods and services in stemming the
decline in the standards of living of working-class families.

The austerity program has particularly affected the role of women in
the Nicaraguan economy. In part as a result of the equal-rights movement
and of the drafting of men for the armed forces, but also as a consequence
of the deterioration in the real wages of traditionally male workers, the
participation of women in the labor force has increased dramatically.
Unfortunately, the data presented in Table 9.4 do not permit a precise
demarcation of the changes before and after 1979.

The general situation in Managua has changed rapidly since the new
economic policy was initiated in 1985. The shift in priorities from
Managua to the countryside has involved a freeing up of the prices of
domestic foodstuffs and the movement of goods (both domestic manufactures and imported goods) that were previously available to the
countryside and to the smaller urban areas located in the war zones.
This attempt to close the town-country "scissors" has had the effect of
increasing the supply of food to the cities, but at significantly higher
free-market prices. The widening gap between the rate of inflation and
increases in nominal wages and salaries has meant that purchasing

TABLE 9.4
Nicaragua: Economic Participation of Women

	1971	1985
Women of working age	614,657	1,002,129
Economically inactive women	504,215	683,547
Students	107,913	200,730
Homemakers	329,135	434,718
Retired	4,252	8,193
Incapacitated	--	29,014
Others	62,915	10,892
Economically active women	110,442	318,582
Employed	106,923	309,039
Full-time	--	172,168
Sub-employed	--	116,210
Others	--	20,661
Unemployed	3,519	9,543
Laid off	1,601	4,494
Looking for first time	1,918	2,642
Others	--	2,407
Participation rate	17.9	31.8
Rate of employment	17.4	30.8
Rate of unemployment	3.2	3.0
Rate of underemployment	--	36.4

Source: Unpublished data from the Secretariat of Planning and Budget.

power had declined by the end of 1986 to less than 20 percent of its 1980 level (see Table 9.2).

At the same time, the government responded to workers' demands by indexing the SNOTS scale to a basket of 54 goods, opening up a network of Workers' Distribution Centers (CATs) and factory-level commissaries, and allowing employers to pay bonuses above the official SNOTS scale.[43] However, the fact that wages and salaries are indexed to the official prices of a basket of goods that does not represent their "typical" consumption pattern, and the fact that goods in the official distribution centers are limited in availability, means that workers' living standards will continue to decline, though possibly at a slower pace than before. Although precise data are not currently available, the economic plan for 1987 noted that most social services—in particular, the "social wage" that was designed to stem the fall in real individual wages and salaries—have stagnated or decreased during the past three years.[44]

This deterioration in customary standards of living in the context of wartime austerity raises a final question: How are the urban workers surviving? Recent research has discovered a wide assortment of survival strategies in the more "popular" neighborhoods of Managua.[45] Basically, working-class families have been forced to find a combination of formal-sector employment (so as to receive nominal wages and, more important, access to the goods available in the CATs and commissaries), informal-sector marketing, and the production of goods and services in informal-sector activities.

Austerity in the Countryside

Agriculture was the key economic sector within the Somozaist pattern of capitalist development. This leading role has not been challenged thus far by the revolution. Moreover, as a result of the concentration of the *contra* war in the countryside, the rural areas have acquired additional prominence during the last eight years. At the same time, government policy and rural social movements have achieved a qualitative transformation of the Nicaraguan countryside.

The nationalization of the properties of the Somoza family (1979–1980) and the first agrarian reform (1981) were the first steps in recharting the course of agriculture. The reorganization of these lands into state farms (the Area of People's Property, or APP) and agricultural cooperatives still left the bulk of both domestic-use and export-oriented land and production in the form of peasant smallholder and capitalist enterprises.[46] Other early measures that directly affected the class landscape of the countryside included the nationalization of export marketing, the reduction of land rental rates, the attempt to replace traditional rural merchants by state marketing boards, the provision of credit from the nationalized banking system, and the expansion of agricultural extension programs.[47]

The key role within the first phase of economic recovery was assigned to the APP—specifically, to the state capitalist farms. Although these state enterprises occupied only 21 percent of the land under cultivation (and although they participated in agricultural production in roughly the same percentage), they were planned to occupy center stage in reactivating agricultural production.[48] This emphasis was reinforced by the raising of rural minimum wages (in an attempt to attract landless laborers and small peasant producers to state farms), by the extension of credit to the enterprises directly under the control of the Ministry of Agriculture, and, later, by the state investment program in agro-industrial projects. These measures were complemented by state support for agricultural producers organized into production, credit, and service cooperatives.[49]

Other forms of production have generally occupied a less-prominent role in state policy, but there has been no attempt to eliminate them. Together, peasant producers of basic grains and capitalist enterprises in both export-oriented production and the production of domestic foodstuffs have accounted for about 65 percent of land and 74 percent of total agricultural production.

From the beginning, capitalist producers have been squeezed between, on the one hand, the decline in international commodity prices and their political role as the "class enemy" and, on the other hand, their traditionally strategic position in the production of agricultural exports and some domestic foodstuffs. One option would have been to eliminate them entirely. However, neither the 1981 agrarian reform nor a subsequent reform law in early 1986 has eliminated capitalist production. Rather, the various phases of adjustment and stabilization during the last eight years have maintained capitalist producers through a combination of state credit and support prices. In the case of agro-exporters, increased price guarantees have meant an implicit rate of exchange above the official rate. These producer prices began to be supplemented in 1985 with a complex procedure of surrendering export proceeds directly in dollars. By 1986 the implicit exchange rate ranged between 1.68 (for coffee) and 7.08 (for sugar) times the official exchange rate.[50]

In the case of peasant producers of basic grains, the situation has been similarly complicated. Again, although the emphasis of government policy has been on state farms and cooperative forms of land tenure, there has been no attempt to eliminate individual peasant producers. Rather, the state has supplied credit, technical assistance, and the legalization of individual land titles in return for state purchases of their marketed output. Thus, between 1981 and 1982, ENABAS was able to increase its purchases of grain (corn, beans, and rice) from 33 to 50 percent of total marketed output.[51] However, this apparent success masked the emergence of a significant problem: The total level of marketed grain production decreased by 29 percent during the same period.

The first attempts to increase grain production were oriented toward the strengthening of cooperative producers (for example, under the aegis of the Nicaraguan Food Program, or PAN, established in 1981) and state production (within, for example, the 1983 Contingency Plan). This emphasis on state and cooperative farms, which was successful in raising the level of domestic-use agricultural production, failed to address the problems of peasant smallholder and capitalist producers of basic grains. The effects of economic stabilization led, therefore, to the formation of a new multiclass organization of agricultural producers, the National Union of Farmers and Cattlemen/Ranchers (UNAG). The UNAG has pressured for expanded individual land reform, increased support prices, and the distribution of consumer goods to the countryside.

The reaction of UNAG bears a close resemblance to the pre-revolutionary response of both peasant and capitalist producers to the monopsonist position of private merchants and banks under the Somoza regime. Its conflict with the Sandinista state—over ENABAS's purchases of basic grains at prices below what the black market would yield, the privileging of state and cooperative ownership of land, and the lack of availability of consumer goods—led its members to resist marketing basic grain output at official prices and, especially in the most remote zones, to their limited support for the *contras*.

TABLE 9.5
Nicaragua: Town-Country Terms of Trade — Basic Grains

	1981	1982	1983	1984	1985	1986
A	1.00	.94	.80	.72	.43	.37
B	1.00	1.03	1.13	.97	.63	1.13

Notes: A is the ratio of basic grain support prices (a simple average of the price index for corn, beans, and rice) and the consumer price index (1981 = 100 for both indices). B is the ratio of the basic grain support price index and the national accounts industry deflator (1981 = 100 for both indices).

Source: Author's calculations based on data from the International Monetary Fund, "Nicaragua: Recent Economic Developments" (June 1987), mimeo.

This dual threat—to starve the cities and to support the *contra* forces—led to a significant reorientation of state policy within the 1985–1987 austerity program. First, there has been an expansion in land distribution (including the transfer of state lands) to individual producers. Second, the state has attempted to improve the distribution of consumer goods (including imports) to rural producers.[52] Finally, the official prices offered to agricultural producers have improved, in part because support prices have been increased (beginning in 1986) and in part because producers have been allowed to market their output through nonstate, private channels (starting in 1987). As a result, the terms of trade, which declined through 1985, began to turn in favor of basic grain producers; a particular reading of the data presented in Table 9.5 makes this clear.

The terms of trade facing basic grain producers can be traced through row A for the years 1981 to 1985 and then in row B for 1985 and 1986. This jumping from one index to another can be explained in the following way: Because manufactured goods at official prices were generally unavailable to rural producers, they had to purchase these goods in private markets; thus, the consumer price index is the relevant terms-of-trade deflator for the 1981–1984 period. The result was that the prices at which producers of basic grains could offer their output through official channels declined steadily with respect to the prices at which they could buy goods from the cities. Between 1985 and 1986, however, support prices rose and manufactured goods became increasingly available at the official prices; hence the national accounts price deflator for industry should be used as the basis of the relevant terms-of-trade index. According to this measure, government policy has succeeded in shifting the town-country terms of trade in favor of producers of basic grains.

Austerity and the
Worker-Peasant Alliance

The Nicaraguan Revolution has captured the imagination of economists and many other observers. Policymakers' flexibility in responding to the ongoing economic crisis and the multiclass nature of the revolutionary movement are two of the reasons Nicaragua has attracted so much attention.

Flexibility in responding to different class demands has been the hallmark of many government strategies, including the various programs of stabilization and adjustment since 1979. In this sense, macroeconomic policy has been based on a series of changing class compromises. The aim of economic policy has been to cement the worker-peasant alliance, and to ally other domestic social groups to the dual processes of revolutionary transformation and national defense. Thus, what may appear at first to be a series of "concessions" to social groups other than workers and peasants—the army, capitalist producers of agro-exports, and so on—may be interpreted as a series of compromises designed to maintain the worker-peasant alliance under difficult and changing conditions.

The austerity program announced in early 1985 may be seen against this background as a response both to the war and to the problems generated by earlier economic policies. Among these "mistakes," two were especially significant in terms of the relationship between the role of the state and the conduct of macroeconomic policy. First, state planners and economic policymakers appear to have been guided by the presumption that market relations had been effectively removed from a large part of the Nicaraguan economy. Macroeconomic balance could be achieved, so it was thought, precisely because private merchants had been ousted and replaced with a state trading system.

A related problem was the presumption that the "correct" functioning of the administrative, banking, and commercial system of the state could control the development of the economy and, ultimately, the terms of the worker-peasant alliance. Implicit in this presumption was the mistake of ascribing a decisive role to the state's economic organs and of one-sidedly emphasizing the development of agro-industry based on investment directly controlled by these organs. This focus on state control has had the opposite effect of putting private, and until recently illegal, commerce and production into an advantageous position. Since efforts to develop the role of the state presumed the existence of more resources than the state could effectively mobilize, private traders and producers were able to step in and replace the role of the state in key economic activities. Minister of Internal Commerce Ramón Cabrales has noted the role of state policy in creating conditions that led to the strengthening of private markets:

> One of the most serious errors was that during each agricultural cycle we obligated the peasants to sell us their production at official prices and in a coercive manner, in an attempt to resolve the distribution problem of everyone in the country. As the peasantry learns that the only thing that matters are the revenues from selling the harvest, it filches the harvest and refuses to sell its products to the state. Therefore, the state enterprise ENABAS is no longer able to collect those products.[53]

This emphasis on the key role of the state, and the tendency to "forget" about the other marketing and production relations in the Nicaraguan economy, ended up driving a wedge between workers and peasants. Peasant producers of basic grains were compelled to increase their self-sufficiency and to market their output through parallel and black markets.[54] Many producers were drawn toward the UNAG in an effort to bargain with the state over higher prices, over the ability to market their output in nonstate markets, and over the improved distribution of industrial goods to the countryside. Others joined with landless rural laborers in demanding more land reform.[55] Workers, on the other hand, were faced with deteriorating living standards as wage goods become increasingly scarce in official channels and available, at much higher prices, only in "free" markets. Calls for increased work discipline and productivity were no solution. Instead, wage-earners responded by pressuring the leadership of the Sandinista Worker Confederation (CST) and by moving into the informal sector.

In brief, post-1985 austerity policies have benefited peasants and rural capitalists (through higher food prices, the distribution of consumer goods, etc.) at the expense of the urban population consisting of both workers and nonworkers alike.

The government's response to this situation, especially in 1987, may be seen as an attempt to recompose the worker-peasant alliance on new terms. The data are not yet available to analyze whether the peasants are responding to the new policies by expanding the area planted and marketing their output to the urban areas. The workers, on the other hand, are still struggling just to survive.

The political costs of this austerity are difficult to gauge. At least one observer has concluded that the counterrevolution has gained at least "passive support" from the peasantry.[56] The situation in the cities is somewhat different. Tensions have increased in the trade union movement and within such mass organizations as the Sandinista Defense Committees (CDS), but there is little evidence of urban support for the "contras." On the contrary, the bulk of the blame for the current situation seems to have been placed squarely on the invading forces. Again, according to at least one report,

> there is no relation between the popular sectors' criticisms of the economic situation and their political position. The economic crisis these people are living through is not translated into domestic political criticism.
>
> The ideology of Managua's popular classes included the clear image of a government which began to aid them in a variety of ways until the war cut off the possibilities for further advancement. This is the base of their understanding of the government's economic campaign.[57]

The short-term solution for this crisis depends in large part on the course of the war and the current regional negotiations for peace. Recent economic problems and the severity of the austerity program imposed on the country also raise questions about the medium- and longer-term strategy for the Nicaraguan Revolution. If the worker-peasant alliance—both the participation of workers and peasants in the revolution and the project of transforming the class structure of society—is to survive in the postwar period, developmental solutions beyond the mere continuation of austerity will have to be forged.

Notes

This chapter could not have been completed without my access to the data and observations offered by a large number of individuals and institutions. Special thanks are due to colleagues in the Nicaraguan Institute of Economic and Social Research (INIES), the Center for the Study of the Agrarian Reform (CIERA), the Nicaraguan Institute of Statistics and Censuses (INEC), the Nicaraguan Central Bank (BCN), and the Economic Research Team of the Regional Coordinator of Economic and Social Research (CRIES) in Managua. Research assistance was provided by Jimmy Campbell and Stephen Francis. The Helen Kellogg Institute for International Studies provided partial travel support. An earlier version of this chapter was presented at the fourteenth International Congress of the Latin American Studies Association, Yale University, and the University of Chicago. Comments from the editors of this volume, Michael Conroy, Michael Zalkin, and an anonymous reviewer are gratefully acknowledged. The author is responsible for the translations and, finally, for the analysis itself.

1. Victor Bulmer-Thomas, "The Balance-of-Payments Crisis and Adjustment Programmes in Central America," in *Latin American Debt and the Adjustment Crisis*, edited by Rosemary Thorp and Laurence Whitehead (Pittsburgh: University of Pittsburgh Press, 1987), p. 302.

2. "Tomás Borge on the Nicaraguan Revolution" (interview with Fredric Jameson), *New Left Review*, No. 164 (July–August 1987), p. 58.

3. The economic situation across the Central American isthmus is discussed by the United Nations Economic Commission for Latin America, "The Crisis in Central America: Its Origins, Scope and Consequences," *CEPAL Review*, No. 22 (April 1984), pp. 53–80.

4. The different adjustment programs adopted by the five Central American countries are surveyed by Bulmer-Thomas, *op. cit.*, pp. 271–317.

5. The coverage and effects on Latin America of IMF-sponsored programs are analyzed by Manuel Pastor, Jr., "The Effects of IMF Programs in the Third World: Debate and Evidence from Latin America," *World Development*, Vol. 15 (February 1987), pp. 249–262.

6. For example, see Rodolfo Delgado C., *Sobre las medidas de ajuste y la crisis económica de Nicaragua*, Ediciones Nicaragua Hoy (Managua: Centro de Investigación y Asesoría Socio-Económica, 1985); and Roberto Pizarro, "The New Economic Policy: A Necessary Readjustment," in *The Political Economy of Revolutionary Nicaragua*, edited by Rose J. Spalding (Boston: Allen & Unwin, 1987), pp. 217–232.

A similar debate was provoked by the new austerity program adopted in mid-February 1988. The latest measures include a substantial devaluation of the córdoba, a currency conversion (1,000 old córdobas to 1 new córdoba), price increases, a wage and salary adjustment, and a 10 percent cut in the state budget. This chapter was completed in late 1987; there is no attempt to analyze the impact of the 1988 measures.

7. Cf. Gerald K. Helleiner, "Balance-of-Payments Experience and Growth Prospects of Developing Countries: A Synthesis," *World Development*, Vol. 14 (1986), pp. 877–908.

8. See Manuel Paster, Jr., *The International Monetary Fund and Latin America* (Boulder, Colo.: Westview Press, 1987).

9. "Simply stated, the core economic problem of the transition is how to transform the inherited economic structure of underdevelopment into one that benefits the majority of the population and at the same time generates acceptable levels of economic growth" ("Introduction," in *Transition and Development: Problems of Third World Socialism*, edited by Richard R. Fagen, Carmen Diana Deere, and José Luis Coraggio [New York: Monthly Review, 1986], p. 17).

10. The role of the state and planning in the Nicaraguan economy is discussed by David F. Ruccio, "The State, Planning, and Transition in Nicaragua," *Development and Change*, Vol. 18 (January 1987), pp. 5–27.

11. For the Chilean case, see Stephany Griffith-Jones, *The Role of Finance in the Transition to Socialism* (New York: Allanheld, 1981); and, for the Soviet experience with the New Economic Policy, see Charles Bettelheim, *Class Struggles in the USSR: First Period, 1917–1923*, translated by Brian Pearce (New York: Monthly Review, 1976).

12. *Stagnationist* is the term used by Lance Taylor, in "Varieties of Stabilization Experience" (Massachusetts: Massachusetts Institute of Technology, April 1987), mimeo, p. 12.

13. This is the sum of net short-term capital movements and errors and omissions for the 1977–1980 period. See the United Nations Economic Commission for Latin America and the Caribbean (ECLAC), *América Latina y el Caribe: Balance de pagos 1950–1984* (Santiago: United Nations, 1986), pp. 182–183.

14. United Nations Economic Commission for Latin America (ECLA), *Economic Survey of Latin America and the Caribbean, 1981* (Santiago: United Nations, 1982), p. 565. The total of damage and lost production for the 1978–1980 period was estimated to be $2 billion, equivalent to the 1980 Nicaraguan GDP. See the World Bank, *Nicaragua: The Challenge of Reconstruction*, Report No. 3524-NI (October 9, 1981), p. 2.

15. The plans had predicted growth rates of 22.5 and 18.5 percent for the two years, respectively. For a comparison of the planned and actual values for a wide variety of economic indicators, see Hugo Cabieses, *Economía Nicaragüense, 1979–1986: Marco global para su analisis* (Managua: Departamento de Economía Agricola/UNAN, July 1986), p. 96.

16. ECLAC, *op. cit.* The mix of multilateral and bilateral loans and credit lines changed considerably during the 1979–1981 period: Multilateral financing fell from 78.4 percent of the total in 1979 to 11.4 percent in 1981. The sources of bilateral external financing also changed during that period: The socialist countries (including Cuba) increased their participation in total bilateral credit from negligible amounts in 1979 to 26 percent in 1981. (The author's calculations were made on the basis of data in Richard Stahler-Sholk, "Foreign Debt and Economic Stabilization Policies in Revolutionary Nicaragua," in Spalding [ed.], *op. cit.*, p. 162). The strategic importance of external finance for the initial stage of socialist transition in peripheral societies is argued by Barbara Stallings, "External Finance and the Transition to Socialism in Small Peripheral Societies," in Fagen, et al. (eds.), *op. cit.*, pp. 54–78.

TABLE 9.6
Nicaragua: Selected Economic Indicators 1980-1986

	1980	1981	1982	1983	1984	1985	1986
Gross Domestic Product (GDP)[a]	100.0	105.4	104.5	109.3	107.6	103.2	102.8
GDP per capita[a]	100.0	102.1	98.0	99.1	94.3	87.5	84.2
Exports[b]	495	553	447	463	430	338	292
Imports[b]	909	1,037	829	925	890	973	955
External debt[b]	1,825	2,566	3,139	3,788	4,362	4,936	5,773
Fiscal deficit/GDP[c]	9.2	12.4	13.6	30.0	24.8	23.3	15.8

[a]1980 = 100
[b]In millions of dollars
[c]In percentages

Source: United Nations Economic Commission for Latin America and the Caribbean, *Estudio económico de América Latina y el Caribe, 1986: Nicaragua* (LC/L. 425/Add. 11, November 1987).

17. See Ruccio, *op. cit.,* p. 79.

18. Ruccio, *op. cit.* These percentages differ only slightly from the corresponding entries in the longer data series presented in Table 9.6.

19. For a discussion of the rural credit program, see Laura J. Enriquez and Rose J. Spalding, "Banking Systems and Revolutionary Change: The Politics of Agricultural Credit in Nicaragua," in Spalding (ed.), *op. cit.,* pp. 105–125.

20. ECLA, *op. cit.,* p. 575.

21. See Ruccio, *op. cit.,* p. 79.

22. The annual average rates of inflation were 48.1 percent (1979), 35.3 (1980), and 23.9 percent (1981); see ECLA, *op. cit.,* p. 582.

23. See Table 9.6.

24. One of the forms of class compromise offered by the Somoza regime had been the free convertibility of foreign exchange. After the revolution, foreign exchange earnings have been controlled by the state, and capitalists' access to foreign exchange has been allowed for either rationed inputs at the official rate of exchange or, at rates considerably higher than the official rate, in the parallel market.

25. See the data on export and imports in Table 9.6. Still, because of the continued payment of interest on the outstanding external debt, the deficit on current account fell by only 8.7 percent during 1982. See ECLAC, *op. cit.,* p. 183.

26. See E.V.K. Fitzgerald, "Stabilization and Economic Justice: The Case of Nicaragua," in *Debt and Development in Latin America,* edited by Kwan S. Kim and David F. Ruccio (Notre Dame: University of Notre Dame Press, 1985), p. 203.

27. The logic of "stabilization with equity" is explained by Fitzgerald, *op. cit.,* pp. 191–204.

j

28. The theory of the transitional state serving as the center of accumulation is presented by E.V.K. Fitzgerald, "The Problem of Balance in the Peripheral Socialist Economy," *World Development*, Vol. 13 (1985), pp. 5–14; and by George Irvin, "Establishing the State as the Centre of Accumulation," *Cambridge Journal of Economics*, Vol. 7 (1983), pp. 125–139; it is critically discussed by David F. Ruccio, in "Nicaragua: The State, Class, and Transition," *Latin American Perspectives*, Vol. 15 (Spring 1988), pp. 50–71.

29. For a comprehensive list of these investment projects, many of which are still under way, see Cabieses, *op. cit.*, p. 75.

30. These figures refer to gross domestic investment, including changes in inventories. For 1979 and 1980, see ECLA, *op. cit.*, p. 568; for 1983, see United Nations Economic Commission for Latin America and the Caribbean, *Economic Survey of Latin America and the Caribbean, 1983*, Vol. 1 (Santiago: United Nations, 1984), p. 474.

31. See Table 9.6.

32. On the evolution of food imports, see Peter Utting, "Domestic Supply and Food Shortages," in Spalding (ed.), *op. cit.*, pp. 137–140.

33. See Table 9.6.

34. A more detailed analysis of the costs of the "contra" war is presented by E.V.K. Fitzgerald, "An Evaluation of the Economic Costs to Nicaragua of U.S. Agression: 1980–1984," in Spalding (ed.), *op. cit.*, pp. 195–213. The evolution of the war and of U.S. policy toward Nicaragua is discussed by Peter Kornbluh, *Nicaragua, the Price of Intervention: Reagan's War Against the Sandinistas* (Washington, D.C.: Institute for Policy Studies, 1987).

35. International Monetary Fund, "Nicaragua: Recent Economic Developments" (June 1, 1987), mimeo, p. 31. This report, an internal document prepared by a May 1987 staff mission, was made available for consultation by my colleagues in Nicaragua.

36. See Table 9.2 for data on the increase in the overall consumer price index during 1985. The price index for food covers eight agricultural products: rice, beans, sugar, coffee, corn, beef, eggs, and milk products. The Nicaraguan Institute of Statistics and Censuses (INEC) graciously supplied the unpublished global indicators for this data in Chapter 2 of *Nicaragua en Cifras 1986*.

37. For data on the fiscal deficit, see Table 9.6; data on defense expenditures as a percentage of GDP are taken from United Nations Economic Commission for Latin America and the Caribbean, *Estudio económico de América Latina y el Caribe, 1986: Nicaragua* (LC/L.425/Add.11, November 1987), p. 16.

38. Unpublished data supplied by INEC, *op. cit.*

39. The accumulated external debt includes the capitalization of payments in arrears. See Mario Arana Sevilla, Richard Stahler-Sholk, and Gerardo Timossi Dolinsky, "Deuda, estabilización y ajuste: La transformación en Nicaragua, 1979–1986" (Managua: Coordinadora Regional de Investigaciones Económicas y Sociales, August 1987), mimeo, p. 46.

40. Unless otherwise stated, information about conditions in the cities refers to Managua. According to recent estimates, Managua's population is growing at an annual rate of 7.04 percent (compared to a national population growth rate of 3.36 percent); the current population stands at 1.3 million (out of a total population of 3.3 million). See *Monitoreo*, No. 3 (August 1987), a publication of the Nicaraguan Institute of Economic and Social Research (INIES).

41. According to unpublished data provided by colleagues in the Secretariat of Planning and Budget, job rotation in the Ministry of Transportation (workers

who left the ministry as a percentage of total ministry employment) reached 57.9 percent during the period from September 1986 and February 1987. For the government as a whole, job rotation (by the same definition and for the same period) was 9.5 percent.

42. These attempts to circumvent the SNOTS scale by making payments in kind were declared illegal by the government in June 1985. See Richard Stahler-Sholk, "Pago en especies" (Managua: Coordinadora Regional de Investigaciones Económicas y Sociales, July 1985), mimeo.

43. The state has also bowed to pressure from professionals and other higher-income formal-sector employees to open up a CAT specifically for those groups. It remains to be seen if the professionals will be successful in achieving their other demand—to release them entirely from the SNOTS scale.

44. Secretariat of Planning and Budget, "Nicaragua: Plan económico nacional, 1987" (December 1986), mimeo, p. 95.

45. The initial results of this research, organized by the Department of Sociology at the Central American University in Managua, were reported in "Managua's Economic Crisis—How Do the Poor Survive?" in *Envío*, Vol. 5 (December 1986), pp. 36–56.

46. The complex class structure of the Nicaraguan peasantry is discussed by Michael Zalkin, "Food Policy and Class Transformation in Revolutionary Nicaragua, 1979–86," *World Development*, Vol. 15 (July 1987), pp. 961–984.

47. The Nicaraguan agrarian reform and associated policy measures are discussed in detail by Carmen Diana Deere, Peter Marchetti, and Nola Reinhardt, "The Peasantry and the Development of Sandinista Agrarian Policy, 1979–1984," *Latin American Research Review*, Vol. 20 (1985), pp. 75–109.

48. Throughout this section, land and production figures are based on Cabieses, *op. cit.*, p. 131.

49. The cooperative sector covered approximately 15 percent of farm land in 1983. This figure grew to 21 percent by the end of 1986, the last year for which data are available. The figures for production are 9 and 26 percent for the two years, respectively. Production cooperatives are distinguished from credit and service cooperatives by the degree of collective ownership of both land and machinery and the collective organization of work. Credit and service cooperatives tend to gather together peasant producers for the purpose of sharing state credit and technical assistance; however, property ownership and the responsibility for organizing work remain at the individual family level. A third, "intermediate" stage of cooperative production is the *surco muerto*, in which barriers between individual plots of land have been eliminated. Their weight in total land use and production is negligible.

50. These figures are based on calculations made by the International Monetary Fund, *op. cit.*, Table 35, p. 57.

51. Zalkin, *op. cit.*, p. 970.

52. The state has guaranteed to distribute the following nine products through the Centers of Rural Distribution at official prices: batteries, lighters, blankets, flashlights, light bulbs, boots, ponchos, grain mills, and kerosene lamps.

53. Ramón Cabrales, "El Abastecimiento en ocho años de revolución" (Managua, 1987), mimeo, p. 3.

54. Parallel markets are legal markets (involving both state and private merchants) in which goods are exchanged at prices higher than the official ones. Black markets are strictly illegal. To the extent that goods and services can be channeled through official and parallel markets, transactions can be accounted

for (i.e., for planning purposes) and taxed. Black-market activities tend to undermine both state planning and government tax revenues.

55. The demand for land reached a peak in the region around Masaya during 1985. According to unpublished data (Ministry of Agricultural Development and Agrarian Reform, Region IV, "Plan Masaya"), land redistribution has affected 13,356 acres, benefiting a total of 1490 families: 460 in individual land-tenancy arrangements and the remainder in cooperative form. The land was redistributed from diverse sources: 22.4 percent from APP enterprises, 50.8 percent from negotiated sales involving private landowners, and 26.8 percent expropriated from a single landowner, Enrique Bolaños Geyer (head of the Superior Council of Private Enterprise and outspoken critic of the government).

56. Peter E. Marchetti, "War, Popular Participation, and Transition to Socialism: The Case of Nicaragua," in Fagen et al. (eds.), *op. cit.*, pp. 303–330.

57. "Managua's Economic Crisis," *op. cit.*, p. 55.

About the Contributors

Werner Baer is professor of economics at the University of Illinois at Urbana-Champaign. He specializes in economic development problems of Latin America and has written many books and articles on Latin American industrialization, inflation, and state enterprises. In 1989 the third edition of his book, *The Brazilian Economy: Growth and Development*, will be published.

Paul Beckerman received his Ph.D. in economics from Princeton University in 1979. He has taught at the University of Illinois and at Fordham University and in 1988 was at the Federal University of Bahia, Brazil, on a Fulbright grant. He has worked in Peru and other Latin American nations on macroeconomic issues.

Dan Biller, a Brazilian citizen, received his B.A. degree from the University of Kansas and his M.A. in economics from the University of Illinois. He is currently working on his doctoral dissertation at the University of Illinois.

René Cortázar received his Ph.D. in economics from MIT. He is a researcher at CIEPLAN and has been a visiting professor at the Catholic University of Rio de Janeiro and at the Kellogg Institute and Department of Economics of the University of Notre Dame. His main research areas are labor economics, labor movements, and macroeconomics.

Edward C. Epstein is an associate professor of political science at the University of Utah, Salt Lake City. He has done research in Peru, Colombia, and Argentina, and has published articles appearing in such journals as *Comparative Politics, Comparative Political Studies, World Development, Economic Development and Cultural Change,* and the *Latin American Research Review*. The volume he has edited, *Organized Labor, the State, and Autonomy in Latin America,* is scheduled to appear in early 1989.

Howard Handelman is professor of political science and department chairman at the University of Wisconsin, Milwaukee. He has conducted research in Peru, Mexico, Uruguay, Ecuador, Venezuela, Cuba, and Colombia. His books include *The Politics of Agrarian Change in Asia and*

Latin America and *Military Governments and the Movement Towards Democracy in South America.* Journals in which he has published include the *Latin American Research Review,* the *Journal of Inter-American Studies and World Affairs,* and *Cuban Studies.*

Kenneth P. Jameson is a professor of economics and a Fellow in the Helen Kellogg Institute of International Studies at the University of Notre Dame. In addition to his work on Bolivia, he has worked in and published on Peru, Chile, Mexico, and Paraguay, dealing with such issues as macroeconomics and agricultural development. His most recent publication is "Education's Role in the Rural Areas of Latin America," in *Economics of Education Review* (1988).

Jennifer L. McCoy is associate director of the Latin American and Caribbean Program of the Carter Center of Emory University. She is on leave from Georgia State University, where she is an assistant professor of political science. Her current research is on social pacts in new and established democracies in Latin America. Her articles have appeared in the *Journal of Inter-American Studies and World Affairs* and the *Journal of Developing Societies,* and she is co-editor with B. Edward Schuh of *Food, Agriculture, and Development in the Pacific Basin* (Westview Press, 1986).

Curtis T. McDonald received his B.A. and M.A. in economics from the University of Illinois and is currently a Ph.D. candidate. He has spent two semesters in Latin America as an exchange student—one in Costa Rica and the other in Brazil.

Miguel D. Ramírez is an assistant professor of economics at Trinity College in Hartford, Connecticut. His research is in the area of economic development, and his articles have appeared in the *American Economic Review,* the *Journal of Economics and Business,* and the *Journal of Inter-American Studies and World Affairs.*

David F. Ruccio is assistant professor of economics and director of Latin American Area Studies at the University of Notre Dame. His most recent publications on Nicaraguan political economy have appeared in *Latin American Perspectives, Development and Change,* and *The Political Economy of Revolutionary Nicaragua* (edited by Rose Spalding). He is also co-director of a joint research project of the Kellogg Institute and the Nicaraguan Institute for Economic and Social Research on Nicaraguan history.

David W. Schodt, Ph.D. (University of Wisconsin, Madison), is associate professor of economics at St. Olaf College in Northfield, Minnesota. He has published various articles on the Ecuadorian economy. Most recently, he completed an economic and political history of Ecuador entitled *Ecuador: An Andean Enigma* (Westview Press, 1987).

Index

3 1542 00113 3150

338.98
H236p

WITHDRAWN

338.98
H236p

DATE DU

Handelman
Paying the
costs of auster-
ity in Latin
America

JUL 1 1993

4611353   LAF

Trexler Library
Muhlenberg College
Allentown, PA 18104

DEMCO